Matthew

CHALICE COMMENTARIES for TODAY

Jeremiah
Jorge Pixley

Matthew

RUSSELL PREGEANT

CHALICE
PRESS
ST. LOUIS, MISSOURI

Cover and interior design: Elizabeth Wright

This book is printed on acid-free, recycled paper.

Visit Chalice Press on the World Wide Web at
www.chalicepress.com

10 9 8 7 6 5 4 3 2 1   04 05 06 07 08 09

Library of Congress Cataloging–in–Publication Data

Pregeant, Russell.
  Matthew : Chalice commentaries for today / Russell Pregeant.
    p. cm.
  ISBN 0-8272-0525-2 (pbk. : alk. paper)
  1. Bible. N.T. Matthew—Commentaries. I. Title.
  BS2575.53.P74 2004
  226.2'077—dc22
                                                              2004005201

Printed in the United States of America

Contents

Series Preface

The *Chalice Commentaries for Today* are designed to help pastors, seminary students, and educated laity who are open to contemporary scholarship claim the Bible in their personal lives and in their engagement with the crucial issues of our time. Although the various authors manifest a variety of interests and theological perspectives, they share a vision of God as a relational being who is passionately involved in the life of the world, whose primary feature is love, and who both affects and is affected by the world. Their intention is to foster a dialogue between the world of the Bible and our own world and to do so in clear, nontechnical language with a minimum of footnotes. The aim of the series as a whole is therefore a better understanding of the biblical challenges to the values, beliefs, and behavior in today's world as well as our own world's challenges to the values, beliefs, and behavior in the biblical world.

It is the conviction of the members of the Editorial Board of *Chalice Commentaries for Today* that the dialogue described here has had no better exemplar than the life and scholarship of William A. Beardslee, a founder of the series, whose original commentary on 1 Corinthians has provided the model for all the volumes to follow. It is therefore with great admiration, gratitude, and love that we dedicate this series as a whole to his memory.

Kathleen A. Farmer
David J. Lull
Russell Pregeant
Marti J. Steussy

Preface

The advent of this book's publication brings with it an almost mystical sense of having come full circle, though I would hope that the route I have traveled is more of a spiral than a mere return to a starting point. This feeling issues in part from the opportunity that this commentary on Matthew has given me to work out in systematic fashion the ideas that I have been in the process of developing since I began work on *Christology beyond Dogma: Matthew's Christ in Process Hermeneutic*, published in 1978. But it also has a great deal to do with the sense of companionship that I have had as I have tried to approach the interpretation of the New Testament from a particular perspective.

William A. Beardslee—to whose memory this entire series is dedicated—served as the editor of that first, rather tentative venture, and he has played the same role with regard to the present volume. My debt to him is incalculable. Far beyond the editorial role, he gave me wise counsel, insightful criticism, and sincere encouragement at every stage of my ongoing work. In addition, his perusal of my manuscript—a remarkable act of dedication—was one of the last projects in which he was involved before his death. More than all this, however, Will Beardslee became over the years a close and valued friend.

In 1977, while I was on sabbatical at the School of Theology at Claremont (Claremont, California), I worked with Will and several other scholars and theologians on developing a theory of biblical interpretation rooted in the process thought of Alfred North Whitehead and Charles Hartshorne. The work of this cohesive team—which also included John B. Cobb, Jr.; David J. Lull; Theodore J. Weeden, Sr.; and Barry Woodbridge—extended far beyond 1977. In 1979, we published a set of essays in the *Journal of the American Academy of Religion* and in 1989 a jointly authored book titled *Biblical Preaching on the Death of Jesus*. Several of us were also active for many years in successive interest groups within the Society of Biblical Literature, where we were joined by Kathleen Farmer, Ron Farmer, and Marti Steussy, all of whom are involved in the present series. So there is indeed a sense of having come a long way with companions who have for many years shared a labor of love. To all these I render my gratitude, acknowledging that I owe much to each one of them, even as I hasten to add that none of them should be held accountable for any shortcomings of the present effort.

I am also indebted, in a rather different way, to the members of the Matthew Group of the Society of Biblical Literature, with which I have been associated for many years. I have learned much from a wide range of scholars in this circle and deeply appreciate the opportunity I have had through the years to enter into discussion with them. I also wanted to thank Gene Boring, himself the author of an excellent commentary on Matthew, for reading the first draft of my Introduction. His scholarship and wise judgment have served as important guides in my work for many years.

Finally, I must express deep gratitude to the entire staff at Chalice Press. It is obvious that they believe in the series as much as do we, the authors and editorial board.

Russell Pregeant
March 4, 2004

to laypersons and pastors I have known,
progressive in thinking, courageous in action, steadfast in intention,
who have kept the faith;
who accept the outsider at the price of their own rejection;
who know the difference between God on the one hand
and country, class, race, creed, or economic system on the other;
and in whom the spirit of the prophets lives;
who open themselves to the world of human knowledge
but can see beyond its surface;
who read with care the biblical texts
but also let the Spirit speak;
and who dare to doubt so that faith might grow.

Introduction

Matthew as Story, Proclamation, and Theology

The gospel of Matthew is a story. This might seem like an obvious point, but biblical scholarship has often obscured the narrative form of the gospels. It has treated them sometimes as doctrinal treatises, at other times as sources for the reconstruction of historical events "behind" the texts. The result, in either case, has been a failure to appreciate the significance of the story format of the gospels. A story is made up of characters, settings, and plot, all of which are conveyed to those who read them through a narrator who is not the author, but rather the voice that tells the tale through both recitation and commentary. The gospels clearly fit this description, but only recently have biblical interpreters, making use of modes of literary criticism drawn from secular scholarship, approached them in light of their character as story.

It is nevertheless important to ask what specific kind of story the gospel of Matthew is. New Testament scholars have devoted a great deal of attention to the question of the genre, or literary type, of the gospels. One view, dominant for the greater part of this century, is that the gospels are unlike any other writings in antiquity, which is to say they constituted a unique genre in that setting. Although they might appear on the surface to be biographies of Jesus, they do more than tell the story of a person's life and teaching. The gospels proclaim; they preach; they declare. They proclaim that through the life, death, and resurrection of Jesus, God brought about a fundamental turn in human history; that the events that comprise the story, in fact, constitute the dawn of the long-awaited rule (or kingdom) of God. Thus, when church tradition encompassed Matthew, Mark, Luke, and John under the designation "gospels," it recognized that these four writings are announcements of the "good news" of God's gracious action in history.

This approach to the gospels made an important contribution, but the focus on proclamation meant neglect of their character as story. In addition, other analysts have noted that the sharp distinction between the gospels and biographies is based more on modern standards for the latter than on those prevailing in antiquity. Ancient biographers knew nothing of the notion of so-called objective or value-free reporting, and it was actually a common practice to write a "life" or biography in order to advance a philosophical point of view. There is thus a strong tendency in recent scholarship to acknowledge that the gospels do after all conform to the broad pattern of the biography known in antiquity. And the value of recognizing the biographical character of the gospels is that it focuses on the figure of Jesus in them and the importance of his character, deeds, and teaching.

It is nevertheless true that the gospels remain in some ways highly distinctive. As much as they concentrate on Jesus himself, their interest is ultimately in looking "through" Jesus to God on the one hand and to humanity on the other, for they consistently present both the deeds of Jesus and his life as a whole as the action of God. This point has little relevance to the gospels' claim of divine status for Jesus. As the theologian Schubert Ogden notes, even at the earliest level of pregospel tradition, which speaks of Jesus "as in every way human and in no sense divine," he nevertheless appears "on the divine side of the relationship between God and human beings generally, not on the human side" (*The Point of Christology*, p. 77). Both in the early tradition and in the gospels, the fundamental point of the focus on Jesus is not simply to laud his admirable qualities or to illustrate the truth of his understanding of life. It is rather to announce that through Jesus, God has initiated the age to come and the final redemption of the world.

If the gospels would have appeared to ancient readers as in some sense "lives" of Jesus, then, they also constitute a distinct subgenre, the nature of which is grounded in their function in the Christian communities. In Matthew specifically, we will find the themes of Jesus' own character and of the redemptive action of God woven together in intricate ways. It is in fact the genius of the gospel form that it carries out its proclamation of the good news precisely through the medium of an account of Jesus' life.

To the extent that the gospels are proclamation, they are also theological in nature. Some proponents of literary approaches to biblical interpretation shun the attempt to identify the theological perspectives of the gospels, since narratives engage the audience in a fundamentally different way than does systematic theological language. Hearers of stories become involved with characters and get caught up in events; they develop expectations that are either disappointed or fulfilled. And their experience is more a matter of feeling than of distanced reflection. Feeling, however, can become an invitation to more systematic thought. Although the gospels are not primarily doctrinal statements, they do make truth-claims and thereby call for commitment on both the affective and intellectual levels. They demand a total loyalty to Jesus and an acceptance of the belief system that underlies the story of his life, death, and resurrection.

Ultimately, of course, the gospels invite their readers to integrate the affective and intellectual components of commitment into action—into lives that are lived, on both the individual and communal levels, totally on the basis of the faith these narratives proclaim. In the present commentary, I will seek to honor both the narrative and the theological dimensions of the gospel of Matthew and also to take note of the concrete demands it issues in terms of living out the gospel message.

Story and History; Author, Text, and Reader

There were good reasons for modern scholarship to focus for so long on the events behind the gospel narratives. On the one hand, if Christianity has boldly proclaimed that Jesus is the Son of God, it has been equally insistent that he was a human being. On the other hand, modern skepticism regarding God's intervention in the world called into question not only the accounts of miracles but also the entire worldview within which notions such as divine sonship had their origin. From either point of view, it made sense to scholars in an age devoted to the use of "scientific" method in the study of history to ask "what really happened" in the life of Jesus. It made sense, that is to say, to reconstruct the "historical Jesus" in distinction from the Jesus Christ of faith presented in the gospels.

Although this search for the historical Jesus continues, in the mid-twentieth century scholars began to identify the different theological perspectives of the individual gospel writers and to value them precisely as *interpretations* of Jesus' life. Thus, for the majority of recent students of the gospels, the ideological commitments of the authors appear no longer as deficiencies but as links in an ongoing process of grasping the significance of Jesus' life in ever-new circumstances. Some scholars and theologians have argued, moreover, that what historians can actually hope to reconstruct "behind" the gospels is not the bare historical figure of Jesus but the earliest understanding of, or witness to, the meaning of his life. That is to say, what we find at the beginning of the tradition is not pure fact, but once again proclamation.

Scholars have long been aware of an extended process of tradition that lies behind the written gospels. Although the early church believed that the authors of Matthew and John were eyewitnesses to the ministry of Jesus and the author of Mark received his material directly from Peter, the weight of modern scholarship counts against both these judgments.

John appears to be a highly meditative and reflective work, containing extended discourses of Jesus that are not the type of material that would have been remembered by an eyewitness. Most scholars therefore believe that it is the product of tradition that developed within a distinctive kind of early Christianity rather than a description of events actually observed by one of Jesus' original followers.

Matthew, Mark, and Luke, by contrast, are composed largely of small units of tradition that are in themselves relatively self-contained. Such tradition has in all probability a generally firmer grounding in historical events than does Johannine tradition. This does not mean, however, that any one of these three gospels is an eyewitness account, for the self-contained nature of the individual units suggests that each story circulated independently and that only at a late stage did someone gather them together into an extended narrative.

A close comparison of the three shows differences that are great enough to suggest that either the writers themselves or earlier bearers of tradition felt relatively free in shaping that tradition to meet the needs of their specific situations. On the other hand, the wording is so close at many points as to make literary dependence of some sort virtually certain. The majority opinion among scholars today is that Mark was written first and that the authors of Matthew and Luke each drew on it but also added material from another document (designated by the symbol Q), now lost, to which they both had access. Some scholars have other views on the literary relationships among the gospels, but few regard any of the four as eyewitness accounts.

The majority of scholars also acknowledge that the names attached to the four gospels—Matthew, Mark, Luke, and John—are the products of tradition. These names appear in the headings of the manuscripts, which were apparently added some time after the composition of the writings, but do not occur in the actual texts of the gospels as claims to authorship. For that reason, I will reserve the name "Matthew" for the gospel itself and will not apply it to the author, who—like the other three—remains unknown to us.

Some interpreters put a great deal of emphasis on the order of composition of Matthew, Mark, and Luke. If, for example, it can be established that the person who wrote Matthew made use of Mark, then it would be possible to gain insight into that author's intentions and theological perspective by focusing on changes made to the Marcan text. A great deal of the most important work done on Matthew in this century is based precisely on this procedure. I will not, however, use this method in this commentary, even though I am convinced that Matthew is indeed dependent on Mark and Q. It will be useful, however, at some points to make comparisons with the other gospels.

My reason flows from my perspective on what it is that an interpreter seeks to interpret. To focus on the differences between the text of Matthew and the sources the author used is to seek to gain insight into that author's mind. That is one way of thinking about what interpretation means, and I by no means reject it entirely. Other approaches, however, focus not on the author but on the written text itself and/or the reader. Although I believe that the author's intentions contribute heavily to the meaning of a text, I would also argue that this contribution is not exhaustive. Language and culture have to some extent lives of their own, so that in both speaking and writing we often say more than we intend. In seeking to set out one particular argument, our word usage and lines of logic often lead us in directions we do not intend and of which we are often unaware.

A text, therefore, has a way of pushing beyond its author's intentions. And readers, because they will come to the text from various perspectives, will interact with it in differing ways and find differing meanings in it. One of the most interesting insights of feminist criticism, for example, is that sometimes a text will take on a different meaning if read by a woman than it would have if read by a man. One needs to add, however, that many other factors affect a person's reading—for instance, race, social class, and individual experience. Any reader, in fact, reads from an exceedingly complex background.

My position is not that a text can mean anything some individual or community experiences it as meaning. One cannot legitimately read Matthew as saying that Jesus was an agent of Satan or that he taught that self-preservation is a higher ideal than service to the neighbor. I do understand meaning, though, as something that does not reside in a simplistic sense either in the author's mind or in the text in isolation from the reader. Author and text provide possibilities for meaning, but actual meaning occurs only in the process through which a reader encounters a text and responds to it.

In approaching the gospel of Matthew, I will focus on the text and the reader, not the author. My assumption is that the text both opens up avenues of meaning and places limits on meaning. I will try to determine how the narrator tries to elicit specific responses from a reader, but I will also explore some of the various ways a reader might in fact react. This means that I will try to be sensitive both to the dominant emphases of the story and to "undercurrents" or "countertendencies" that might suggest other legitimate ways of understanding it. But I will treat the story as a relatively coherent whole rather than concentrate on the points at which it departs from the sources the author used.

My emphasis will also be on the story that the gospel of Matthew tells, not on the earlier story constituted by the witness of Jesus' earliest followers and not on the mind of the author. I will therefore give somewhat less attention than most commentators do to the question of the specific historical situation in which the author wrote. Unlike some text and reader-centered interpreters, however, I do not think we can adequately interpret a writing in complete isolation from its broad historical context. The simple fact is that the gospel of Matthew shares the culture, worldview, and language of the first-century world in which Judaism interacted with the Greek-speaking world and in which Christianity was born. Because the text itself presupposes certain items of knowledge, it is important that we inform ourselves regarding that broad context to the extent that we can. However, our goal is to understand the story, not to learn about the author or to write the history of the specific group for whom that author wrote.

Matthew: Past Influence, Problematic Aspects, and Contemporary Potential

Of the four canonical gospels, Matthew was the most widely used in the ancient church. It alone employs the word that we usually translate as "church" (*ekklesia*), and its emphasis on the life of the Christian community has made it a valuable resource throughout the centuries. Its influence has not ended there, though, for it contains the segment of Christian tradition that has without a doubt appealed to a wider range of persons, both within and without the church, than has any other: the Sermon on the Mount. The sayings of Jesus contained in Matthew 5—7 (only partially paralleled in Luke's Sermon on the Plain, Luke 6:17–49) have touched the hearts of countless millions, challenged them to the highest standards of human behavior, and confronted them with almost unbearably poignant images of the nature of authentic human life.

Nevertheless, some aspects of the gospel of Matthew are problematic for readers in our time. Matthew's story of Jesus purports to be a crucial link in the larger story of God's interactions with the world. But this notion of human history as the scene of divine activity, moving toward some final resolution, does not fall easily on the late twentieth-century Western ear. It is generally easier for persons in our life situation to think of the divine (insofar as they can think of it at all) in terms of an inward spiritual presence than of an active agent in the world of actual events on the political and social planes. Equally problematic are the assumptions lying behind the concepts of God's covenant with Israel, "Messiah," and "Son of God." Theologians of an earlier phase of modernity agonized over what they called the "scandal of particularity," the offense to "enlightened" sensibilities that accompanied the suggestion that God should favor Israel over other people with a covenant or that one human being could in some unique and exclusive sense claim divine sonship.

The difficulties do not end there. Although Matthew understands the story of Jesus largely within the framework of the broader story of God's covenant with Israel, it also contains bitter invectives against Jewish leaders and a number of other passages that have played key roles in the long and shameful history of Christian hatred of Jews. Some readers find Matthew problematic on other issues as well. Along with the New Testament as a whole, it partially reflects the patriarchal structure of the ancient world, a structure that has become increasingly suspect in light of a feminist consciousness that rejects any claim to truth that denies the "full humanity of women" (Rosemary Ruether, *Sexism and God-Talk*). Moreover, to the extent that it focuses on Jesus' death and resurrection, interprets those events in terms of the atonement for human sin, refers to Satan and demons, and looks beyond this earthly life to a world to come, it plunges the reader into an age-old tension. Are we to understand Christianity primarily as a system of otherworldly salvation from sin and death or as a word of empowerment for the renewal of life and society in this world?

If the gospel of Matthew is essentially a story, then it is one that demands a thoughtful reading from contemporary interpreters—a reading, that is, in which the interpreter is an active partner, free to ask probing questions. Such a reading is a major goal of this commentary; and in pursuing it, I will draw heavily on the notion, sketched out in the preceding section, that a story can legitimately be read in more than one way.

Approaching the text this way will involve an attempt to avoid two pitfalls. One of these is allowing the desire for contemporary relevance to foster distortion of the text itself—to "make" it mean something it cannot legitimately be said to mean, or to force aspects of the ancient worldview and the social system it reflects into our own frame of reference. The other is suppressing the legitimate concerns of contemporary readers by imposing the presuppositions of the ancient world on them, insisting that responding to Matthew's proclamation means the uncritical acceptance of ancient ways of understanding the world.

In contrast to both these approaches, I will employ a model of interpretation that takes it to be a kind of dialogue rather than a one-way communication. This will mean, on the one hand, trying to allow the text its own integrity and not reading into it the point of view we might want to find there. On the other hand, it will also mean allowing our concerns their due. The goal is a genuine conversation in which we allow the text to question us even as we give ourselves permission to question the text. Perhaps there will be points at which the contemporary reader will need to reconsider aspects of an ancient worldview that modernity has tended to dismiss.

Perhaps there will be others at which a contemporary perspective can open up creative avenues of meaning by noticing undercurrents in the text that might have remained opaque to the author and original readers.

The Reader in the Text

Every writing presupposes some preliminary knowledge. It should therefore be helpful to specify some central aspects of the knowledge the gospel of Matthew assumes. To put the matter in terms of the reader, this means attempting to identify the "implied reader," the hypothetical interpreter the text of this gospel presupposes as its audience.

The implied readers of the gospel of Matthew are able to understand Greek and are thoroughly familiar with the Septuagint—the Greek translation of the Hebrew Scriptures. (Although it is probable that the majority of the actual "readers" of Matthew in the first century were illiterate, they would have been acquainted with the scriptures through hearing them read aloud in communal settings.) They accept the Israelite worldview, which means that they are monotheists who believe that God made a special covenant with the people of Israel and that the Hebrew Scriptures constitute divinely inspired writings. They also know something of the geography of Jewish Palestine and of the various leadership groups that had existed in Israelite society early in the first century—the priesthood and temple hierarchy, the Sadducees, and the Pharisees. These hypothetical readers are also, apparently, aware of political events that had taken place later than the period described in the story. Most specifically, they would know about the destruction of the temple by the Roman army in 70 C.E. (C.E. and B.C.E., Common Era and Before the Common Era, mark the same periods as A.D. and B.C. without imposing a Christian framework on secular history).

Many scholars have tried to derive from the text (along with some external sources) specific knowledge about the situation of the actual first readers of Matthew, as well as about the actual author, but their opinions are varied. Matters of current debate are whether the Matthean community has fully separated from the religious life of the larger Jewish community, whether the author was Jewish or Gentile in background, what the precise ethnic makeup of the community was, and the date and place of composition.

I will enter this debate only tangentially, confining myself to what I think the text itself presupposes and what the contemporary reader needs to know in order to play the role the narrator expects. It seems clear, to start with, that the implied readers are members of a community that accepts Jesus as Messiah, sometime between 70 C.E. (that is, after the destruction of the Jerusalem temple) and the end of the century, most likely circa 80–90.

They feel a strong connection to an Israelite heritage but are also aware of a mission to the Gentiles that is either in its initial stages or fully underway. They are apparently close enough to the wider world of Jews who do not accept Jesus to be influenced by it and to wonder about the authority of the leaders of that wider Jewish world over their own lives as followers of Jesus. Yet they also have a strong sense of identity based on their attachment to Jesus and some sense of distinctiveness as his "church." And they have concerns about how they, as his followers, should live their lives and order their community.

The narrator presupposes that the readers know the story of Jesus and accept the gospel; but their faith and understanding need nurturing, and there are problems within the community. The narrator therefore tells the story in such a way as to preserve its sequential quality—building up tension and creating anticipation—and thus treats the reader as someone who in some sense comes to the story afresh, ready to experience it as if for the first time. In the following analysis, I will try to help the reader of the present book play the role of the narrator's implied reader, coming to the story afresh, without presupposing the outcome.

To the extent that this attempt is successful, the reader will be engaged in an experience that should in some measure parallel that of any competent reader of Matthew at any time. But one of the most important insights of much recent literary interpretation is that part of what a reader is called on to do is to engage the text through certain kinds of mental actions. Because the story doesn't tell everything, the reader has to fill in certain gaps. And because the story engages the imagination, the interested reader will constantly be anticipating what is to come, gathering up and rethinking what has already occurred, and also reflecting on the meaning of what is taking place. Thus, the reader will actually contribute to the meaning of the story by entering into it from a perspective influenced by her or his own time and circumstance. Along with attempting to guide the reader through the story, then, I will also seek to foster reflection from a specifically contemporary point of view.

Signposts in the Text

Many interpreters have proposed outlines of the gospel of Matthew. In keeping with my intention to treat Matthew as a story, I have followed here a scheme, endorsed by a number of scholars, based on two turning points in the plot that are signaled by clear linguistic markers. At 4:17 and 16:21, the narrator uses the exact same Greek construction, translated in the NRSV as "from that time Jesus began to …," in order to introduce a new phase in Jesus' ministry. The first instance indicates the point at which Jesus begins his proclamation: "Repent, for the kingdom of heaven has come near." At the second, Jesus focuses on the disciples specifically and begins to teach them that "he must undergo great suffering at the hands of the elders and chief priests and scribes, and be killed, and on the third day rise."

Everything before 4:17 is in some sense preliminary. The narrator relates Jesus' genealogy, gives account of his birth and his parents' settlement in Nazareth, introduces John the Baptist, and tells the story of Jesus' baptism and victory over Satan in the wilderness. At 4:12–16 Jesus returns to Galilee from the encounter with Satan, and verse 17 informs the reader that his public ministry is now beginning. From this point until the dramatic scene at Caesarea Philippi in chapter 16, where Peter acknowledges Jesus as "the Messiah, the Son of the living God," Jesus pursues his activities in Galilee with occasional treks into Gentile territory. He preaches, teaches, heals, casts out demons, performs other miraculous deeds, and engages in controversy with the scribes and Pharisees.

Immediately following Peter's acknowledgment, Jesus informs the disciples of his coming death and resurrection (16:21–23), and this theme dominates the remaining chapters. Twice again, Jesus predicts his death, and in all three instances, his announcement is followed by extended interchange with the disciples. At 19:1, Jesus leaves Galilee for the region of Judea beyond the Jordan, and at 20:17 the reader learns that he and his entourage are now headed directly for Jerusalem. Then in chapter 21, Jesus enters the city, initiating the final phase of the drama in which he is crucified and resurrected and appears to his followers.

The narrative thus falls into three major parts: preparation; public ministry/proclamation; death and resurrection. But there are other markers that point to Jesus' teaching rather than the sequence of the story. Five times we find another Greek construction, rendered in the NRSV as "When Jesus had finished ...." In each of these instances, the clause ends by referring to some kind of teaching that Jesus has been engaged in, and in each case the formula is preceded by an extended discourse that has thematic unity. We thus find superimposed on the threefold narrative sequence a scheme of five major discourses: (1) 5:1—7:27: The Rule of Heaven in the Community of Faith (The Sermon on the Mount); (2) 10:1—11:1: Instructions and Encouragement for Mission; (3) 13:1–52: Parables and the Rule of Heaven; (4) 18:1–35: Life in the New Community; (5) 23:1—25:46: The Judgment of God and the Close of the Age.

The five discourses play a crucial role in the Matthean scheme: They are a clear indication that the reader is expected to understand Jesus' role in large part as that of teacher and, more specifically, as in some sense of a teacher of the Jewish law. Nevertheless, the discourses occur precisely in the context of an ongoing narrative—a fact that interpretations of Matthew as a kind of teaching manual tend to ignore. As I will try to make clear, the teaching aspect of Matthew in some ways stands in tension with the story aspect; and a recognition of this tension can lead to some fruitful reflection on the meaning of this gospel for our own situation. It is important, however, to remember that The Gospel According to Matthew is above all a *story*.

Language, Feeling, Belief, and Faith

The preceding reminder of the narrative quality of the gospels brings our discussion full circle and invites some final reflection on the broader question of the nature of the language we find in the gospels and in the Bible generally. We have seen that the gospels are not eyewitness reports and are not intended to convey bare factual material. They stand within a long chain of tradition, beginning in the oral stage, in which followers of Jesus have expressed their faith in Jesus as the one through whom God has acted decisively for the salvation of the world. Like many of the earlier links in that chain, the author of Matthew shaped various received traditions into a statement of faith, intended to nurture those who had begun the Christian journey and perhaps to engender faith in those who had not.

The language this author employed makes no pretense to be the language of neutral reporting or distanced analysis. It is the language of faith, and as such, it is a primary form of religious language, different from the secondary, reflective language of systematic theology that tries to order religious concepts into a self-consistent whole. It is the language, in other words, that flows more from the "heart" than from the "head." It expresses feelings, seeks to engage the imagination, and tries to evoke human responses from the deepest center of one's being.

It is important, on the other hand, to note that this language also *leads toward* reflection on the intellectual level in an attempt to give conceptual coherence to the deep-seated response that it evokes. Although it is rooted in the "heart," it moves toward the "head," encouraging that secondary form of verbal religious expression that is more explicitly rational and ordered.

Now, what does all this mean with respect to the interpretation of the gospels? It is essential that we not confuse the roles of feeling and belief and that we develop a sense of how the text functions in relation to each of these responses. The problem is that people often mistake the imaginative and evocative aspects of a biblical text for language designed primarily to convey information and/or to assert doctrinal truth. The result is that they think the proper response is to accept the supposed information as literally true in the historical sense and/or to give assent to certain doctrinal propositions.

Let us take as an example the language in Matthew that concerns the coming of God's rule. In 24:29–31 that language is particularly graphic:

> Immediately after the suffering of those days
> the sun will be darkened,
>   and the moon will not give its light;
> the stars will fall from heaven,
>   and the powers of heaven will be shaken.
> Then the sign of the Son of Man will appear in heaven, and then all the tribes of the earth will mourn, and they will see 'the Son of Man coming on the clouds of heaven' with power and great glory. And he will send out his angels with a loud trumpet call, and they will gather his elect from the four winds, from one end of heaven to the other.

What are we to make of this passage? It is clear, to begin with, that it employs highly imaginative, emotionally charged language. It invites the reader to imagine a situation in which the existing cosmos is dismantled and the Son of man (whom Matthew's reader will identify with Jesus) will finally take charge, vindicate his followers on earth, and initiate God's rule. The key word here is "imagine," for the initial function of the passage is to provide a powerful word of encouragement to Christians who feel beleaguered in the world. The details of the description are valuable first of all for their emotional impact, not their literal detail; it is difficult, in fact, to know just what they are intended to mean in terms of some actual set of future events. What is most important is that the reader *experience* hope and assurance that God will not abandon the world to the forces of evil. In imagining a final vindication of the righteous, the reader is able to nurture just such a hope.

Clearly, then, the passage operates primarily in relation to the preintellectual or affective aspect of the human psyche. But it cannot stand alone as pure poetry, engaging the imagination only; for unless the reader can make some actual affirmation about God and human history, the comfort is groundless. Thus, the imaginative aspects of the language encourage the reader to engage in a secondary kind of reflection, seeking just such an affirmation.

The difficulty arises, however, when we try to specify just what that affirmation should be. At this point, the interpreter's task becomes more difficult. If we ask how the author of Matthew intended this language, or how the first readers would have understood it, the truth is that we simply do not know. An essential step, of course, is to read Matthew as a whole and see if it expresses a consistent point of view. But what one often finds in the attempt to trace down the theological perspective of a biblical writing is that considerable ambiguity remains.

Here, then, is the problem. The comfort the passage offers depends on a movement from feeling to belief, but because of the imaginative character of the language we cannot easily identify what specific affirmation on the rational level is necessary to honor its force. Must the reader take the passage as actual information about the end of the age? Must one, that is to say, believe the details of description of the cosmic breakup? Or is it sufficient to affirm that God will eventually bring human history to a close and usher in a heavenly rule? And is it really necessary to conceive that rule as heavenly, or we can honor the deepest intention of the language by hearing in it the assurance that God will one day bring genuine peace and justice to human society?

According to the model of religious language that informs this commentary, there is no one answer to such questions. It remains for the reader, bringing to the text her or his questions, concerns, and worldview, to participate in a process that begins from the imaginative dimension of the text and extends to the conceptual. Because the text does not outline a systematic belief system, but contains numerous crosscurrents and intellectual gaps, this reflective process is a necessary part of the reader/ interpreter's work. In commenting on specific passages (see "The Imaging of Evil," pp. 33–36; "The Coming Rule of Heaven," pp. 41–44; and "Thinking Today about Matthew 21:1—22:46," pp. 160–64), I will suggest a way of appropriating its language that is somewhat different from any of the options given above. My point, however, is not that this will be the "correct" option but only that it is one way of bringing Matthew's world into conversation with our own.

In summary, we may say that the language of the gospel of Matthew is the language of faith. It issues from the faith of the Christian community and is intended to nurture faith in the reader. As faith-language, it is at base imaginative and evocative rather than systematic, and we read it as logically ordered conceptual language only at our peril. We must not think that what it demands of us in the first instance is the acceptance of factual details or assent to doctrinal propositions. Our job is rather to grasp its images precisely as images, to read its story precisely as story, and to hear its proclamation precisely as proclamation.

Part of the way we honor the intention of this writing to engage us as whole human beings, however, is to enter into a process of theological reflection on it. At this point, we do not simply reproduce the conceptual scheme in which the gospel of Matthew presents its message; we wrestle with the questions with which it wrestles. In all of this, in moving back and forth between imaginative engagement and secondary reflection, we open ourselves to the possibility that this gospel will in fact accomplish precisely what it intends—which is to engender and nurture our faith and thereby transform our lives.

1:1—4:16

The Origin and Preparation of Jesus the Messiah: Genealogy, Infancy, and Inaugural Events

1:1—2:23 The Preparatory Events

1:1–25: Genealogy and Birth of the Messiah

In the opening section of the gospel, 1:1—4:16, the narrator prepares the reader for the story of Jesus' ministry through a series of accounts that attest to Jesus' identity and place in God's ongoing action in history. This agenda appears immediately in the title the narrator has provided in the text: "The Book of the Origin of Jesus the Messiah, the Son of David, the Son of Abraham" (my translation). Although many interpreters understand this title as applying only to the genealogy, and others view it as a heading for the section that ends at 4:16, there is good reason to believe that it applies to the gospel as a whole.

The argument hinges in part on the translation of two Greek words in 1:1. It is virtually certain that the term *biblos* means "book," for it does so in every other instance in the New Testament and in almost every instance in the Septuagint, the Greek translation of the Hebrew Bible. The second term, *genesis*, presents more of a problem. Its primary meaning is "beginning" or "origin," though it can be used to mean "genealogy." However, there is a third usage that is relevant in the present context: In the Septuagint it also takes on the force of "story" (Boring, *The Gospel of Matthew*, p. 126). When we consider, further, that it was customary in some types of ancient Jewish writings for the author to begin a work "with an independent titular sentence announcing the content of the work (Davies and Allison, *The Gospel According to Saint Matthew*, I, p. 151), it seems most likely that we should interpret 1:1 as a title for the entire narrative that is to follow.

In any case, the reader enters the story under the influence of the proclamation that the subject of the narrative, Jesus, is Messiah, Son of David, and Son of Abraham. It is therefore immediately apparent that this is a story that stands within the Israelite tradition and draws on the category of Messiah Son of David. To say that Jesus is Son of Abraham is to say that he belongs to God's covenant people; to say he is Son of David is to attest that he has the proper lineage to qualify for the title Messiah. But a subtler note is also present in the reference to Abraham, because according to Genesis 12:3 the promise God gave to Abraham would ultimately extend to all humankind.

The first part of the story proper is Jesus' genealogy, and it is important to note the specific form in which it appears. One negative effect of translating *biblos* as "record" (NIV), or "table," to fit a reading of *genesis* as "genealogy," is that it obscures the fact that verses 2–16 take the form not of a list (as in Luke 3:23–38) but of a narrative. The narrative quality is further weakened by recent translations that render the Greek verb that links father to son throughout the account as "was the father of." The King James Version captured the sense more accurately with the (now archaic) verb "beget": "Abraham begat Isaac …." Already one gets a sense of movement. Knowing that at the end of the chain will be Jesus the Messiah, the reader will understand the repetitive account of "begettings" as moving toward a divinely ordained goal.

The genealogy supports the claim to descent from David, but it is virtually impossible that we have here a historically/biologically accurate account. To begin with, it seems dependent in large part on genealogical materials in the Hebrew Scriptures yet differs from them in important ways. It omits three kings from the list in 1 Chronicles 3, and it makes Josiah the father rather than the grandfather of Jeconiah. Beyond that, it allows an insufficient number of generations to cover some periods. It also differs at numerous points from Luke's version, tracing Jesus' ancestry through a completely different branch of the Davidic line for a significant period.

From a modern perspective, then, one might pronounce the genealogy a fraud. But studies of genealogies in ancient societies suggest that they functioned more as testimonies to, rather than as historical proofs of, a particular person's lineage. This attitude is manifest in the fact that a person could actually have more than one genealogy, each serving a different purpose. It is fair to say, then, that in the same spirit in which early tradition shaped the stories about Jesus in order to proclaim the Christian message in new situations, the author of Matthew gathered and arranged genealogical materials with a theological intent. And that intent was to express the conviction that Jesus stood within God's continuing action in the history of Israel through the house of David.

This broad conviction comes to the fore in verses 17–18 in the schematization of Israel's history from Abraham to Jesus into three sets of fourteen generations—a scheme, by the way, that is not supported by an actual count of the generations listed. Scholars have proposed several more specific interpretations of the significance of the numbers, though none has found wide acceptance. But the fundamental point is clear enough.

A subtler note is also present, however, for the witness to God's action in history receives some enticing nuances from the unusual role played by women. After tracing Jesus' lineage through Joseph in a consistently patrilineal pattern, the narrator concludes the account by relegating Joseph to a secondary status as "the husband of Mary, of whom Jesus was born, who is called the Messiah." This move pushes Mary's role to the fore in a way that is striking in the context of a patriarchal society. But the reader is already prepared to recognize her prominence by the earlier references to four women—references that are unnecessary in a patrilineal account.

This recognition of women stands as a tensive undercurrent within the mainstream of a history defined in male terms. And the tension is increased by a note of irregularity surrounding each woman. Although some commentators argue that all the women before Mary were in some way sinners, this is not at all clear with respect to Ruth; and in any case Jewish tradition found ways to honor all of them as having served God's purposes. Nevertheless, there is something unusual about each of them. Ruth and Rahab were Gentiles, and Bathsheba was married to a Gentile. Both Ruth and Tamar took strong initiative—Ruth by insisting on following her mother-in-law back to the land of Judah, and Tamar (Genesis 38) by posing as a prostitute in order to conceive sons by her father-in-law.

As Elaine Wainwright argues, all these women stood as anomalies within the patriarchal system and therefore in dangerous situations. Although the patriarchal narratives of the Hebrew Scriptures worked them into their overall pictures to some degree, each in some way constituted a threat to the social system. Their presence in Matthew's genealogy "functions, therefore, as a critique of patriarchy and introduces a point of tension into the narrative that must guide the reader as the story unfolds" (Wainwright, *Towards a Feminist Critical Reading of the Gospel According to Matthew*, p. 68).

Through the genealogy, the narrator draws the reader into a story marked by both continuity and discontinuity. If the overarching point is that the birth of Jesus is the climax to God's ongoing activity, this activity does not follow a smooth trajectory. For the mention of the Babylonian exile in verse 17 is also a subtle reminder of a point in history in which human unfaithfulness threatened to thwart God's plan, because a strong strain of biblical tradition taught that the exile was the result of Israel's sin. God's action therefore consists partly in rescuing human beings from their own mistakes—a prominent theme in the Hebrew Scriptures.

There is a stronger note of discontinuity in the implication that God's activities transcend established precedent, traditional boundaries, and existing social systems. If this note is present in the references to Tamar, Rahab, Ruth, and Bathsheba, it is even more clearly evident in verse 16. Here the entire patrilineal account defers to another woman who stands outside the patriarchal structure in a dramatic way that is only hinted at in the grammatical structure of the verse. The patriarchal point of view remains dominant, however, because even her story will in the following verses be encased within an account that focuses on her husband.

The removal of Joseph from the string of "begettings" subtly prepares the reader for a story (vv. 18–25) that describes Joseph's actions in the face of Mary's virginal conception of Jesus. The miraculous character of the conception is not the point of the account, but only provides its framework. Legends of divinely initiated births surrounded numerous heroic figures of the ancient world, and the special pleading of Christian interpreters regarding the unique qualities of the gospel birth narratives is hardly to the point. The story simply assumes the miraculous conception without making it a central attestation to Jesus' status. Nor does the story actually narrate the birth. The references to both conception and birth function primarily to lead up to the naming of Jesus. And this action accomplishes two tasks. When Joseph names Jesus, by adoption he includes him in his family and thus in the line of David. This completes the point made in the genealogy. The angel's explanation of the name "Jesus," on the other hand, combines with the quotation from Isaiah to give a preview of the role Jesus will play as the narrative unfolds. He will save the people from their sins, because he will in fact be "Emmanuel."

It is important to note that the stress is on Jesus' role rather than his identity in some abstract or metaphysical sense. It is, of course, by virtue of his identity that he is qualified to play the role; the force of the narrative up to this point is that he is in fact *born* Messiah. But the reader will soon see (4:1–11) that he must live up to that identity precisely by fulfilling his role. The epithet "Emmanuel," moreover, should probably be taken in the sense of "God *is* with us" (NRSV) rather than of "God with us" (*Revised Standard Version* [RSV] and most translations). This would be in keeping with the usual sense of Hebrew names that incorporate God's name. In any case, Jesus' birth not only fulfills prophecy, as the narrator emphasizes in verse 22 ("All this took place to fulfill …"), but also points forward to a ministry in which he will through his actual words and deeds manifest God and bring salvation.

The narrator gives little specific help about the nature of this salvation. Some commentators note that the phrase "from their sins" tends to play down the sociopolitical dimension (traditionally expressed in Israel's hope for deliverance from concrete, historical enemies) in favor of a moral/ "spiritual" emphasis. There is validity in this observation, but the distinction between the "outward" sociopolitical realm and the "inward" world of moral and spiritual qualities is largely a modern imposition. The phrase "his people" leads the reader in the direction of the more traditional Hebrew view of a collective salvation that cannot be abstracted from sociopolitical realities. The reader will have to proceed through the story as a whole to know more precisely what it means by sins, what salvation is, and how and in what sense Jesus brings it about.

At this point, the reader gets only a hint of what Jesus' ministry will be. It is Joseph's action that receives the most attention. That action does not come without a moment of uncertainty, though: Joseph initially decides to dissolve the betrothal (a highly formalized arrangement) because of Mary's pregnancy. His attitude embraces an interesting conflux of values. The narrator's notation of Joseph's wish to avoid Mary's shame, reinforced by the adjective "righteous" (or "just"), attests his good character. Yet from a broader perspective, Joseph's righteousness is shortsighted because the angel has to lead Joseph past his well-intentioned resolution so adoption can in fact take place.

Although Mary is a passive character, her anomalous pregnancy links her to the other women in the genealogy and intensifies the challenge to the social system. For Mary's situation puts her in a precarious position with respect to the patriarchal order and a value system revolving around honor and shame. The fact that she bears in her womb the Davidic Messiah, but does so apart from the activity of a male member of the Davidic line, constitutes an undercurrent of meaning that resists the larger patriarchal framework.

Joseph's action is the focal point of the story, but the force of that action is precisely to legitimate the child, so that Jesus himself—who like Mary is at this point a passive character—stands in some sense at the center of the broader narrative. To get the full force of the story, however, the reader will have to discern action on another level. Jesus' conception is the work of the Holy Spirit, not human beings, and Joseph acts only because of divine prompting through a dream. All that is happening, moreover, is taking place in order to fulfill prophecy. Although Jesus is the subject of the ongoing narrative, it is God who is the active agent in the sequence of events.

2:1–23: The Magi, Herod, and a Sojourn in Egypt

By stressing Jesus' place in the Davidic line, the narrator has brought the reader into the world of royalty, and the opening scene in the infancy cycle reinforces that emphasis. Matthew's narrative is not a variant of Luke's but is simply a different story, and it is important not to read Lucan elements into it: there is no stable here, nor are there humble shepherds. The magi who visit the child are not kings, as later tradition made them, but neither are they simple folk. The term *magos* could refer to a range of figures, from magicians and sorcerers to wise men (so most translations) and astrologers, and could have either positive or negative connotations. Despite the negative use of this and related terms in Acts 8 and 13, however, Matthew's magi appear in a positive light. Their discovery of the star suggests (surprising) approval of their astrological knowledge, and the expensive gifts they bear suggest a connection with the elite of their society. These gifts, moreover, are fitting tributes to a royal figure.

The emphasis on Bethlehem as the place of the Messiah's birth, as predicted in scripture, also reinforces the connection to the royal house of David. Within the Matthean account, which again has no hint of the Lucan motif of the parents' journey from Galilee, Bethlehem—the city of David—is clearly their home. The main point of the concluding segment of the infancy cycle (1:19–23) is to explain how it came about that Jesus grew up in Nazareth, whereas Luke's story explains how he came to be born in Bethlehem.

Despite the regal aspects of the story of the magi, there are motifs that undermine a simplistically positive valuation of royalty. In Bethlehem, David was not a king, but a shepherd-boy. As Brian Nolan has documented (*The Royal Son of God*, pp. 158–69), Jewish piety of the first century focused on David less as a powerful and majestic figure than as a prophet and a model of spirituality and fidelity to God. The revised quotation of Micah 5:2 in Matthew 2:6 would thus have a complex set of nuances for the reader familiar with this tradition. The Hebrew addresses Bethlehem as "one of the little clans of Judah," and the Septuagint reads similarly except for "thousands" instead of "clans." But Matthew has "you, Bethlehem … are *by no means* least among the rulers of Judah." Part of the effect is to emphasize that it is a small, unassuming village that paradoxically plays a powerful role in God's redemptive plan. David was a king, by virtue of God's choice, but God's choice for the founder of a royal line for perpetuity was in fact a shepherd. It is into such a royal line that Jesus is born, and the Matthean narrative will eventually confirm that he will exercise a rule marked precisely by humility (see especially 11:25–30; 12:18–20; and later in this book, commentary on 21:1–27, pp. 151–54).

Significantly, the narrator indicates that when the magi find Jesus, they worship him. Understanding this action as proper, the reader will associate Jesus even more closely with God and will look for further specification of who Jesus is. That identification will come shortly, but an immediate effect of the narration of the magi's worship is to add further qualifications to the positive use of royal imagery. It is not human, but divine, rule that the narrator approves, and insofar as God's rule is nascently present in the child Jesus, it threatens existing human governmental authority. Thus Herod, the vassal king of Judea, fears for his own reign when the magi ask about the location of "the child who has been born the king of the Jews." The narrator thus creates a scenario in which the birth of Jesus pits God's own rule against the existing power structure in Jewish society, and the degeneracy of that structure is manifest in Herod's response. He is filled not with joy but with fear, and he responds not with faithfulness but with deceit. Already the theme of conflict is evident.

Because the reader will recognize the magi as Gentiles (probably connecting them with Arabia, Babylonia, or Persia), their interaction with Herod creates a strong note of irony. Although the king who ostensibly rules over God's people gives no thought whatsoever to responding to the birth as God's gift of salvation, foreigners journey from afar to find the Christ child and acknowledge him. The scene not only reinforces the narrator's earlier hints about the inclusion of Gentiles but also contrasts these particular Gentiles with Jewish leaders.

Many commentators see an anti-Jewish motif at work in the story of the magi, but the matter is not so simple. Herod does in some sense stand for the Jewish leadership. The "chief priests and scribes of the people" are readily at his service, and they, too, apparently give no thought to acknowledging the rival king. In assuming knowledge of the actual King Herod, however, the narrator also presupposes a reader who would know some further specifics. Herod was called King of the Jews (or Judeans) but was in fact a native of Idumea (an originally non-Israelite territory annexed during the Hasmonean dynasty, which preceded his rule) whom the people regarded as a brutal agent of Roman rule. Therefore, the reader would likely view his reign as illegitimate to begin with. Although it is clear that a sharp critique of the power structure of Jerusalem is in view, that is precisely because it is in fact a false leadership.

The more difficult question is whether there is also a subtle condemnation of the Jewish people as a whole in this story. The phrase "of the people" could point in this direction, and it is not only Herod but also "all Jerusalem" that is disturbed by news of the Messiah's birth. The people of Jerusalem, however, are by no means the equivalent of the Jewish people as a whole, and the positive image of "the people of Jerusalem and all Judea" and "all the region of the Jordan" flocking to John the Baptist to confess their sins, which the narrator will provide in 3:5, forms an important counterbalance to the negative portrayal of the Jerusalem populace in 2:3. Moreover, if we understand that populace as representing specifically the city itself, then another contrast appears, reinforcing the point of the quotation regarding Bethlehem in 2:6. Although the Messiah is rejected in Jerusalem, the center of corrupt power, he is accepted in humble Bethlehem. So at this point, at least, we cannot speak of a blanket condemnation of the Jewish people as such (see also pp. 156–58 on 21:41, 43, and "The Crowds"/ "The People," pp. 191–92).

It should also be said that the inclusion of Gentiles is itself in no way anti-Jewish, because there was a significant strain in Hebrew thought itself that envisioned such inclusion at the time of Israel's restoration. And the image of the magi prostrating themselves before the Christ child is a reflection of this Jewish hope. The fact that worshipers have appeared from among the Gentiles means that the coming age, in which God's salvation will be made available to all, is even now beginning.

However, the image of Gentile worshipers of the Israelite Messiah also raises questions about how Gentile wisdom and God's special disclosures to Israel relate to one another in Matthew. Clearly, the gospel as a whole operates within the framework of Hebrew covenantal thought, and even here it is finally the biblical prophecy that discloses the child's location rather than the visitors' own calculations. However, it is apparently the "pagan" practice of astrology that led them to discover the star in the first place. This implies that the birth of the Messiah does not (despite some commentators) simply negate, but in some sense fulfills, the broad religious consciousness that exists among human beings generally. Contrary to the theology of many, mostly Protestant, interpreters, the line between the human quest for God on the one hand and God's quest for humanity on the other is not so clear in this story.

The account of the magi ends on a note that once again reminds the reader of God's activity in the whole sequence of events. They return home without fulfilling Herod's request for the location of the child, precisely because they are warned in a dream. The theme of divine guidance resounds even more clearly in the following scenes. Joseph himself has three additional dreams (2:13, 19, 22) in which he receives divine instruction.

The narrator's emphasis throughout the infancy cycle on the fulfillment of prophecy, moreover, reinforces a sense of the broader scope of God's action. At 2:15, in relation to the escape into Egypt, the same Greek construction found at 1:22 reappears, translated in the NRSV as "to fulfill what had been spoken by the Lord through the prophet …" Later, at 2:23 an equivalent construction explains the family's settlement at Nazareth: "so that what had been spoken through the prophets might be fulfilled." One effect of such repetition is to familiarize the reader with a formulary grammatical construction that will recur. The more important effect is to reemphasize the point that in the events of Jesus' life, God is fulfilling the promises made in the prophets' writings.

The introduction to the quotation in 2:17 contributes to this reinforcement but also adds subtle qualifications. For here the narrator replaces the purposive conjunctions of the other three constructions with an adverb of time, resulting in the rendering of the NRSV, "*Then* was fulfilled what had been spoken." Although the reader is supposed to accept the escape to Egypt and the settlement at Nazareth as fulfilling not only prophecy but also God's intentions, this is apparently not the case with Herod's murder of the male children in an attempt to exterminate his rival. The narrator apparently wants to say that this horrific act was anticipated by prophecy but not that God caused it to happen.

The account of Herod's slaughter of the children serves a number of narrative functions. First, it confirms the necessity of the flight to Egypt, which in turn sets the stage for the return to Israel and eventual settlement in Nazareth. It also brings more fully into view the theme of conflict, and it does so in such a way as to alert the reader that Jesus' life is in danger. And, finally, it not only reinforces the reader's negative view of Herod but also confirms the view that he is not the *true* King of the Jews.

The reader will hear a number of echoes in the motifs of danger, flight, and return. The theme of the endangered royal child was widespread in ancient literature, and the reader will notice parallels with the early life of Moses—who escaped danger in childhood and who later fled the place of his birth and returned. Subtler but no less important is the hint of a parallel between Jesus and Israel itself. Not only does the return of Jesus from Egypt call up the image of the exodus, but Hosea 11.1—the passage quoted at

2:15 in conjunction with the fulfillment formula—is also in its context in the Jewish Scriptures a direct reference to that event. It is uncertain whether the reader is expected to make that specific association or simply to accept the Messianic reading as the meaning of the text, but it would be consistent with ancient ways of interpreting scripture to embrace both meanings. The parallels with Moses invite the reader to understand Moses as a typological foreshadowing of Jesus—that is to say, as a "type" or pattern to which Jesus conforms—and Jesus as in some (superior) sense repeating the deeds of Moses. Similarly, the reader can view Jesus the individual Son of God as somehow embodying the entire experience of God's collective child Israel.

The narrator, however, does not quite call Jesus Son of God at this point. The quotation from Hosea is only a hint. But it does build on the image of the magi's prostration before the Christ child and, more importantly, foreshadows the narrator's later explicit use of the title.

The typological correspondence between Jesus and Moses or Jesus and Israel is foreign territory to the modern reader but familiar ground to the ancients. Its force is to play up the continuity of God's action in history. When Joshua (along with other figures in the Jewish Scriptures and later tradition) performs deeds similar to those of Moses, or when Peter and Paul do the same in relation to Jesus in Acts, the reader learns how to recognize a pattern in the way God acts through human representatives. With that recognition comes a sense of assurance: Joshua's Moses-like deeds attest that he too represents God, and the continuity between the events in Jesus' life and God's actions in the past give further testimony to his identity. It is important to note that the typological correspondence defines Jesus' identity precisely by stressing God's activity *through* Jesus and not by proposing any abstract or metaphysical understanding of his status. It is still true to say, however, that in Matthew, Jesus is born Son of God, and the narrator will have much more to say about his identity as the story proceeds.

Thinking Today about Matthew 1:1—2:23

The Power of God as Problem

The opening chapters of Matthew present the action of God in a way that is likely to strike some readers in our own time as quite naïve. The world of these chapters is one in which divinely inspired dreams guide human actions to accomplish God's purposes, history proceeds in such a neatly ordered way that it conforms to a precise mathematical pattern, and both ancient prophecies and the actions of individuals in the past foreshadow what is happening in the present.

Such credulity is not absent from our own culture. Persons of all ages soak up television "documentaries" or tabloid accounts that interpret current events as literal fulfillments of predictions made in past ages, without regard to any standards of logical consistency or sound methods of historical investigation. We have even produced the astonishing phenomenon of persons who neither identify with the Christian or Jewish faith, nor even believe in God, but who are perfectly willing to entertain the notion that the apocalyptic segments of the Bible contain a reliable outline of our collective future! The question, however, is the extent to which such credulity constitutes a genuine openness on which we can build and the extent to which it is a barrier to genuine engagement with the biblical text.

A particular challenge of Matthew 1—2 is how to make sense of the proclamation of God's guidance of the historical process. The most creative wrestling with this problem, in my opinion, will not result from an insistence that a faithful response to Matthew means a literal acceptance of such notions as Jesus' Davidic ancestry or God's unilateral control of history. If, however, we simply dismiss Matthew's witness to God's action in history, we completely deface the story as it stands written and replace it with a more convenient, but less compelling, story of our own. Our task is to integrate a variety of notions: the biblical sense of God's activity in the world, our contemporary perceptions of our own free will, and the reality of powerful causal forces beyond our control.

This task will demand reflection on the nature of the language of the biblical text, and some of the elements in Matthew 1—2 can in an indirect way provide important assistance in this process. Rather than viewing the blatantly unhistorical nature of the genealogy and the "manipulation" of passages of the Jewish Scriptures as embarrassments in need of apology, we ought to see these phenomena as important clues regarding the mode of meaning that the texts themselves call forth.

The genealogy provides a good illustration of how religious language speaks first of all to the imaginative and intuitive aspects of the psyche and secondarily to the rational and empirical. Apparently unconcerned about historical fact, it presents a broad witness to Jesus' Davidic lineage because it operates within the thought-world of Davidic messianism. It is one of many attestations to Jesus' identity as the one through whom God initiates the divine Rule in the world. But what if the contemporary interpreter should conclude that Jesus was not in fact of Davidic ancestry? Although at some level the text demands that the reader integrate its witness into a coherent understanding, such an understanding need not be that which is presupposed in Matthew itself. Is biological Davidic or royal lineage a literal prerequisite for the messianic role, or can it serve simply as a metaphorical witness to the claim that in Jesus God does in fact in some way accomplish the messianic task?

Similar considerations should inform our approach of the story of Herod's murder of the children. M. Eugene Boring has noted that, although the revision of the fulfillment formula in 2:17 absolves God of causing this atrocity, it does not speak to the deeper question of why God saved only Jesus and not the others. This is a question, Boring argues, that must be approached by taking note of the nature of religious language. He therefore distinguishes the truth function of such language from its strictly literal and logical sense:

> Such language becomes problematic if it is objectified as though it reported a literal event that a spectator could observe and from which logical inferences could be drawn…The truth function of such language is that it serves to confess authentic faith, but cannot legitimately be made a link in a chain of inferences in the objective world. (*The Gospel of Matthew*, 149)

I would add only this: Although it is a misunderstanding of the language of the story to extend its logic beyond the bounds of its story-world, actual readers do live beyond that story-world and bring to it their own concerns and questions. We should therefore honor the power of the story to invite an engagement with the problem of theodicy—the justice of God. Behind the images of divine intervention on behalf of Jesus stands the notion of a literally all-powerful deity who works in human history by way of direct intervention. Is it possible, however, that a dialogue between Matthew's world and our own could help conceive of God's action in terms of a different model—perhaps that of a persuasion rather than a coercion—that avoids the logical conundrum of a loving deity who saves one child but not another? (for further reflections on the problem of divine power, see "The Power of God Revisited," pp. 119–22).

Patriarchy, Monarchy, and Undercurrents

Similar dialogue is also crucial in dealing with the tensions surrounding the role of women in Matthew 1—2. In many ways, the gospel of Matthew remains within the world of patriarchy and male domination, even though at various points it makes a partial break with it. It is therefore important to claim neither too much nor too little for Matthew in relation to the contemporary struggle of women for full equality. To the extent that the material in Matthew 1—2 remains tied to patriarchal values, it is fair game for a feminist critique that exposes the ways in which those values permeate the biblical texts. But to the extent that elements in the text depart from those values, they create competing strains of meaning that the reader must consider. It is therefore appropriate for the experiences of contemporary persons in the struggle for women's rights to draw on the presence of women in Matthew's genealogy and on the motif of the virgin birth itself as resources in that struggle.

If the patriarchal framework of the story is problematic from our contemporary perspective, this is no less the case with regard to Matthew's royal imagery. It is arguable that the persistence of such imagery in Christian worship has dulled our sensitivity to the more prophetic, egalitarian, and liberating dimensions of biblical thought. We should therefore pay attention to the way in which elements of Matthew's narrative stand in tension with hierarchical ways of thinking. The Davidic ideology was one of the powerful strains of meaning that gave strength to the Jewish faith of the period, and it is not surprising that early Christians drew on it. The royal imagery served as assurance that the human person and group are not alone and abandoned in a sea of conflicting forces. The ideal king cares for the people, and many persons through the years have felt this aspect of the imagery. Nevertheless, the presence of tensive undercurrents even in stories that draw heavily on this mode of thinking should warn us against viewing that tradition as monolithic and sensitize us to its oppressive aspects. These undercurrents should also encourage the contemporary interpreter to find ways of expressing the announcement of God's rule that do not perpetuate the legitimization of hierarchical structures.

3:1—4:16 The Inaugural Events

Although 3:1 brings a shift of scene, and although the reader will soon discover that much time has passed because Jesus appears as an adult in verse 13, the narrator has drawn a close connection between chapters 2 and 3 through a conjunction (*de* = "and" or "but") that does not usually find expression in English translations. Although the phrase "[i]n those days" in the Jewish Scriptures often designates the beginning of a new period, in the present case that new period has already begun with the life of Jesus. What follows immediately is still in some sense preparatory.

The preparatory character of 3:1–12 is in fact evident in the story's conclusion: John the Baptist points beyond himself to the greater one who will come after him. The figure of John, however, is not insignificant, for all the details about him—his words, his personal appearance, and the scene of his ministry—contribute to the reader's understanding of the broader narrative.

Immediately, the narrator sets the stage by locating John in the wilderness. Outside the bounds of organized society, the wilderness was a place of danger, populated with demons. Yet Hebrew tradition also knew the wilderness as the scene of God's early encounters with the people of Israel—a place where they were tested and failed, but where God was present with them. The description of John's dress and diet reinforce the sense of being outside social boundaries and is consistent with the narrator's later identification of him with the prophet Elijah (11:14).

John's message—repentance in the face of the imminence of the rule (or kingdom) of heaven (an alternative term, preferred in Matthew, for rule of God)—intensifies a theme already in the genealogy and infancy cycle. We may characterize this theme as "eschatology," which is commonly defined as the "doctrine of the last things," but it does not necessarily indicate "the end of the world" as popularly understood. It has to do with the dramatic end of one age and the beginning of another, in which God completely reorders human society.

In this passage, in combination with the rich symbolism of the wilderness, the call to eschatological repentance suggests a major social upheaval. Although the contemporary reader's image of repentance is likely shaped by the individualistic presuppositions of modern society, the ancient reader would have understood John's call as directed to Israel as a whole and therefore involving a challenge to existing social structures. Preaching and baptizing in the wilderness, John stands as a symbol that something is so radically wrong that the very foundations of society must be shaken. The depth of the problem is evident in that when the Pharisees and Sadducees appear (whether they are seeking baptism is unclear), John sends them away with a bitter insult and a warning that lends a negative tone to his entire message. The emphasis is clearly on God's wrath and judgment; even John's description of the one coming after him is focused on the latter's role as judge.

This note of judgment is subtly linked to the hints in chapters 1—2 regarding the inclusion of Gentiles in God's plan. Through John's pronouncement in 3:9 that "God is able from these stones to raise up children to Abraham," the narrator suggests that God is free to work beyond the bounds of the covenant community when that community fails. It would be wrong, however, to interpret it as a simplistic rejection of Israel as a whole, for although John directs the statement to the Pharisees and Sadducees, it is not a programmatic statement on the status of Israel before God. And, as will be increasingly apparent, the same principle applies to the community of Jesus' followers (see pp. 94–96 on 13:24–30, 36–43 and pp. 155–56 on 22:1–14).

Despite the emphasis on judgment, the notation in verse 6 that those who receive John's baptism confess their sins will remind the reader that it will be the mission of Jesus himself to save the people from their sins (1:21). There is no indication of which specific sins are in view, but John's injunction to "bear fruit" coaches the reader to understand them as concrete negative behaviors that must be replaced by positive deeds. The reader will therefore know that repentance is possible and expresses itself in action; but one still comes to the end of the account of John's preaching focused on the theme of coming judgment.

The reader is also focused, however, on the figure to whom John points and will, based on chapters 1–2, easily identify that figure as Jesus. It is thus no surprise when in the next scene Jesus appears and John implicitly recognizes him as the coming one by resisting Jesus' request for baptism.

John's resistance (which occurs only in Matthew's version) calls attention to Jesus' superior role in God's scheme of things and gives the narrator the opportunity to explain why the Messiah submits to baptism by the lesser John. Commentators through the centuries have found here an indication of an early form of the notion of the sinlessness of Jesus. Many have therefore argued that Jesus must have received baptism not as an act of repentance from sin but either as a sign of solidarity with sinful humanity or as a commissioning for his mission.

Although almost all New Testament scholars believe that the historical person Jesus was actually baptized by John, our interest here is only in the meaning of the story in Matthew. The theme of John's resistance in this story may in fact stem from a strain of Jewish thought according to which the Messiah must not be tainted by sin. The more evident issue, however, is that of lesser/greater status. As to the specific significance of the act, the narrator gives little help, and the reader must depend entirely on Jesus' reply in 3:15: "it is proper for us in this way to fulfill all righteousness." The simplest explanation of this statement is that Jesus justifies the act solely on the grounds that God has commanded it. Thus, the main point is that Jesus' first public act is one of submission to the will of God. But Jesus' reply also gives a preliminary indication of how important the concept of righteousness will be in the narrative.

This theme of Jesus' obedience is reinforced in the climactic ending of the story, when the voice from heaven announces that God is pleased with him. Because the only action of Jesus of which the reader has knowledge at this point is his submission to baptism, this must be at least the primary basis of the divine evaluation. But the more dramatic elements in the story are the voice itself, accompanied by the descent of the Spirit, and the pronouncement by God's own voice attesting to Jesus as the beloved Son.

Here for the first time Jesus' status as Son of God becomes fully explicit. The narrator has named him Messiah (Christ), Son of David, Son of Abraham, and Emmanuel; and the reader knows that his birth was by the action of the Holy Spirit. Now, however, the testimony is directly from God and the designation of Jesus' status is the highest imaginable: he is God's beloved Son.

It is important, though, to notice that the narrator does not present Jesus' status as Son of God in a merely static way. Although Jesus is born to that status, it nevertheless remains for him to actualize the role. He must fulfill all righteousness, obeying God's will; and the depiction of his action lacks any real function in the plot if the reader takes it as a given, a foregone conclusion. For the story to carry power, one must imagine that Jesus could have acted disobediently, even though in one sense it is evident that he will "do the right thing." In addition, if this is the case with the act of submission to baptism, it is far more so with the scene that follows: the encounter with the devil.

This story of this encounter is generally referred to as "The Temptation," a title that captures only part of the story's substance. The Greek verb *peirazein* can mean either "to tempt" or "to test," but translators usually opt for the sense of temptation in 4:1, because it is the devil who is the active agent. This is probably the best decision, but we must remember that it is the Holy Spirit who drives Jesus into the wilderness, precisely in order to force the confrontation. Thus it is clear that God is in fact testing Jesus, putting him through a kind of initiatory rite whereby he can prove himself worthy of the role he is about to play. This means neither that God and Satan are in league with one another nor that God appears as a harsh and punitive parent; the point—a theme familiar from countless epics—is that the hero is not ready for battle without undergoing a preliminary test of great magnitude.

This theme of testing reaches beyond an emphasis on the individual hero, however, because the story also has clear signs of the Israel-typology that appeared in the account of the escape to Egypt. There is already a subtle suggestion of this typology in the baptism scene, where Jesus' immersion (*baptizein* means "to immerse") in the water has faint overtones of Israel's deliverance at the sea. But it becomes quite transparent in the temptation story, where Jesus' forty days of fasting in the wilderness parallel Israel's forty years of wandering in the desert.

Readers familiar with that tradition would know that this period was for Israel a time of trial or testing (see Deut. 8:2–3) and that the people in many ways failed the test. They grumbled when faced with hunger (Ex. 16:3); they "tested" God (in a reversal of roles!) by quarreling with Moses when faced with thirst (Ex. 17:1–2; Deut. 6:16); and they actually succumbed to idolatry (Ex. 32). Thus, when Jesus himself faces three parallel temptations but resists them, the readers understand that he reverses the earlier failure. He rejects any source of sustenance other than God, he refuses to put God to the test, and he overcomes the temptation to worship something other than God.

From the beginning, the narrator has couched the story in a cosmic framework that presupposes a Hebrew understanding of God as active in human history and related to Israel through a special divinely initiated covenant. So far, however, the opposition to Jesus has appeared only in earthly manifestation, and the theme of conflict has been present only in muted form. Now, however, the narrator locates the seat of opposition in the cosmic source of evil itself and thus invites the reader to focus on all-out confrontation between good and evil with Jesus at its center. From this point, continuing conflict is to be expected; yet the reader already has a sense of the final outcome, because Jesus' victory in the battle of wills seems utterly decisive. For that victory to fulfill its dramatic role, however, the reader must take Jesus' temptations seriously—that is, as confronting him with a genuine choice. The whole point of the story is that Jesus passes the test through which God puts him and thus shows himself worthy and ready to fulfill his role. The narrator in fact plays on the sense of suspense by a skillful buildup, beginning with the legitimate human need of hunger and ending with the blatant offer of power and demand for idolatry.

The focus of the story is thus on Jesus as the Messiah, with a ministry to pursue, who passed successfully through the inaugural stage of that ministry. But there are also lessons for the reader. For not only do Jesus' obedient action and use of scripture model an authentic relationship to God but the narrator's concluding comment also demonstrates that God does not abandon those who trust in the divine promises. Having refused sustenance from another source, Jesus now receives God's own: "and suddenly angels came and waited on him."

For lessons such as this to have impact, however, the reader must accept Jesus as a human being. The hunger must be real; the temptations to test God and commit idolatry must represent meaningful possibilities. Otherwise the victory of obedience is meaningless and its exemplary quality nil. Without any attempt at conceptual clarification, then, the narrator presents Jesus as a human being who is born Messiah and Son of God and whose fulfillment of that role depends on his righteous compliance with what God requires. The reader cannot simply equate Jesus with God but must accept him as God's son—the one through whom God acts to save the people from their sins. How he is to do the latter, however, remains to be seen.

Because Jesus has proved himself obedient, the reader will assume that he is ready to act; and the occasion comes when Jesus learns in 4:12 that John has been arrested (NRSV; more literally, "handed over" or "delivered up"). The final segment of the introductory section, 4:12–16, may appear on the surface as an innocent geographical and chronological notation. It plays an important role, however, in both the plot and the thematic structure of the narrative. The notation about John's arrest stands at this point without elaboration, leaving the reader to speculate on the reason. An explanation will eventually come in 14:1–12, in a retrospective account of John's death, in terms of a personal affront to Herod the tetrarch (Herod Antipas, who assumed the rule of Galilee and Perea at the time of his father Herod the Great's death, when another son, Archelaus, assumed the rule of Judea). For the present, however, the reader will draw on earlier plot elements and understand the arrest against the broad background of developing conflict. John's call to repentance constituted a challenge to the existing order, as did his condemnation of the Pharisees and Sadducees; and as an infant Jesus himself—standing in the royal line of David—had been the object of the wrath of Herod the Great. Thus in the context of the story's announcement of the appearance of the Messiah, both John and Jesus pose clear threats to the established power structure.

John's arrest therefore casts an ominous shadow over Jesus himself, and the narrator will later use the same verb, "handed over" (*paradidonai*), many times in relation to Jesus' own deliverance to the authorities and crucifixion (17:22; 20:18, 19; 26:2; 27:2, 18, 26). The foreboding quality of this event also appears in Jesus' response: "he *withdrew* to Galilee." Later usage of the verb "to withdraw" (*anachorein*) confirms that it carries the full weight of a tactical retreat in the face of opposition; in order to carry out his role, Jesus goes back into Galilee and establishes a base in the village of Capernaum.

Commentators often express puzzlement at this strategy, because Galilee is under Herod Antipas' jurisdiction. But the point is primarily theological: Jesus must base his ministry in Galilee because it provides a symbolic counterpoint to Jerusalem, which is the seat of the opposing power structure. Historically speaking, there was considerable tension between Judea and Galilee. Following the destruction of the northern monarchy of Israel in 721 B.C.E., the conquering Assyrians had settled much of the land with a Gentile population. And although in the first century C.E. it was clearly Jewish territory with some sense of loyalty to Jerusalem, Judeans apparently tended to view the northern region with a bit of condescension and suspicion. Thus in playing up Galilee as the seat of Jesus' messianic activity, the narrator makes an ironical point that picks up on similar notes in chapters 1 and 2.

The fulfillment of God's promises does not necessarily happen in expected ways.

The notation that Jesus begins his ministry not in Nazareth but Capernaum gives an explanation for what the readers would have known as historical fact. More importantly, it provides the opportunity for the use of a scriptural quotation (4:15–16) introduced by the fulfillment formula: Capernaum lies within the region designated by Isaiah 9:1–2, whereas Nazareth does not. The quotation, however, concerns Galilee as such, and it is rich with connotations for the thematic structure of the narrative. The phrase "Galilee of the Gentiles" reinforces earlier hints of the inclusion of non-Jews in God's rule, and the contrast between darkness and death on the one hand and light on the other plays into the broad theme of the dawn of the age of fulfillment—a notion further underscored by the introductory formula itself.

At 4:16, then, the narrator brings the reader back to the beginning point: This is the time in which God's promises will be fulfilled; this is the time of salvation. The reader is thus well prepared to hear the announcement of Jesus in 4:17: "repent, for the rule of heaven has come near" (author's translation). The testimony of narrated events, scripture, the storyteller's commentary, the words of John the Baptist, and even the voice of God from heaven combine to make a bold and powerful claim. The royal Messiah has been born and adopted into the line of David the king. He has, moreover, proved himself obedient to God and victorious over the temptations of Satan. Thus the hope of the Jewish people is now coming to fulfillment, even if paradoxically so, with Gentile magi acknowledging Jesus as Messiah while false Jewish leaders seek his death. He will truly be "God is with us" (see p. 19) and will save the people from their sins—for he is, indeed, the royal Son of God. It is with such thoughts in mind that the reader moves from the introductory phase of the narrative to the narrator's account of the messianic ministry of Jesus.

Thinking Today about Matthew 3:1—4:16

The Imaging of Evil

Heavens opening; descending Spirit and the voice of God; a real, live personal devil who spirits the hero away to temple and mountaintop; calls to repentance in the face of the prospect of unquenchable fire—hardly the stuff of rational conversation in the world in which we live. Yet a remarkable number of contemporary persons, including some well-educated ones, are perfectly willing to take all of this at face value. Why? Because, I think, such persons have looked into the heart and soul of modernity and have found a gaping abyss, an utter vacuum. Given the option between two incompatible worldviews, one that denies all transcendent grounding for meaning in life and support for human values and one that affirms such grounding, they instinctively opt for the latter.

Simplistic acceptance of the ancient worldview brings problems of its own, however. Internal contradictions threaten its coherence, and the discrepancy between its presuppositions and our own concrete experience creates a dissonance that has the potential for genuine pathology. Yet the appeal of a transcendent grounding is enormous. So one challenge in this section of Matthew, as to some extent in the narrative as a whole, is to find ways to honor and appropriate the witness to transcendent reality without negating our own experience.

How meaningful for us is the narrator's attempt to document Jesus' status with a voice from heaven and his worthiness with the story of a temptation by Satan? How meaningful to us are John's call to repentance and his images of a coming judgment? Everything hinges on how we deal with the question of sin and evil. The modern tendency to apply a mental-health model to all destructive behavior has blunted both the reality of evil and the biblical understanding of sin as rebellion against God. Although a psychological approach to the human situation can find some points of contact in the Bible, when we make it the sole category for understanding our problems, we create a reductionism that is in the end incompatible with the most central witness of the scriptures: that God is at work in the world, redeeming it from sin and death. (See also later, "Christian Witness and Social Morality," pp. 76–77.) On the one hand, the human situation is defined precisely by a refusal of God's love that creates a fundamental alienation from our own true nature and from one another. On the other, God enters the world, defeating the forces of evil and restoring the divine Rule of peace and justice. There are perhaps many ways in which one might interpret and elaborate on this point, but apart from some kind of affirmation of it, one does not in fact appropriate the biblical witness.

Only in the context of such an affirmation do the themes of repentance and judgment make sense, but in that context, they are utterly indispensable. If the human problem is in fact sin—if human beings have in fact distorted their relationship to the source of their being and the meaning of their lives—then a fundamental act of reconciliation or redemption is needed. They stand in need of God's forgiveness and are called to a fundamental reorientation of their lives. On the other hand, if there is nothing from which the world needs genuine redemption, as opposed to mere adjustment, then the whole framework within which Jesus appears as Savior collapses.

We will see later ("Sin, Suffering, Society, and Nature," pp. 70–72) that medical metaphors can help us get in touch with some aspect of the gospel of Matthew. But it is no accident that the Matthean narrative establishes the broad context of a conflict between absolute good and absolute evil before telling stories in which Jesus heals the sick; nor is it accidental that these stories are surrounded by tales of the exorcism of demonic spirits.

The figure of the devil plays the crucial roles of symbolizing concretely the cosmic character of the conflict that drives the plot and of giving evil a name and a face. In the encounter in the wilderness, Jesus' victory over this concretized enemy speaks to the reader at a level much deeper than the rational mind. So the question of whether this story can be meaningful to a modern reader hinges on whether one is prepared to acknowledge the reality of evil.

That question brings the reader back to her or his own experience in the world. Attention to some aspects of that experience makes it problematic to accept the framework within which the Bible presents its images of evil and redemption. Nevertheless, those images present an important challenge to a worldview that has either dismissed transcendence altogether or reduced it to a vague sense of spiritual presence. Hellfire, a final judgment, and a personal devil probably make little sense in our world if we understand them literally. But the very fact that many people still try to do that should remind us of their imaginative power.

Our contemporary experience warns us against treating evil too simplistically, for two primary reasons. First, what appears evil from one perspective might not from another. Second, there is strong evidence from both biology and psychology that much of what we could once pronounce as moral evil is in fact largely the result of factors beyond the control of individual human will.

Nevertheless, the modern tendency to deny evil is equally simplistic. To write off our aversion to instances of mass murder such as the Holocaust and other blatant violations of human rights as a matter of mere taste, cultural conditioning, or biological predisposition is to deprive the human conscience of its very base. It is to deny the irreducible claim on our lives made by the very presence of others in the world and to render any moral or religious witness utterly meaningless. Likewise, to push our recognition that all human actions are influenced by biological, social, and psychological factors to the point of denying our freedom and responsibility altogether is to opt for an oversimplified account of our own experience. We know ourselves to be subject to influence, but we are also aware of a measure of free will. When we are completely honest with ourselves, we find it necessary to admit responsibility for our actions even as we acknowledge forces that weigh heavily on us. And with acceptance of responsibility comes the necessity to face the reality of evil.

Thus it is precisely because our experience is complex that the ancient images of a devil and a Messiah who defeats him can speak to us. To know ourselves as free and responsible on the one hand but fragile and malleable under the influence of destructive forces on the other is to find ourselves reaching out for a kind of help that neither mere moral injunction nor psychotherapy alone can remedy. If our contemporary experience discourages acceptance of a personal devil, it also contains elements that force recognition of tendencies within ourselves and our social systems that can and do work themselves out in ways that do blatant harm to human persons and the environment. In that way it is perhaps not so different after all from the experience of our ancient forebears who spoke more easily of evil.

The Point of the Christological Claim

Appreciation of the imaginative power of this material does not preclude critical assessment. The whole point of this segment of material is to attest Jesus as the Son of God who has proved himself obedient to God's will and victorious over Satan's temptations. Wherever skeptical modern readers come down on the question of evil, they will hardly find these stories convincing in any literal sense as proofs of Jesus' status. So, at this point, the critical reader comes on the problem of how to appropriate Matthew's christological scheme and such concepts as Messiah, Son of David, and Son of God. This question will demand repeated attention throughout the commentary, but a preliminary statement is in order.

It is extremely unlikely that ancient writers intended material such as this to constitute anything like what we mean by "proof" in the modern world. These stories had significant meaning and power only within the life of an ongoing community in which faith in Jesus as Son of God was proclaimed in worship and lived out concretely on both the personal and collective levels. In such a context, "proof" was hardly to the point, but witness was. Even in the ancient context, such material functioned primarily on the level of metaphor and proclamation. To present a story in which God declares Jesus' identity from heaven is not to amass "evidence" but to offer this story as a representation of a truth of which one is convinced largely on other grounds.

But what specific value might such a story have for us? The crucial point is that the gospels present Jesus as acting on God's behalf. In one sense, the overriding question is that of his identity; in another sense, however, this is not the question at all. For acceptance or rejection of Jesus is above all a statement on who one understands God to be—that is, on what specific characteristics one ascribes to God. The tantalizing vagueness in the gospels about what it means for Jesus to *be* the Son of God shows that something more is at work than the issue about whether Jesus should be plugged into preexisting categories defined by the titles the New Testament assigns him. The fact is that the proclamation of Jesus as the Christ entails considerable disruption of earlier "messianic" expectations, which were of broad and diverse character. One hallmark of all four gospels is that Jesus does not in fact fit standard expectations.

The issue of whether Jesus is Messiah and Son of God opens into the question of what God is truly like. And this means that a decision about Jesus is utterly dependent on the concrete stories in which he manifests a particular understanding of the character of God and God's will for the world. The whole story is thus important; one does not grasp the significance of the mythically adorned scenes of the baptism and temptation apart from the tales yet to come of his teachings, deeds, death, and resurrection. It will take all of this for the narrator to say who God is, according to the story of Jesus.

4:17—16:20

The Public Ministry of Jesus

4:17–25 The Ministry Begins

The initial phrase in 4:17, "[f]rom that time," indicates a turn in the narrative, and the remainder of the sentence defines the direction of that turn. Jesus has now begun his public ministry, which is defined by his proclamation, "Repent, for the kingdom of heaven has come near."

This summary of Jesus' message repeats the message of John the Baptist in 3:2, giving the reader a strong sense of continuity between these two agents of God. But a closer reading reveals discontinuity also. In John's subsequent words in 3:7–10, the emphasis is on repentance in the face of the coming judgment; and in verses 11–12, John characterizes the one coming after him as eschatological judge. The words and deeds of Jesus that follow immediately after 4:17, however, are far from judgmental. In 4:18–22, he calls four disciples to follow him, without mentioning repentance, and in verses 23–25, the narrator summarizes his activities in terms of "proclaiming the good news (*euangelion*, gospel) of the kingdom" and healing people plagued by various maladies and possessed by demons.

Although John and Jesus preach the same message, then, they play up different aspects of it. If John's words of judgment build on the sequential structure of the message—the call to repentance precedes the announcement of the coming of the kingdom of heaven—Jesus' actions focus on the logical structure. The at-handness of the kingdom is actually the basis of repentance, as is expressed in the conjunction "for." This means that the themes of repentance and judgment are secondary to God's gracious action. Jesus calls disciples without reference to any prior qualifications, and he heals people freely, with no hint that their faith or righteousness has made them worthy. He thus not only preaches the good news of the imminent kingdom but also acts it out, delivering its benefits to suffering humanity.

The term "kingdom of heaven" is a circumlocution for "kingdom of God." Both phrases reflect the language of imagery and symbolism, not of systematic thought. Behind them lies the rich Hebrew notion of God's activity (analogous to that of a monarch) in ruling the universe and, secondarily, the sphere of that activity. Recent interpreters have suggested such terms as "reign" or "rule" as better renderings; but what is most important to understand is that the phrase has a long history and suggests a wide range of meanings.

Early on, Hebrew thought recognized God as the ruler of the universe, and one strain of thought that eventually developed used the terminology of God's rule to refer to the continual activity through which God wielded cosmic power. But the notion of God's rule was closely associated with the ideals of justice and peace. And when in the course of history the hope for the realization of the vision of a world wholly responsive to God was repeatedly dashed, some religious visionaries in Israel came to think of God's rule as lying in the future, beyond a dramatic divine intervention into history. Thus by the time of Jesus there was a strong strain of apocalyptic teaching that drew heavily on imagery depicting a cosmic breakup and renewal in speaking of that future rule of God. Also belonging to this strain were the innovative notions—not earlier known in earlier Hebrew thought—of the resurrection of the dead, eternal life, Satan, and eternal punishment for the wicked.

Nevertheless, the notion of God's rule never lost its connection to concrete, this-worldly reality and the hope for peace and justice in actual human society. It is only if we insist on taking images literally and seeking conceptual consistency in imaginative language that we are forced to think of the rule of God/heaven as a purely futuristic, other-worldly reality utterly distinct from the concrete world of human experience.

When we seek to interpret Jesus' announcement in Matthew 4:17 that the rule of heaven has come near, we will distort the text if we think it refers in simplistic terms either to "the end of the world" on the one hand or to a humanly designed just society on the other, for 4:17 cannot be reduced in either direction. It does point forward to a dramatic action of God, but it also refers to the present; and Jesus' first discourse in chapters 5—7 will describe the process of living in God's rule in the here and now. The reader's task is not to develop a systematic concept of that rule or to lay out a timeline for its arrival but to recognize its meaning for human existence.

The healings in verses 23–25 spell out one dimension of that meaning—human well-being—and also serve as a subtle indicator of the mode through which the rule of heaven actually dawns. In verses 18–22, Peter, Andrew, and the sons of Zebedee make the decision to follow Jesus, and in the subsequent verses, the people of Galilee bring to him the sick and demon-possessed. The reader will thus be aware that the concrete manifestations of the rule appear precisely when human beings respond to Jesus' words through their own concrete actions.

If verses 18–25 address the meaning of God's rule through narrative, Jesus' first discourse in chapters 5—7 will do so through explicit teaching. That discourse, as we will shortly see, is a tightly organized body of material that can be, and often is, read as an isolated unit. It is also, however, fully integrated into the Matthean story, and we miss its function in that writing if we do not pay attention to its context. The most important point is that it is spoken against the background of 4:17, 23, the narrator's summaries of Jesus' message as centered on the rule of heaven. But it is also crucial that the reader comes to the discourse with two sets of images fresh in mind. The first of these concerns those who are following Jesus. He has called four disciples, and all immediately leave what they are doing and come after him. The radical character of their action is underscored by the notation that James and John leave their father. The second set of images are those of the various people Jesus has healed. Thus when the narrator indicates in verse 25 that, in addition to the disciples, great crowds follow him, the reader will assume that it is because of these acts of mercy and power.

The net effect of this preparation for the discourse is that the reader will approach it not only as teaching related to the imminent rule of heaven but also as directed especially toward those who intend to follow Jesus. More specifically, church members will see in the disciples prototypes of themselves, whereas perhaps those who are not yet Christians will identify with the crowds. In either case, the reader will be prepared to hear Jesus' words as spelling out more explicitly the meaning in the here and now of his announcement that God's rule has drawn near.

Thinking Today about Matthew 4:17–25

The Coming Rule of Heaven

The image of the rule of God/heaven has been one of the most powerful elements in Christian testimony through the centuries, but it has also been at the core of many a controversy and has spawned dangerous and destructive attitudes. A major source of inspiration for both the social gospel and a liberation theology, it has also formed the basis of otherworldly ideologies that either remove Christian communities from the concrete world of sociopolitical realities or lead them into severely separatist mentalities that can result in outright hatred of human culture.

Much of the difficulty stems from an exclusive identification of God's rule with a particular form of eschatology, or doctrine of the "last things"— the belief in a literal end of history that will take the form of a cosmic upheaval. There is, to be sure, much language in the New Testament that suggests such a notion; indeed, Matthew 24 is an example. But one of the more important insights regarding the rule of God in recent scholarship is Norman Perrin's identification of the phrase rule of God/heaven as a symbol rather than a concept (*Jesus and the Language of the Kingdom*, p. 5). We should therefore resist the temptation to give a precise definition of the term and explore instead its intended impact on ancient audiences in an effort to discover potential meaning for our contemporary world. So it is important to get a sense of how it actually functions in specific contexts.

In our present passage, the phrase is connected to repentance and leads into brief narratives describing the disciples' response to Jesus and Jesus' gracious actions of healing. It also comes shortly before the Sermon on the Mount, which defines the ethics of God's rule in concrete terms. In addition, it follows Jesus' victory over Satan in the desert and the narrator's claim that Jesus' actions fulfill a prophecy of Isaiah and constitute a light that shines in the midst of death. It is thus neither a pallid reference to human efforts at building social structures nor a simplistic announcement of the "end of the world" but rather a rich metaphor for God's action that is both continuous with past divine action and dramatically new.

The image of the rule of God/heaven cannot be disconnected from the themes of peace and justice, but neither can it be abstracted from the notion of God's past, present, and future action in the world. It is inherently eschatological in that it looks forward to an action of God that results in the reordering of human society, but it is also focused on the concrete realities of human life in the actual world. It is thus important to find ways to relate this image to the world we know without falling into any of these three common pitfalls: a purely futuristic reading that tends to allow the hope for divine intervention to negate the need for social activism, a "modernist" approach that reduces the announcement of God's action to a call for human endeavor, an individualism that locates God's rule in one's heart and thus ignores its collective dimension.

If the rule of God/heaven is understood as symbol or metaphor, the contemporary reader can interpret Jesus' announcement of its imminence as a witness to the conviction that God has acted, is acting, and will act in order to repair that alienation in all its forms. The image of Jesus healing the sick and demon-possessed in verses 23–25 portrays that divine action concretely, just as that of the disciples' decision to follow Jesus portrays the human element in the equation. The coming of God's rule is not the result of human effort, but it calls forth a human response.

Despite the symbolic/metaphorical nature of biblical language regarding God's rule, contemporary Christians may also want some conceptual clarity in their appropriation of it. It is important to dispel the notion that such language conveys a hard and fast concept, precisely in order to encourage contemporary but provisional ways of making sense of it. A fruitful way of fostering a dialogue between the biblical worldview and our own would be to ask whether we should understand God's rule as a final and changeless state that we expect in the future (whether in this life or beyond it) or as an ongoing process.

Our habit is to think more in terms of a changeless state, but that habit is rooted less in genuine attention to biblical texts than in certain Greek thought patterns that Christians adopted soon after the New Testament period. The Greeks held changelessness as an ideal, whereas the Hebrews had a more dynamic understanding of reality. And that dynamic understanding is in some ways similar to visions of reality that have developed in the twentieth century. Our contemporary thought-world is largely determined by images of evolutionary process and pulsating energy, but when we approach the Bible, we unconsciously shift gears and try to think in terms of changelessness—whether about God or God's rule. Perhaps, however, we should experiment with understandings of both that make use of the category of creative and purposeful change rather than static perfection. How would the image of the coming of the rule of heaven affect our thinking and acting if we would cease to imagine it as a far-off state of absolute perfection and envision it as the ongoing process through which God creates peace and justice in creation?

Another aspect of 4:17–25 that merits serious reflection is the relationship between the coming of God's rule and our own response. If the priority of God's action in Jesus' proclamation at 4:17 indicates that human beings do not "build" that rule through their own efforts, the subsequent verses nevertheless indicate the crucial role that Jesus' followers play in the drama. There is thus a subtle tension between God's action in inaugurating the rule of heaven and the implicit dependence of its coming upon human response. In addition, this tension offers a fruitful point of departure for those willing to rethink traditional models of divine power, for one way of honoring the complexity of the text is to conceive of God's rule and human decision in fully reciprocal terms. Granted the logical priority of the action of God, it would capture much of the spirit of the text to say that although human response depends on God's decision to bring the rule of heaven near, that rule in fact dawns precisely when human beings decide to enter it (repent). Whereas it is thoroughly unbiblical to speak of "building God's rule," it is a legitimate appropriation of the symbol "rule of God" to invite one's hearers to foster that rule by allowing it to become manifest in one's own personal/communal experience in the world.

For comments on the broader question of how contemporary persons can understand the notion of an act of God without either falling into a naïve understanding of God's action or depriving the text of a powerful component of its witness, see, "The Power of God as Problem," pp. 24–26).

5:1—7:27 The First Discourse

The Rule of Heaven in the Community of Faith (The Sermon on the Mount)

5:1–16 The Beatitudes and Metaphors of Salt and Light

In 5:1, the narrator indicates that Jesus ascends a mountain because of the crowds following him, implying that he is trying to escape them, in order to teach his disciples. Following the sermon, however, the reader learns in 7:28 that the crowds too have heard the teaching and are astonished by it. The reader must thus recognize two audiences: the disciples, already enlisted in Jesus' cause, and the crowds, who remain interested but neutral. The crowds command the reader's attention in two ways. First, within the framework of the plot, suspense emerges as one wonders whether they will eventually become disciples. Beyond their role in the plot, they stand for all persons—whether in Jesus' time or in the time of the church—who remain outside the community of Jesus' followers as a potential mission field.

Jesus has as yet called only four of the twelve who will constitute an inner circle and whom the narrator will term *apostles* at 10:2. Thus he addresses them as followers per se and not as a leadership group; and the reader may legitimately imagine, based on verses 23–25 and knowledge of a broader use of the term *disciple,* a wider circle of committed followers than those named explicitly. The reader will therefore accept the primary audience as prototypes of members of the later community, not of church officials. In any case, the teaching reaches beyond its narrative function and addresses the reader directly: the point is to hear not only what Jesus taught someone else but also what he says to the reader now.

The nine "beatitudes" that begin the discourse place everything that is to follow in the context of God's gracious gift. Having already described Jesus' ministry as involving both the proclamation of the rule of heaven and the performance of works of mercy (4:25–27), the narrator now has Jesus begin his first discourse with the pronouncement of God's blessing. And that blessing consists not of "happiness" in the merely psychological sense but of a deeper assurance of God's approval. This gift is explicitly associated with the rule of heaven in the first, seventh, and ninth beatitudes, and the future tense in verses 4–9 attests that this rule is not yet present in its fullness. Nevertheless, the blessings apply to the present, and the reader will understand that a foretaste of the future reward is operative now.

Many scholars have puzzled over the difference between Matthew's version of the first beatitude and that of Luke 6:20. Because Matthew has "poor in spirit" in place of "poor," most interpreters have argued that the author Matthew changed the Q (see Introduction, p. 1) text in order to "spiritualize" its meaning, so that it no longer refers to those who are literally poor but to those who recognize their own spiritual poverty. A number of recent interpreters, however, have proposed alternatives. Most convincing to my mind is the suggestion of Mark Allan Powell (*God with Us*, pp. 119–144).

Powell argues that the first four beatitudes refer to persons in unfortunate circumstances. The poor in spirit are not the spiritual elite but those so beaten down by circumstances that they are unable to hope. Similarly, in verse 5 the Greek term *praüs*, generally rendered "meek" or "humble," takes on the sense of "the humiliated" as it does in the Septuagint version of Zechariah 3:12. The humiliated "inherit the land" (*ges*, land, earth, ground) precisely because they are presently disinherited, just as mourners in verse 4 appropriately receive comfort (see also p. 82 on 11:29). Finally, in verse 6, the specific connotations of the term *dikaiosyne*, which is usually translated here as "righteousness," are best captured by the alternative "justice." Those who "hunger and thirst" are not seeking progress in piety but liberation from oppression. Good deeds do figure into the equation, however, in the fifth through eighth beatitudes in which Jesus commends those who do works of mercy and peace, perform them with integrity (purity of heart), and suffer in the process (v. 10).

At its beginning, then, the discourse combines a declaration of God's grace, in the form of blessings, with an implicit demand. Jesus pronounces blessings first on those who suffer; but in extending the blessings to those who seek to alleviate suffering, he invites the hearer/reader to join that latter group. The invitation becomes even clearer in the ninth beatitude (vv. 11–12), for here he shifts from the third person to the second ("Blessed are *you*") and personalizes both the blessing and the persecution that attend his followers.

Verses 13 and 14 underscore the personalizing effect of the final beatitude by using a Greek construction that emphasizes the second person plural pronoun: "*You* are the salt of the earth/ *You* are the light of the world." The effect is to underscore that Jesus speaks specifically to his followers and by implication to the later community. The communal context of the readers is further indicated by the familial phrase in verse 16: "your [plural] Father in heaven." In the context of Jesus' announcement of the imminent rule of God/heaven, the invitation into the circle of his followers is also an invitation into the household in which God rules precisely as father. Because Jesus has already been identified as the Son of God (2:15; 3:17), the reader will understand that those who follow him share his familial relationship with God.

The indicative mood that prevails through verse 15 again suggests the operation of God's grace, but with the appearance of the imperative in verse 16, the quality of the discourse as radical demand becomes explicit. The thrust of the salt/city/light metaphors in verses 13–16 is that Jesus' demand consists precisely in good works that will give glory to God, mirroring the fifth through eighth beatitudes and the description of Jesus' ministry in 4:25–27. Whatever specific qualities of salt the reader is to imagine, the general point is clear: the role of the community is to minister to the world in which it finds itself and thus witness to the goodness of God. This role is consistent with the ninth beatitude, which compares the persecution of those who follow Jesus with the treatment of the prophets of old. In its attempts to function as salt and light within the larger society, the community must expect opposition.

5:17–48 Jesus and the Jewish Law

Opposition to Jesus' message is presupposed in the verses that follow. His disclaimer in verse 17, "Do not think that I have come to abolish the law or the prophets," implies that someone has accused him, and by extension also the later community that witnesses in his name, of doing precisely that. Thus the strong endorsement in verses 18–19 of the continuing validity of the law refutes this charge and reaffirms the link with the Israelite tradition that has been evident from the beginning of the story.

This link involves more than the Torah per se. Jesus denies abolishing either the law *or the prophets*, thereby pointing to the Hebrew Scriptures as a whole. Although the precise meaning of the verb "fulfill" in this passage is debated, it seems to entail two elements. As verses 21–28 will show, Jesus fulfills the law through his teaching; but the reference to "the prophets" reinforces a point made earlier in the fulfillment quotations (1:22; 2:23; etc.): His life and ministry bring about precisely what the prophets foretold. The broad context of a lengthy discourse nevertheless makes the teaching aspect primary.

As a further defense against criticism, the phrase "I have come" in verse 17 stresses Jesus' authoritative status. But verse 20 concludes the passage with a counterattack. By contrasting the righteousness expected of his followers with that of the scribes and Pharisees, Jesus implicitly disputes these groups' own reading of the Law. The point is that what he is about to say brings out the true intention and meaning of the Law, and this teaching—not the teaching or practice of his opponents—should be his followers' guide to behavior.

The final emphasis of verses 17–20 is thus on the practical issue of what is required of disciples. In the immediate context of a discussion of the law and the broader context of the discourse as a whole, the term *dikaiosyne* in verse 20 must refer to right/just action in the specific sense of human deeds in conformity with God's will. By demanding a "righteousness" exceeding that of the scribes and Pharisees, Jesus asks for a particular quality of obedience to God. This emphasis on right action is in my estimation the clue to the difficult phrase at the end of verse 18: "until all is accomplished." Far from an indication that the Law is after all abolished by Jesus' fulfillment of prophecy, it means that the law remains in order that the will of God will finally be done. That is to say, the Law remains so that human beings may at last—now that the full meaning of the Law is in view—render true obedience.

It is immediately apparent at 5:21, however, that Jesus' teaching does more than merely explain the Law. If verses 17–20 show that Jesus neither negates the Law nor replaces the "old" one with a new (messianic) one, the striking formula, "You have heard/But I say unto you," shifts the locus of authority from the Law to Jesus himself. The Greek construction of the second part of the formulation is emphatic ("*I*, however, say to you…"), and the first part ("it was said to those of ancient times") sets Jesus' words in tension not merely with scribal interpretation but with the words of the Torah itself. The conjunction *de*, usually translated here as "but" (I say unto you), does not necessarily indicate sharp contrast, and it can even be translated "and." Nevertheless, the content of the six "but I say unto you" pronouncements in verses 21–48 goes beyond the Law in various ways.

Scholars debate the appropriateness of descriptions such as "interpretation" of the Law on the one hand and "transcendence" of it on the other. Clearly, Jesus requires more than the Torah requires. In some instances, this means simply looking behind deeds in order to address motivation and disposition, and there is no hint of contradiction of the Law. In others, however, Jesus' pronouncements close off provisions that the Law explicitly makes (divorce, swearing/vows, retribution), and thus in some sense they contradict it. However, this means neither that Jesus' teaching annuls the Law nor that it merely stands above it as another category. Rabbinic interpreters themselves, who believed that the Law was unchanging, sometimes gave innovative interpretations that amounted to revision. Perhaps, then, we can say that in Matthew, Jesus interprets the Law, but he does so by seeing through it to God's primordial will to which he, as Messiah, has access. If he transcends the Law, he does so not by introducing an alternative category but by dealing with its true meaning and intention. On a theoretical level, the Law remains in all its details; yet it is Jesus' own pronouncements, in some instances at odds with the actual wording of the Torah, that are functionally authoritative.

It is important, however, to clarify the sense in which the teachings in verses 21–48 appear as authoritative. Because they address concrete situations with specific commands, there is a tendency to take them as literal and simplistic rules of behavior. Their severely limited scope, however, shows that they do not function as an exhaustive statement of Jesus' messianic teaching or interpretation of the Law, but as examples. This means that the community of readers must be responsible for the extension and application of this teaching.

This insight is in keeping with Robert Tannehill's classic analysis of 5:39b–42 as an example of "focal instance" (*The Sword of His Mouth*, pp. 67–77), which involves two points that are crucial for understanding how these verses function. First, "[b]ecause the four commands are formally parallel, they constitute a series. The effect of such a series is to establish a pattern which can be extended to other instances." Second, the very nature of the commands resists literal application and pushes the hearer/reader into an imaginative mode of thought. The slap on the right cheek indicates an extreme insult, and the situation envisioned in verse 40 is that of a very poor person, sued for an inner garment, who now gives up the outer garment (protected by law) and stands naked before the court. Verse 41 counsels a person to go beyond the Roman Empire's requirement to carry a soldier's equipment a stipulated distance when so ordered. The final verse commands almsgiving and lending in absolute statements that make no attempt to differentiate between different types of circumstances and degrees of need. All these actions are barely possible, but their extreme and unqualified character suggests that their function is less to prescribe specific behavior than to provoke reexamination of normally accepted ways of acting.

What is generally accepted in human societies is to exercise some reason and discretion in generosity, to recognize enemies and oppressors as such, and to meet aggression at least with self-defense if not retribution. Retribution, in fact, was an important component of the ancient Mediterranean social system, in which it was necessary for the maintenance of honor. To allow an enemy or outsider to get the best of one would bring shame on one's whole household or family.

By breaking radically with the prevailing value system and presenting demands so extreme as to stand on the far edge of possibility, Jesus' words call into question not simply individual actions that human beings normally pursue but the very principles by which persons and societies structure themselves. "Normally" self-defensive, "normally" loyal to those within a well-defined inner circle, the hearer/reader meets in these extreme demands a challenge to view human relationships, both personal and social, in an entirely different perspective.

The prohibitions of swearing/oath taking and divorce function somewhat differently, especially because verse 32 adds a specific qualification to the latter. It seems likely, in light of the New Testament evidence, that the historical Jesus did in fact take a position against divorce and that Matthew's community followed suit but added the exception in the case of adultery. When interpreting Matthew, however, it is important not to remove these injunctions from the context of verses 21–48, which offer examples rather than exhaustive teaching and call for imaginative rather than literal application.

This entire series is bracketed by the injunction against anger in verse 22 and the command to love one's enemies in verses 43–48, and the section as a whole is permeated with a call to reconciliation (note vv. 23–26). In effect, then, all the teachings are brought together under the rubric of cooperative life within the community of Jesus' followers and between this community and the larger society. Even the prohibition of swearing, which to some extent revolves around the sanctity of God's name, embraces a social component, because it impacts business relations, in which oaths were common. The question of divorce relates to the relationship between not only the husband and wife but also the former and future husbands of the divorced woman. The intention of the injunctions is therefore not to state commandments in abstraction from human circumstances but precisely the opposite: to specify the ways in which God's demand for human reconciliation and cooperation can take place. In the end, of course, there is tension between that attempt at specification and the broad function of verses 21–48 as calling for imaginative interpretation.

Following verses 21–48, the reader is in a better position to understand Jesus' declaration in verse 17 that he "fulfills" the law. His call for a "higher righteousness" in verse 20 has begun to take on concrete meaning. It is a demand not for more meticulous attention to the details of the Torah but for a radical commitment, guided by Jesus' own words and deeds, to discern and implement the will of God in every aspect of life. Moreover, the ideals of love and reconciliation stand at the very center of God's desire.

Commentators often identify "inwardness" as the special quality of the "higher righteousness." There is truth in this designation, but two cautionary notes are in order. First, it is important not to caricature the emerging Judaism of the time as "legalistic" and devoted to external details—that is, to assume that because Jesus and the gospel of Matthew focused on fundamental motivation other interpreters of Israelite tradition at the time did not. Second, the concept of "inwardness" is in some measure misleading. Anthropologists who study the ancient Mediterranean world note an understanding of personality that involves three "zones of interaction": that of "purposeful action," centered in the "hands, feet, fingers and legs"; that of "self-expressive speech," centered in the "mouth, ears, tongues, lips, and throat"; and that of "emotion-fused thought," involving the "will, intellect, judgment, personality and feeling" (Malina and Rohrbaugh, *Social-Scientific Commentary on the Synoptic Gospels*, p. 56). Clearly, in speaking to fundamental motivation, the words of Jesus are distinguished by attention to this latter zone. But it would never occur to an ancient person to think that actions could somehow be split off from feeling and will as separate categories altogether. In fact, the injunctions in the Sermon on the Mount speak to all three zones and are distinguished by a relentless attempt to address the person as a whole. Thus "wholeness" may be a more appropriate term than inwardness, and in any case, one should remember that other teachers in this tradition were as concerned about it as Jesus and Matthew.

Some interpreters view the commands in these verses as strategies directed either toward the conversion of opponents or toward undermining their power. Others insist that such approaches distort the focus on the will of God and the grounding of these radical demands in the rule of God that breaks into worldly reality from beyond. But the dichotomy is unnecessary. The demands are in fact absolute and uncompromising, without the slightest consideration of effect; and this issues from a sense that God's rule stands over against the standards of human society. However, the concrete nature of the demands results in an image of God's rule that necessitates expression in actual social relationships, and one cannot ignore the altered position in which the radical actions that are demanded places opponents. The intention of "turning the other cheek" or "going the extra mile" is indeed neither survival nor conversion of the other, but neither is it obedience to God in some merely "inward" or "religious" sense narrowly defined; it is the manifestation of God's rule in the concreteness of human social relations. And that manifestation confronts opponents with a different "reality" and opens up new possibilities for them.

6:1–18 Instructions on Almsgiving, Prayer, and Fasting

In 6:1–18, Jesus defines more specifically the "higher righteousness" of 5:20. The RSV and NRSV render *dikaiosyne* in 6:1 as "piety," rather than "righteousness," because the following verses address three traditional expressions of religious devotion—almsgiving, prayer, and fasting. The broader sense of the term, however, is "right action," and "piety" tends to obscure the link to verse 20 and, indeed, the connection between almsgiving and the first beatitude where (as I have argued) the term has the specific connotation of "justice."

Strictly speaking, Jesus does not enjoin these actions; he presupposes them as aspects of authentic community life, but as in verses 21–48, looks behind the deeds to fundamental motivation. Now, however, he creates this deepening effect by contrasting his expectations of his followers to the practices of "the hypocrites." Given the reference to the scribes and Pharisees in verse 20, the reader will understand these as prime examples of the wrong attitude. Yet because Jesus warns his own followers against such an attitude, the ultimate reference is to hypocrisy wherever it manifests itself—the community of his followers included.

As in verses 2–4, Jesus contrasts proper almsgiving to the practices of "the hypocrites," so in 5–8 he introduces the Lord's Prayer as a model over against the practices of both "the hypocrites" and the Gentiles. Here the distinction is rooted explicitly in his followers' experience of God as father (v. 6), a theme introduced in 5:16. Because they know God as one who already knows their needs and cares for them, they can pray in confident simplicity with no need of elaborate incantations or manipulative devices.

The introduction to the prayer thus sets the stage for the simple and intimate address, "Our father in heaven," and indeed for the prayer as a whole. This tone is not only intimate but also eschatological, because it is as participants in the inbreaking rule of God/heaven that Jesus' followers know God in familial terms. Appropriately, then, the first two petitions are for God's name to be hallowed and God's rule to come (in its fullness). These two requests are virtually synonymous, because in Hebrew thought name and being are inseparable and full glorification of God will come only in the fullness of the rule of heaven; and, indeed, even the petition that God's will be done on earth as in heaven reiterates the point.

The specifically eschatological thrust of the last three petitions is less certain, but most commentators view them in that light. The interpretation of verse 11 is difficult because of the uncertain meaning of the term *epiousios*, usually translated "daily." Some interpreters interpret it as "for today," but the majority opinion is that it means "for tomorrow" and is a reference to the messianic banquet associated with God's rule. Many likewise associate the plea for forgiveness with eschatological acceptance by God and interpret *peirasmos* not as "temptation" but as the testing associated with the period of "messianic woes" that would precede the consummation of history. Along similar lines, many interpret the ambiguous phrase at the end of the prayer as "the evil one" (Satan) rather than "evil."

The eschatological interpretation of the prayer is probably for the most part accurate, but I join Donald Hagner (*Matthew 1–13*, p. 150) in suggesting that this interpretation does not exclude reference to the present. Thus the petitions for the "bread" of the eschatological banquet and for God's final acceptance also imply requests for daily necessities and ongoing forgiveness. The plea to be spared the final testing applies to ongoing trials as well.

Many Christians through the centuries have been bothered by the suggestion in verse 12—made even more explicit in verses 14–15—that God's forgiveness is dependent on its human counterpart. There can be no doubt that Matthew presents a link between the two, and verses 14–15, reinforced in the strongest terms by 18:23–35, also show that the continued operation of grace is in fact dependent on the willingness of Jesus' followers to exercise forgiveness in their own relationships. It must be noted, however, that the Sermon on the Mount begins with a note of grace and is preceded by Jesus' announcement of the coming of God's rule. Divine grace is thus clearly prior to any human response, and verse 13 rules out any sense that those who pray the prayer can do what is right(eous) by sheer force of will: The petition to be delivered from testing is a clear recognition of human weakness. The link between divine and human forgiveness, far from a reflection of human autonomy, is rather another indication of the communal context of the prayer: Apart from the ongoing practice of reconciliation, those who follow Jesus can in no sense manifest the coming rule of heaven.

This reconciliation, moreover, includes a very "material" dimension. In the petition for forgiveness, Matthew's version uses the term *opheilemata* (debts) rather than Luke's *hamartia* (sins) in relation to both divine and human forgiveness. The verb translated "forgive" (*aphienai*), moreover, often refers to the cancellation of loans. The forgiveness of debts on the human level undoubtedly takes on a broader meaning here, but it also probably includes the specific sense of amnesty with respect to loans that the poor cannot repay to the rich. Such a nuance is fully in keeping with the emphasis on justice in 5:6 and with the communal context of the Sermon on the Mount.

The Lord's Prayer is a literary unit that resists total assimilation into its context, but the prefatory material in verses 7–9a provides a link to the theme of right motivation in verses 2–4 and places the prayer together with those verses under the general instruction about right motivation. Then, following the prayer, verses 14–15 reinforce the prayer's emphasis on forgiveness.

Verses 16–18 relate back to the broader context and make their own contribution to the unity of the section. The reference to God as father reinforces the feeling of familial relations, whereas the language about secrecy, recalling verses 4 and 6, reiterates the theme of wholeness and fundamental motivation: Jesus' followers fast not to impress others but to express their deeply experienced relationship to God. Thus, with respect to three pivotal signs of devotion, Matthew's Jesus demands undivided attention to the will of God rather than the approval of human beings.

6:19—7:12 Further Injunctions

At 6:19, Jesus initiates a series of injunctions and related materials that falls into two subsections, 6:19–34 and 7:1–12, each of which ends with a strong proclamation of God's protective care (6:25–34; 7:7–11). Then at 7:12 comes Jesus' version of the Golden Rule, which combines a broad injunction with another reference to the Law and the prophets and thus delineates 5:21—7:11 as teaching on the "higher righteousness" enjoined in 5:17–20. Because 7:13 then turns exclusively to warnings that continue to the end of the sermon, 7:12 stands as a summary of the teaching from 5:17 on. And the combination of exhortation and proclamation of God's care in 6:19—7:12 mirrors the dialectic between grace and demand that has characterized the sermon from the outset. This section, then, brings the teaching part of the discourse to a summary conclusion; only the reinforcement provided by the warnings remains.

The first subsection concerns human wealth as a threat to undivided loyalty to God, and here again the theme of wholeness is prominent. As with much of the material in 5:21–48, both the injunctions and the supporting statements are absolute, making no attempt to deal with the specifics of actual life. Thus many interpreters have agonized over whether Jesus here condemns wealth altogether, and practical-minded critics have found the statements on God's care hopelessly and even destructively naïve.

Like 5:21–48, however, this material functions primarily on the imaginative level. It is left to the reader to work out how to implement the injunction to take no care for material needs when one knows perfectly well those needs are real. And when verses 25–34 are read in light of the entire Matthean narrative, they do not foster naïveté but contribute to a creative dialectic. It is already clear from 5:11–12 that following Jesus entails persecution. The reader will not only encounter the theme again (10:16–26, 34–39) but also eventually learn that discipleship is inseparable from accepting for oneself Jesus' own path to the cross (16:24–26). This subsection itself closes with an acknowledgment that troubles will in fact come (v. 34).

The poetic references to "the birds of the air" and "the lilies of the field" reflect a style of thought, pursued both in Israel and the broader environment, known as "wisdom." One of its characteristics is the attempt to arrive at truths about human existence through observation of the natural world and/or normal human activities. Because this type of thinking stands in tension with the more characteristically Israelite notions of God's covenant and action in history, many interpreters are reluctant to recognize its full weight in the biblical writings. Here the appeal to the natural world is clear enough: God's providence manifests itself in the mysterious way plants and animals are cared for. The presupposition is that one can know something of the ways of God by observing the operations of the cosmos. The argument ultimately reaches beyond the naturalistic level, however, by employing a formal mode of reasoning used both in Greek philosophy and rabbinic thought: "from the lesser to the greater." By stating that because God cares even for birds, lilies, and grass (all of lesser value) it is only logical to believe that God will care even more for the community of believers, Jesus assumes a prior knowledge of and commitment to God.

That the argument is directed specifically to members of the community is clear from the term "you of little faith" (*oligopistoi*) in verse 30. Matthew uses this word two more times in relation to the disciples as a group (8:26; 16:8) and once in relation specifically to Peter (14:31). Then in 17:20, he uses the related term *oligopistia*, which designates deficient faith itself, again in relation to the disciples. The function of such terminology is to distinguish Jesus' followers from those who reject him but also to point out that their faith is partial, still very much in process of maturation. In emphasizing God's care, then, Jesus assures those seeking to follow him and do the will of God that as difficult as it is to be single-minded in one's faith, given the mundane worries that always accompany human life, God will not abandon them.

The imaginative character of the language requires that the reference to *mammon* (the Aramaic term for property or wealth) in verse 24 stands for any worldly concern that can divert one's attention from God's demands, but it is significant that it is wealth specifically that plays this role. The Greek adjective applied to "eye" in verse 23 is *haplous*, which carries the connotation of "simple" or "single" but also of "generous," because the related noun *haplotes* can mean "generosity." The NRSV is thus probably wrong in translating *haplous* as "healthy"; the point is that if one's eye—which is to say one's fundamental disposition—is open and generous, focused solely on God rather than on grasping after material goods—then one's life is full of light rather than darkness. Thus the same spirit that motivates almsgiving (vv. 2–4) must pervade one's total life.

Verses 32–33 bind the whole subsection to its context in the discourse by references to God as Father and the phrase "the kingdom of God and his righteousness." Once again, the reader is reminded that the subject of the sermon is the ethic of God's rule—that is to say, the right action that is demanded for participation in it—and of the familial relationship Jesus' followers have with God.

The second subsection begins (7:1–2) with an injunction against judging others that is graphically reinforced through the comic and hyperbolic image of a log (as compared to a speck) in the eye of the judgmental person. Christians through the centuries have struggled with such questions as whether the prohibition is absolute, forestalling all judgments whatsoever in personal relations and extending even into public arenas such as courtrooms. To ask these questions, however, is to reduce imaginative language to the level of legalisms. Here again, as in much of the preceding material, the function of the sayings is not to prescribe the minute details of behavior but to confront the reader/hearers with a fundamental challenge and leave them to work out the details of application. The broad point is the condemnation of a judgmental attitude that focuses on the faults of the other while overlooking one's own.

The seriousness of this tendency is indicated in verse 5 by the application of the term "hypocrite"—used in 6:2 of persons outside the community—now to the followers of Jesus themselves. The distinction between insiders and outsiders is thus blurred, but it is still retained because in 7:5 Jesus says that after removing the log from one's own eye one can then see clearly to remove the speck from the "neighbor's" (NRSV). The term for "neighbor" here is *adelphos* (literally, "brother"), which in Matthew usually means member of the community of Jesus' followers. This verse not only underlines the community context of the discourse but also signals the evocative rather than the literal nature of the original injunction. One can, after all, make judgments about others' behavior, but all such discernment must take place in the spirit of communal caring, which is the exact opposite of judgmentalism.

Verses 1b–2, which reinforce the injunction in verse 1a with the threat of being judged oneself, probably have a double force. It is a commonplace on the human level that a judgmental attitude invites reciprocation from others, and an endless chain of accusations can destroy community life. In the eschatological context of the sermon as a whole, however, "you will be judged" is undoubtedly a divine passive: The ultimate judgment against judgmental persons is the eschatological condemnation by God.

The specific function of verse 6 (on not giving what is holy to dogs) in this context is highly uncertain, and many interpreters find no thematic links to the surrounding material. One interpretation views it as a qualification of verses 2–5: Even though one must guard against judgmentalism, some persons make themselves "swine" or "dogs" and are no longer worthy of the proclamation/teaching of the community. It is in any case an acknowledgment of the unreceptiveness of some persons, presumably to the proclamation of the rule of God.

The use of the imperative in verse 7 ("Ask...search...knock") places the material that follows alongside the other injunctions in the sermon; it is thus in part a call to persistence. The primary function of verses 7–11, however, is assurance. Here again Jesus employs the lesser-to-greater mode of argument to demonstrate God's loving care for the community members. In this case, the argument rests on the designation of human beings as evil, and theologians have often invoked verse 11 to support a doctrine of original sin. It is important, though, to distinguish between a formalized doctrine and a broad assumption. Rabbinic teaching recognized an "evil tendency" alongside a "good tendency" in human nature, and apocalyptic thought viewed the world as under Satan's sway; so it is not surprising to find here a recognition of the pervasiveness of evil in human hearts and human society. But this in itself does not indicate the specific notions of "original sin" or the "fallenness" of humanity that developed in later Christian theology (see also "The Imaging of Evil," pp. 33–36).

The Golden Rule was widely known, in several variations, in both Hellenistic and Jewish teaching of the period. But it is not found in the Hebrew Scriptures, and in itself it is—as philosophers through the ages have noted—lacking in specific moral or religious content, for the phrase "as you would have them do to you" leaves wide latitude for personal preferences. The explanatory statement in 7:12b, however, provides an interpretive background. To say that this injunction "is the law and the prophets" links it not only to the Hebrew Scriptures but also to Jesus' interpretation of the latter, the spirit of which has been spelled out in the sermon as a whole. Against the background of 5:21–26 and especially 43–48 (the opening and closing segments of Jesus' "rereading" of the Law), it becomes an equivalent of the love command itself (22:34–40). Moreover, in the broad context provided by the beatitudes, it embraces the ideal that love seeks: justice.

If the context helps interpret the rule, it is equally true that the rule itself functions as an interpretive key. In 22:40, Jesus will state explicitly that the Law and the prophets "hang" on two great commandments, and 7:12 is a preliminary statement of the same point. Strategically placed at the close of the teaching section of the sermon, the Golden Rule stands as a guide for the community as it wrestles with all the gaps and ambiguities left by the imaginative language in Jesus' ethical teaching. Its open-ended and all-embracing quality is underscored, moreover, by the Greek phrase *panta…hosa ean* ("all things," "whatever"), with which it begins. The principle to which Jesus' followers must always look—in all matters, whether addressed specifically in the sermon or not—is precisely that of love, and of its referent, justice.

7:13–27 Warnings

Having begun with blessings in 5:1–11, the sermon now closes with a series of warnings. As the future tense and the references to the rule of heaven in the beatitudes placed the discourse in the context of eschatology, so now the warnings reiterate that emphasis. They also underscore the concern of the entire section with right action, obedient response to the words of Jesus. The net effect of the closing verses is thus to provide a final reminder that the hearer/reader's fate hinges not on right doctrine but on actual deeds of righteousness/justice. But this emphasis will appear as a legalism only to those who miss the note of grace that initiates and underlies the discourse and who also ignore the open-ended and imaginative nature of Jesus' commands.

Both the first (vv. 13–14) and the third (vv. 24–27) sets of warnings set up absolute dichotomies that serve as powerful rhetorical devices for demanding fundamental choice. Both also draw on stock images from the Jewish and Hellenistic environments. There are only two roads to travel on one's life journey, and each leads through a different gate into a different destiny. There are only two ways to build one's house, or construct one's life, and only one of them can withstand the tribulations of existence or the final terrors of the end-times. And it is this way that Jesus has presented in the discourse.

Between these two sections, there is a lengthy warning (vv. 15–23) against false prophets, those who could potentially divert Jesus' followers from the true, or "narrow," path. Many interpreters have speculated about actual persons the author of Matthew or earlier bearers of tradition might have had in mind (ranging from Pharisees to Paul and/or his followers), but from a literary perspective such speculation is unnecessary: The text functions broadly enough to cover any group whose actual lives do not measure up ethically. The fact that at least some of the false prophets call on Jesus' name (7:21), however, means that the reader will think in terms of internal rather than external threats. Those who come in sheep's clothing (7:15) are probably persons within the community itself.

The production of "good fruit" (7:16–19) is of course an extremely broad criterion for distinguishing between true and false prophets, but for its specific content one can look back to the teaching in the main body of the discourse. That means, finally, that one can look primarily to the Golden Rule that closes it at 7:12. The ethical concern, moreover, receives even further reinforcement from the fact that those Jesus rejects at 7:23 bring impressive credentials in terms of acknowledging his authority, prophesying, exorcisms, and "deeds of power." All this counts for nothing in the face of their failure to bear fruit.

The discourse thus closes with an interesting juxtaposition of themes. Mere acknowledgment of Jesus gives way to ethics. Yet Jesus is in fact the one who possesses the power of acceptance or rejection. At this point (v. 21), he speaks of God as specifically his father, thus reminding the reader of his status as Son of God. Therefore, insofar as Jesus defines right action in verse 21 as "the will of my Father in heaven" and has cast his own teaching as in some sense interpretation of Torah (5:17–20), the reader will also know that Jesus' authority is not his own possession; it comes from God.

This dialectic between the authority of Jesus and the will of God has the effect of encouraging the reader not only to understand Jesus in terms of God but also to understand God in terms of Jesus. The teaching of Jesus in the first discourse contributes to the reader's evaluation of his character. That is, the reader can now see that Jesus stands for uncompromising obedience to the will of God, which is summarized in the equivalent of the command to love (7:12) and has justice (5:3–6) as its referent. The reader also gains insight into God, who appears not only as the one who commands love and justice but also as the loving father whose care is manifest in the natural order itself (6:25–34), as well as in a special relationship to those who follow Jesus. To the extent that readers grasp the imaginative character of the language in which Jesus states the will of God, they will also recognize God's relationship to them as more dialogical than legislative. That is to say, although human beings are clearly subject to God's will, the community of believers is given a remarkable degree of freedom in applying the broad contours of that will to concrete situations.

In the end, of course, the readers of the gospel are themselves drawn into the dialectic between Jesus and God. By interpreting Jesus in terms of God and vice versa, they also come to understand who they are called to be.

They are the ones who are promised blessedness and the unending care of God even as they are commanded to pursue love and justice in the face of life's ongoing difficulties, persecutions, and the coming eschatological woes.

The narrator's statement in verses 28–29 signals the reader that the discourse has ended (by employing the formulary closing for the first time), and the reaction of the crowds adds further emphasis to the theme of Jesus' authority. These verses also advance the plot in a subtle way, gently leading the reader back into the story line. At 5:20, Jesus mentioned the scribes and Pharisees in a negative light, and in 6:1–18, he made several references to the "hypocrites." Thus when the narrator explicitly contrasts Jesus' authoritative teaching to that of the scribes and Pharisees, this alerts the reader to the possibility of an ensuing conflict. With Jesus' ethical teaching in view, with the band of disciples in the process of formation, and with "the crowds" as a buffer zone between Jesus and his emerging opponents, the stage is set for that conflict to erupt.

Thinking Today about Matthew 5:1—7:27

Struggling with Radical Demands

If the Sermon on the Mount has inspired millions through the centuries, both within and without the church, its stringent demands have also fostered varying interpretations. Although some (notably Tolstoy and Gandhi) have accepted these demands as literal expectations of all who would follow Jesus' way, others have viewed them differently. To interpreters influenced by Luther's interpretation of Paul, the sermon has often seemed to present a works righteousness that leaves no place for God's saving grace. They have saved its place in Christianity only by finding in it an impossible ethic designed to drive the reader to despair to open the way for a faith based on faith in God's redemptive act in Christ.

Joachim Jeremias opposed both these approaches by arguing that the sermon should not be understood as pure demand, because it presupposes Jesus' preaching of the rule of God. Eduard Thurneysen expanded on Jeremias by arguing for a full-blown christological interpretation. On this view, Jesus himself "fulfilled" (5:17–20) the Law by accomplishing its demands, and his followers are called to "partake of his fulfillment."

Other interpreters have met the problem by limiting the sermon's application. A strain of Roman Catholic teaching viewed it as a higher, more demanding ethic for the "professionally" religious only, and Albert Schweitzer thought it presented an "interim" ethic specifically designed for the short period between Jesus' announcement of the apocalyptic rule of God and the final consummation.

There is no indication within the sermon itself or the gospel of Matthew, however, that its application should be limited either in terms of audience or temporal frame. Nor is there the slightest hint that the reader should view the demands as impossible. As for Thurneysen's christological approach, it hinges on an interpretation of 5:17–20 that few contemporary scholars would accept. For better or worse, then, it would seem that the Sermon on the Mount calls for radical, uncompromising obedience by all who seek to take it seriously. And although it is set against an eschatological background, its demands present themselves as God's primordial will for human beings, not special rules for special times.

This does not mean, however, that the "perfectionist" approach of Tolstoy is the "right" one, for recent scholarship's emphasis on the imaginative and open-ended character of much of the language of the sermon calls a purely literalist reading into question also. But one must be careful in evaluating this latter insight too, because it can easily lead to a reduction of the biting demands to broad principles.

The challenge for interpretation in our day is to preserve the truly radical character of the sermon's demands without falling into a severe, world-denying rigorism on the one hand or a vague, purely situationist ethic on the other. The force of much of the material is to call into question both a narrow legalism and wishy-washy conformity to the norms and values of society in general on the other.

We thus find in Matthew 5—7 an important opportunity to exercise the kind of dialogue between worldviews discussed earlier (see "The Power of God as Problem," pp. 24–26). In this case, divine intervention is not directly at issue, but the "otherworldliness" of the text does come through in the way in which its ethic clashes with modern presuppositions. We need to take seriously some of the criticisms of the sermon's demands even as we allow the uncompromising character of the language to speak back. To do so will create a tension, but one that is in keeping with the open-ended character of the sermon's language and can serve as an invitation to a creative process of discernment.

A related point is that it is very easy to use Matthew 5—7 to issue demands, but far more difficult to incorporate such demands in a genuine word of grace. The sermon itself, however, does contain that word of grace, and its most significant impact will in my estimation come as readers refuse to import that grace from "outside"—for example, in the atonement motif— but seek to discover its operation within this material itself.

On one final note, it is fashionable to play down that the Sermon on the Mount has an appeal beyond the bounds of Christianity. My own interpretation, in fact, has stressed the function of this material within

Matthew's total narrative, its eschatological orientation, and its primary applicability to the community of Jesus' followers. It is nevertheless shortsighted to overlook the way in which this discourse tends to stand out of the narrative context and certain teachings tend to transcend a specifically Christian context. My intention is not to invite readings that fall into a "religion-in-general" mode but to argue that because of the inherent appeal (or, conversely, offense) of its radical ethic, the sermon has the ability to engage human beings in a primary, existential way, apart from prior confessional commitments.

This quality, moreover, actually operates within the narrative itself, because even though in this context it is backed by a prior understanding of Jesus' authority as Son of God, it also defines Jesus' character. Thus both within and without the narrative the sermon provides a point of contact that gives the reader/hearer a "reason" (existential, not intellectual) to want to follow Jesus in the first place.

8:1—9:38 Jesus' Messianic Deeds

When in 11:2 the narrator refers to "the deeds of the Christ" (RSV; NRSV="what the Messiah was doing"), the reader will readily call to mind the momentous events recounted in chapters 8—9. This narrative section, which follows the Sermon on the Mount, includes nine miracle stories (involving ten miracles), arranged in three triads separated by brief transitional sections. It concludes with material that recalls the verses immediately preceding the Sermon. Matthew 9:35 is, like 4:23–25, a summary of Jesus' activities; and verse 36 begins with the same phrase that set the stage for Jesus' ascent of the mountain in 5:1: "Seeing the crowds..." The narrator thus marks off chapters 5—9 as a distinct block of material, which falls naturally into two segments: Jesus' messianic words in 5—7 and Jesus' messianic deeds in 8—9.

In terms of plot, Jesus here presents himself to Israel as Messiah, encountering faith on the part of some but opposition on the part of others. Thematically, the stories in this section stress Jesus' status and authority expressed in his miraculous deeds, his call to discipleship, the centrality of mercy to his messianic mission, and the contrast between those who respond to Jesus in faith and those who do not.

8:1–17 Three Stories of Healing

The first triad includes three stories of healing, involving a leper, the servant (or son) of a Roman centurion, and Peter's mother-in-law. The last of these concludes with a summary of various healings in Peter's house, with an emphasis on exorcisms, and a fulfillment formula (see pp. 23–24) introducing a quotation from Isaiah. The quotation, "He took our infirmities and bore our diseases," coaches the reader to understand the preceding miracles precisely as messianic deeds, predicted in a prophetic scriptural book. It also lays the groundwork for a motif that will receive further development later: Jesus' compassionate nature. The point here is not that Jesus will die to redeem humanity from sin, although this theme will appear in time, but only that through his actions he rescues human beings from all the forces that wreak havoc on their lives.

These forces are both otherworldly and ordinary: Jesus casts out demons on the one hand and on the other heals illnesses that the narrative traces neither to Satan nor to God's punishment. Social and religious constraints are also in view, however, because all three major recipients of Jesus' mercy are in some way marginalized. Lepers were regarded as ritually unclean and were subject to severe social restrictions; the centurion was of course a Gentile; and as a woman, Peter's mother-in-law would have had a secondary status in Israelite society. In actually touching the leper, Jesus breaks the purity code, and the story of the centurion adds to the hints regarding the inclusion of Gentiles that appeared in chapters 1—2. Jesus' actions thus to some extent challenge traditional social and religious barriers.

Nevertheless, these stories also present Jesus as sensitive to the demands of the Law. By commanding the leper to show himself to the priest and present an offering, thus regaining the right of social interaction, Jesus recognizes the law of Moses. And although he grants the request of the centurion, he complies with the supplicant's request to perform the healing at a distance. This motif not only demonstrates the extent of Jesus' powers but also avoids having Jesus enter a Gentile home—a point that is consistent with the instructions Jesus will give in chapter 10, limiting the mission during his lifetime to Israel itself.

Jesus' actions in these stories thus reflect the viewpoint of 5:17–48, in which he both affirms the continuing validity of the Law and transcends it through his own radical interpretation. But just as Jesus' new reading of the Law is the controlling element in 5:17–48, so the story of the centurion ends with an emphasis on Jesus' breaking down of barriers rather than on his conformity to ancient patterns and expectations. In 8:11–12, he proclaims, "many will come from east and west and will eat with Abraham and Isaac and Jacob in the kingdom of heaven." Although it is probable that this saying originally referred to the eventual gathering of Israelites from the diaspora, in its present context it clearly signals the inclusion of Gentiles.

Complementary to the motif of inclusion is that of exclusion. As outsiders will be included, "the heirs of the kingdom will be thrown into the outer darkness" (8:12). The combination of this imagery with that of Abraham's banquet shows that the issue is eschatological judgment. Because Jesus contrasts the centurion's faith with what he has found in Israel, the reader finds here the same irony present in the contrast between Herod and the magi in chapter 2 and the same principle that was at work in John the Baptist's condemnation of the Pharisees and Sadducees in 3:7–10: God is free to work beyond the bounds of the established covenant community. Nevertheless, Jesus finds some degree of faith among Israelites. Disciples are following him, crowds of people are at least interested, and the leper has shown faith by kneeling before Jesus and declaring confidence in his power. The reader will eventually learn, moreover, that God's freedom is exercised not only over against Israel but also against the new community of Jesus' followers (see pp. 95–96, 155–56).

The specific force of verse 4, where Jesus commands the leper to say nothing, is a matter of dispute. The author of Matthew has, through extensive reworking of Mark's tradition throughout the gospel, played down the theme of the "messianic secret" that is so strong in Mark. Thus some commentators argue that this command no longer carries the connotation of secrecy that it has in Mark 1:44, but simply means that the leper should go straight to the priest. A crowd, after all, has already witnessed the event. Nevertheless, the command is consistent with a theme that will become increasingly important as the story develops—Jesus' humility and meekness, which contrast with triumphalist images (see, e.g., 11:25–30; also 12:16, where the author again preserves a Marcan command to secrecy regarding his activity).

The notation of various healings and exorcisms in 8:16 rounds out the triad with an emphasis on Jesus' power and the extent of his merciful deeds. He heals "many" who were possessed and "all" who were sick; and he casts out the demons "with a word." The reader must conclude that Jesus has presented himself before the people of Galilee as a very powerful figure. The faith that the leper and the centurion have placed in him will thus seem justified to the reader, who has the advantage of the "inside information" the narrator has presented from the beginning.

8:18—9:7 A Call to Follow Jesus and Three Miracle Stories

With three miraculous deeds in the background, together with a well-established pattern of both disciples and crowds following Jesus on his journeys, the narrator now develops the theme of discipleship in two brief accounts of would-be followers in 8:18–21. As Jesus is about to embark to the other side of the Sea of Galilee, a scribe declares that he will follow Jesus wherever he goes. Jesus' reply in verse 20 is not an explicit rejection of the offer, but the narrative's prior treatment of the scribes predisposes the reader toward a negative valuation of this character. In addition, his approach conforms to the standard Jewish practice of disciples choosing their teachers but not to the gospel pattern wherein Jesus always takes the initiative in calling his followers. The implication is that when confronted with the image of a homeless, wandering teacher, the scribe will in fact exclude himself, for it is clear that the life of the disciple must correspond to that of Jesus himself, and a life of insecurity is probably not what the scribe had in mind. Thus his self-confident offer will carry some of the irony of the declaration of the sons of Zebedee and their mother in 20:22: "we are able." In neither case are the petitioners aware of the sacrifice discipleship entails. The scribe's story will evoke a sense of tragedy similar to that in the story of the rich young man (19:16–22).

The disruptive, paradoxical character of Jesus' image of his own messiahship and the lifestyle required of his followers is underscored by Jesus' use of the term "Son of Man" as a self-designation. Speculations about whether and in what sense the historical Jesus used this term are irrelevant to an understanding of Matthew, because in the gospels it is clearly a christological title. Jesus will later use it in relation to his return as eschatological judge (e.g., 16:27; 24:30; 25:31–46; 26:64), and the reader will connect it with the imposing figure of Daniel 7. In describing the Son of Man as homeless, Jesus thus offers a radical reinterpretation of tradition that overturns triumphalist expectations. For the present, both he and his followers are confined to the margins of society and human existence.

The second petitioner is identified as "another of his disciples." The implication is that he is one of a larger circle of followers, not one of those whom Jesus will name as the Twelve in chapter 10. It is an interesting twist that whereas the scribe begins with an unqualified but naïve declaration of intent, this person begins with a request for a temporary deferral; yet it is only this second petitioner to whom Jesus issues an invitation: "Follow me…"

The narrator does not say whether he answers this call, but the possibility that he does so is left open. The net effect of the account is thus to encourage reflection on the implications of the choice. Having first introduced the categories of insecurity and sacrifice, the narrator now gets to the crux of the matter. The reader must imagine that the man's father has just died and he is obligated by Jewish law to see to the burial immediately. That is to say, one must imagine the most legitimate of all reasons for a temporary deferral, and the force of the story is lost when interpreters speculate that the father is still alive and the son wants to wait until his death. The point is that Jesus' demands are absolute and that nothing—neither "religious" tradition nor family obligation—can stand in the way. Like the provocative material in the Sermon on the Mount (see pp. 44–59), the injunction to "leave the dead to bury their own dead" functions as shock treatment, an intentional flouting of socioreligious obligation in order to play up the unqualified character of Jesus' claim on those who would follow him.

With this thematic statement on discipleship in the background, the narrator introduces the second triad of miracle stories with a tale that focuses on the disciples: the calming of a storm on the sea. Here the reader gets the first chance to reflect on how they are progressing in their assigned roles, and the accurate evaluation will be a double-edged one. On the positive side, they turn to Jesus for help, and they ask the right question in verse 27: that of Jesus' identity. Negatively, they are unable to answer that question, and they manifest a fear that reveals a wavering of confidence in Jesus. He thus dubs them "you of little faith," and this phrase should determine the reader's evaluation: Those whom Jesus has called into his inner circle are indeed persons of little faith—faith that is real but still flawed in significant ways. Their understanding is partial and their courage wanting; and yet they are there, following the homeless one on perilous seas.

The readers of Matthew in the early church would tend to view all the stories in the gospel on two levels, understanding them as both accounts of past events and lessons for the present. But the story at hand will have a particular appeal from the latter point of view. Readers will more naturally identify with the disciples than with Jesus, and Matthew's presentation of the Twelve as complex characters struggling toward complete faith (in contrast to the harshly negative portrayal in Mark 4:35–41 enhances their appeal.

The calming of the storm adds significantly to the theme of Jesus' awesome power, because it implies his authority over nature. The sea is symbolic of chaos, and it is of course God who in Hebrew thought ordered chaos in the process of creating the world (Gen. 1:1). The final story of the healing of the paralytic, moreover, adds yet another dimension to Jesus' image. The scribes' reaction to Jesus' pronouncement that the man's sins are forgiven (they accuse him of blasphemy) encourages the reader to interpret Jesus' statement not as a mere declaration such as a priest might issue but as an actual act of forgiveness. Jesus thus seems to exercise God's own prerogative, and it is consistent with this heightening in the depiction of Jesus' powers that in 9:4 he knows the thoughts of his opponents.

The narrator's injection of the issue of sin does more, however, than enhance Jesus' status. It also places the miracle stories in perspective, demonstrating that the most fundamental issue is not illness but separation from God. The spiritual character of humanity's plight is of course evident in the exorcisms, but Jesus' act of forgiveness makes this dimension explicit and ties the whole miracle cycle back to the early descriptions of the message of John the Baptist and Jesus—a message in which the dawn of God's rule necessitates repentance (3:2, 8; 4:17).

The story of the healing of the Gadarene demoniacs contributes to the escalation in the depiction of Jesus' power and authority: Although the narrator has reported exorcisms earlier, this is the first actual description, and it is powerful indeed. Jesus has absolute authority over the demons, so that their attempt to weasel out of their fate comes to naught. Their initial reaction, moreover, emphasizes his status. They recognize him as Son of God and acknowledge that his role is in fact to defeat them in the eschatological hour, but their testimony to his status and power reflects fear rather than faith. They know him not because their hearts are open to him but because, like him, they are agents of a cosmic power beyond the visible world and privy to special information.

The reaction of the townspeople, too, must be distinguished from faith. This story takes place on Gentile soil, as is emphasized by the presence of the herd of swine, so that the positive image of the centurion in 8:5–17 is balanced by a negative portrayal. These people view Jesus' miraculous deeds only as an occasion for resentment and fear. He has disrupted their economy by destroying the herd, and they have no idea what to make of the power he manifests. So they do not in any sense engage the issue that the presence of Jesus raises. Moreover, this is appropriate in the context of the narrative, because Jesus is presenting himself specifically to Israel and these folk stand not only ethnically and religiously but also geographically outside Israel— unlike the centurion, whom Jesus encountered in Capernaum.

When Jesus is back on Galilean soil for the final story of the triad, however, the narrator turns explicitly to the issue of faith. Jesus commends those who have brought the man for healing (and possibly the man himself) for their faith, and the story concludes with the notation that the crowd's response was to glorify God, even though they were filled with fear. In contrast to both the supplicants and the crowds, however, the scribes appear totally closed to the possibility that Jesus does in fact exercise the power of God and thus they react with the accusation of blasphemy.

Jesus' response to the scribes in 9:6 makes explicit the issue of his authority, which is a crucial theme in the gospel as a whole. This motif is implicit also in that Jesus himself is always at the center of the miracle stories. The issue is never faith in God per se but whether Jesus specifically is acting in God's stead and does in fact manifest God's own authority.

Nevertheless, verse 8 shows that the issue of Jesus' authority does not stand absolutely alone but also involves the question of who God is (see "The Point of the Christological Claim," pp. 36–37), for the response of the crowds is to glorify God, and the implication is that they are impressed that Jesus, as God's representative, performs a deed of mercy for a human being. (The granting of authority would be no cause for celebration if it were used for ill rather than good.) Thus the other side of the question about whether Jesus represents God is the question of what kind of God the deeds of Jesus imply. In marveling over God's mercy, then, the crowds—who after all are following Jesus physically—show an early tendency to understand something of his mission and an interest in discipleship. This is consistent with the narrator's treatment of them as potential disciples by having them hear the Sermon on the Mount. This is not to say, however, that they actually become disciples or even manifest genuine faith. The narrator gives no further indication of where they stand and will have much more to say about them as the story develops.

Their response nevertheless contributes to the reader's understanding and also provides a subtle link between the story-world and the world of the reader. They are impressed that God has given such authority "to human beings." The consistent emphasis through the story is that it is specifically Jesus who has received God's authority. What the reader will eventually see, however, is that as Jesus has received authority from God, so he passes it on to his disciples (28:18–20). The readers in the later community thus will hear in this story a subtle reference to their own situation, in which they perform their worship and carry out their mission in the name of Jesus. In doing so, they exercise his very own authority that comes ultimately from God.

9:9–38 Controversies, Healings, and Calls to Discipleship

Between the second and third triads of miracles, the narrator relates three stories that weave together the themes of discipleship, inclusiveness, mercy, and the radical newness engendered by Jesus' mission. The story of the call of Matthew (9:9) parallels the accounts of Jesus' would-be followers in 8:18–22, underscoring the discipleship motif by providing the image of one who responds unquestioningly to Jesus' call. The designation of Matthew as a tax collector also provides a link to the following story in which Jesus eats with "tax collectors and sinners" and encounters the Pharisees' challenge. In turn, Jesus' unorthodox behavior regarding table fellowship leads into the controversy over fasting, which ends with the brief parables of the wedding guests and the wineskins. The parables refer to the novel situation presented by Jesus' presence in order to explain the disciples' failure to fast, but the reader will apply this explanation to the question of table fellowship as well. Thus the three brief accounts justify both radical inclusiveness and departure from traditional religious obligation based on Jesus' unique role in the eschatological drama. Things are different now because the "bridegroom"/Messiah has appeared.

The person of Jesus thus stands at center stage, but here again the issue of the character of God emerges through the portrayal of Jesus' words and deeds. The quotation of Hosea 6:6 in verse 13 refers to *God's* valuation of mercy over sacrifice (which seems to stand here in Matthew for all cultic/ritual obligation), even as it is buttressed by Jesus' remark that *he*, Jesus, has "come to call not the righteous but sinners." The effect of this juxtaposition is clear: In his radically inclusive behavior—his acceptance of sinners and other marginalized persons—Jesus acts for God.

In linking Jesus' behavior to the will of God, the quotation also reaffirms tradition even as it paradoxically endorses departure from accepted practice. As unexpected as Jesus' behavior is, it is in accordance with God's will as expressed in scripture. The narrator thus holds the old and the new together in a creative tension that becomes explicit in 9:17. The dominant thrust of the saying on wine and wineskins is to justify Jesus' "new" behavior and to show that it must not be judged by "old" standards. The final clause "and so both are preserved" (which appears in neither the Marcan nor the Lucan parallels; cf. Mk. 2:21–22; Lk. 5:36–39) qualifies this emphasis on the new. It does not mean that both the new wine and the new skins are preserved but that the old skins can be retained if they are not used to stifle the new.

Here again the thought is parallel to that of 5:17–48: Matthew's Jesus affirms the continuing validity of the "old," but the teaching and practice of Jesus constitute the real center of the life of the new community. Those who read the story in the post-resurrection community will see a reflection of their own situation in the reference to Jesus' disciples. Even though they, strictly speaking, no longer live during the earthly lifetime of the "bridegroom," they will understand themselves as free from fasts that are endorsed by the Jewish leadership. As 18:20 and 28:20 will make clear, they retain a sense of Jesus' presence with them. Nevertheless, they will also understand that there can be a time and a place for fasting, as indicated in the second half of verse 15, such as the period immediately following Jesus' death.

This allusion to Jesus' death, of course, encourages anticipation of the eventual outcome of Jesus' ministry. The theme remains undeveloped at this point, but 9:15 subtly reinforces the sense of conflict that is emerging as the scribes and Pharisees appear in opposition to Jesus.

The four miracle accounts in the final triad enhance the themes of Jesus' power/authority and of the necessity for faith. The first story (9:18–26), in which the account of the woman with a hemorrhage is embedded in that of the raising of the daughter of the leader of the synagogue, dramatically illustrates both motifs. The faith of the synagogue leader is so strong that he comes to Jesus even though his daughter has already died, and the woman has confidence that merely by touching Jesus' garment she will be made well. The overwhelming character of Jesus' power is prominent, of course, in the resurrection account, and it is not diminished but enhanced by Jesus' comment in verse 24: "the girl is not dead but sleeping." The narrator has already pronounced her dead; the comment thus serves only to indicate that Jesus sees and acts not from the point of view of human beings but from that of God, who alone holds the power of life and death. Jesus' encounter with the woman, on the other hand, sounds a subtler note: She is not in fact healed by the touch that she initiated, but only by Jesus' word, in combination with her faith, as the latter half of verse 22 makes clear.

The story of the healing of two blind men (9:27–31) emphasizes the theme of faith by having Jesus ask explicitly if they believe he can do what they ask and also making an explicit link, as he does also in speaking to the woman, between their faith and the miraculous result. Their address to him as Son of David reaches back to the beginning of the gospel (1:1) and reminds the reader that Jesus' role is partially comprised of his Davidic identity—a point that helps secure the interpretation of Jesus' miracles as his messianic deeds.

The command to secrecy in verse 30 is, like that in 12:16, a hint regarding Jesus' humility, but it also serves as a foil for verse 31. Despite his efforts to the contrary, Jesus' fame spreads: such is the majesty of his power.

Powerful deeds, however, are ambiguous and subject to interpretation. The final story of the triad, the healing of a mute demoniac, plays on this note to conclude the entire cycle of miracle stories with an incident that makes a theme of the conflict that has been bubbling and draws together other motifs as well. The Pharisees, in contrast to those who have received Jesus' merciful deeds in faith, attribute his power to "the ruler of the demons." And once again in the middle category, the reader finds the crowds, who neither reject Jesus nor express explicit faith but manifest amazement: "Never has anything like this been seen in Israel."

In the summary passage in 9:35–38, the narrator not only reiterates Jesus' various deeds but also reemphasizes the motivation behind them. Verse 36 asserts Jesus' compassion for the crowds, who appear to him like "sheep without a shepherd." What this phrase shows, however, is that the physical ills Jesus has healed are but symptoms of a deeper malady. A spiritual homelessness, brought on in part by the failure of Israel's leadership, is the real problem. That is why in 9:2 Jesus pronounced the paralytic's sins forgiven before performing the healing.

The summary also points forward, integrating the miracle cycle more closely into the plot of the story. Given the helpless state of the people to whom Jesus has ministered through his messianic deeds, there is need for more laborers in that task. Verse 38 thus leads into the discourse in chapter 10 in which Jesus will commission his disciples as such laborers. And in the background stands the image of the harvest, which is a clear reminder of the context of hope, the eschatological framework in which the whole story is set.

Thinking Today about Matthew 8:1—9:38

Sin, Suffering, Society, and Nature

The question of the character of God as seen in Jesus (see "The Point of the Christological Claim," pp. 36–37) underlies this entire section in the form of a consistent emphasis on mercy. The theme becomes explicit at 9:13, but it is implicit as well in the miracles of healing. The healings are connected, however, to a number of other strands in Matthew's thematic pattern. The exorcism at Gadara and the healing of the paralytic are reminders that all of Jesus' activity takes place against the background of a cosmic struggle against evil and that the fundamental human problem is not disease but sin. Thus, the stories and sayings in 8:1—9:35 invite reflection on the difficult question of the relationship between sin on the one hand and disease and suffering on the other. And the difficulty is compounded by chapter 10 when Jesus discloses that discipleship, far from exempting one from suffering, makes it inevitable.

The dangers in linking sin with disease or suffering are great. One danger is "blaming the victim"—adding to the agony of those who suffer by holding them responsible for the ill fortune that has befallen them. Another is undercutting the declaration of God's mercy with a harsh and punitive image of the divine. Neither the New Testament as a whole nor the gospel of Matthew itself falls headlong into these traps. Nevertheless, the present section presumes a connection between sin and suffering at some level, for Matthew's whole scheme of sin and redemption is set within an apocalyptic framework that sees Satan in control of the present age and at least implicitly views human suffering as in some sense flowing from a fundamental corruption that pervades the cosmos.

Such a presupposition, however, is problematic in our contemporary context. For apart from the dangers mentioned above, it cuts against one of the most profound and hopeful aspects of recent cultural developments and theological reflection: an appreciation of nature as valuable in itself and pervaded with spiritual presence. It is therefore important to bring our current worldview into conversation with that of the text.

Those who suffer mightily from disease do not need the further burden of having their condition linked with sin. Nevertheless, because the New Testament makes such a link, however vaguely, we must ask whether this link can still communicate something of importance in our time.

Part of our difficulty stems from our tendency to treat sin subjectively, to see it only in terms of individual transgression. This tendency stems from the extreme commitment to individualism that pervades Western society. The ancient world, however, thought in more holistic fashion and focused on the community. Even though the New Testament, along with Jeremiah and Ezekiel, reflects a departure that emphasizes individual responsibility, it retains the collective element and creates a more balanced perspective that all modern individualists should consider.

The healing accounts in Matthew 8:1—9:35 need to be seen against this balanced background. The stories are concerned with individuals, but in no case does Jesus blame the individual for an illness. Both the sick and the demon-possessed are seen as victims of forces beyond themselves, not as persons who are reaping the fruit of evil deeds. Jesus' mercy thus consists in alleviating the effects of *oppression from without*. It may be appropriate in some contexts to emphasize the ways in which human beings bring trouble on themselves, and the insights of modern psychology are an important resource as long as one is aware of the dangers mentioned above. The more distinctively biblical word, however, is that human suffering results from an evil that we do not in a simplistic sense create ourselves.

This line of reflection, however, does nothing to reconcile the biblical perspective with our own sense of the essential goodness of nature. Can an apocalyptically based message speak to those who reject the notion of nature as literally "fallen"? There is some neutral ground in recognizing the ways in which our sociopolitical environments manifest a connection between sin and suffering. One may think, for example, of the effects of industrial pollution on human health, particularly that of the poor, or of the ways in which the pressures of an achievement-, competition-, and production-oriented society ravages the minds and bodies of working people. Indeed, the "translation" of the New Testament sense of the corruption of creation into social/political/economic categories is a profound way of capturing a fundamental insight that lies behind apocalyptic materials, which have justly been termed the "literature of the oppressed." Segments of the human community have always known that their humanity is under attack from forces beyond themselves.

Not all illness or suffering falls into this category, however, and we are still faced with the discrepancy between the New Testament approach to nature and the more positive view that is emerging in our time. It is important to note the ways in which the newer, more holistic understanding of our relationship to nature coheres with some aspects of biblical thinking even though at other points the two modes of thought seem incompatible. These holistic views, for example, are highly compatible with the biblical notion of the goodness of creation. It is also important to remember that much biblical imagery makes its most powerful witness in our age when it is valued primarily as metaphor. We can understand the corruption of nature, for example, as an imaginative way of pointing to the connectedness of all things without thinking that disease literally stems from sin.

Miracles: The Authority of Jesus and the Character of God

Another role the miracles play in Matthew is to demonstrate Jesus' authority, and here again biblical presuppositions are in tension with our contemporary worldview. From our perspective, reports of miracles are themselves in need of substantiation and can hardly function as evidence that Jesus acts for God. At just this point, however, it is important to remember that the question of who Jesus is cannot be separated from the issue of who God is, according to Jesus. Perhaps the issue for contemporary Christians, then, is not whether an external form of the miracles validates Jesus' identity but whether the image of God that is implicit in these stories strikes an intuitive chord. That is, one can value the stories for their ability to raise the question of whether human experience attests the presence of a God who is merciful and inclusive and who in some sense bears human infirmities. What is most important from such a perspective is to allow these stories to encourage readers to reflect on their own experiences of grace and mercy.

If Matthew 8:1—9:35 is rich in its explicit presentation of Jesus and implicit characterization of God, it also has important potential regarding the issue of faith. The faith of the recipients of healing is explicit in some of the healing stories and thus probably implicit in all. The striking phrase "you of little faith" is particularly important. It expresses the Matthean view of the disciples as works-in-progress, showing a nascent faith in need of development—an image to which persons struggling to maintain or increase their faith can easily relate.

Closely related to faith is the theme of discipleship, which emerges powerfully in 8:18–22. The potential here is similar to that in the radical components of the Sermon on the Mount, but the context of the surrounding miracle stories provides a somewhat different background. Here the call to single-minded devotion comes in the midst of the powerful deeds through which Jesus manifests both his own authority and the mercy of

God. The call is thus not for an arbitrary decision but for one that is both informed by Jesus' manifestation of the character of God and empowered by Jesus' mediation of God's presence. Early in the gospel (1:23), the narrator gave Jesus the title "God [is] with us." In both word and deed, Jesus is fulfilling the role that the title entails.

10:1—11:1 The Second Discourse
Instructions and Encouragement for Mission

The summary passage 9:35–38 employs two metaphors to set the stage for the discourse in chapter 10. The narrator notes Jesus' compassion for the Israelite crowds who were "harassed and helpless, like sheep without a shepherd," and Jesus tells his disciples to pray for God to send additional laborers for the harvest. The harvest symbolizes the last judgment, and the image of the shepherdless sheep portrays the crowds of Israelites as abandoned by their leaders. Thus when Jesus gives the disciples instructions for mission in chapter 10, he is speaking to those whose task it is to announce the dawning of the rule of heaven to the community of Israel; and the presupposition is that the people's response to this announcement will determine their final destiny.

The hope of the people lies in their willingness to respond to the missionaries' message. But Jesus' words make it clear that the usual response will be rejection, so that the missionaries must be prepared for persecution and possibly even death. This pessimistic projection about the mission thus not only foreshadows the later turn of the narrative, when the people will finally reject Jesus, but also points beyond the narrative to the experience of the postresurrection community. And it builds on the negative portrayal of the scribes and Pharisees earlier in the narrative: It is they who have left the people helpless. In keeping with this focus on Israel as a whole, the phrase "lost sheep of the house of Israel" refers not to a segment of society but to the community collectively.

The narrative to this point has recounted the specific calls of only five disciples, and 10:1–4 is the first time the reader encounters the notion of a core group of twelve. This specific number is important, however, because the word *twelve* occurs three times in the first five verses. The symbolism is transparent: Sent exclusively to "the lost sheep of the house of Israel" (10:6), the twelve disciples stand for the reconstitution of the whole house of Israel. The naming of each, even though only a few figure as individual persons in the development of the narrative, underscores the disciples' importance as a definable group.

The limitation of the disciples' mission to Israel is consistent with Jesus' direction of his own ministry to Israel, and in 15:24, he will describe it in a way that parallels 10:6. This limitation, however, creates a complex task for the reader. From the beginning of the narrative, there have been clear indications of the wider significance of Jesus' messiahship, and at two points (8:5–13, 28–34), Jesus himself has had dealings with the non-Israelite world. The story in which 15:24 occurs, moreover—Jesus' encounter with a Canaanite woman—concludes with the healing of the woman's daughter. Finally, and most importantly, the gospel ends with Jesus' explicit injunction to the disciples to "make disciples of all nations" (or Gentiles). What, then, is the reader to make of the Israelite/Gentile dialectic in the Matthean understanding of mission?

It is the final passage of the gospel that must control interpretation of the narrative as a whole, and the universalistic thrust of 28:16–20 is consistent with the hints of Gentile inclusion throughout the story. Nevertheless, 10:6 and 15:24 must be taken seriously, as the theme of a limited mission plays a crucial role in the narrative. Jesus' own encounters with the Gentile world are brief and are clearly exceptions to his dominant practice. Thus the story of Jesus' ministry is a story of the ministry of Israel's Messiah to Israel. And chapter 10, presented as Jesus' instructions to the Twelve during his lifetime, describes a parallel ministry similarly limited because Jesus is specifically Israel's Messiah, and the message of the dawn of the rule of heaven must come first to God's covenant people. This emphasis is consistent with the various ways in which the narrator explicitly presents Jesus as standing in continuity with the Jewish Scriptures and Hebrew tradition.

The reader will thus approach the discourse in chapter 10 on one level as an account of an incident in the past that no longer applies in all details to the present. The discourse, however, functions on more than one level, for in various ways it actually forces the reader to look beyond the Twelve and their role in the story line. To begin with, the narrator never actually relates the mission on which Jesus sends them, which subtly encourages the reader to apply the instructions to the present. More importantly, the instructions themselves reach beyond the narrative context at various points.

The reader in the Matthean community, for example, will recognize in the initial instructions in verses 9–15 and 40–42 the lifestyle of the wandering missionaries of the early *postresurrection* communities, which may in some degree still prevail in that reader's time. In addition, the phrase in 10:22 "because of my name" likewise suggests the period after Jesus' death. Even more striking is verse 18, which speaks of the missionaries' testimonies before governors, kings, and "the Gentiles." Because such events do not occur in the narrative, the reader will necessarily hear in the verse a reference to later times. However, the reader will not just transpose the instructions to the situations of later missionaries because much in the discourse, especially in the latter part, will speak to Christians in general.

One theme that is particularly applicable in all times and places is the correspondence between Jesus and his disciples. On the one hand, Jesus empowers them with his authority to perform the same works he has performed as Messiah. On the other, he explicitly links their anticipated persecution to his own rejection: "If they have called the master of the house Beelzebul, how much more will they malign those of his household" (10:25). Although readers in the Matthean community will think of the later careers of the Twelve, they will also understand "disciple" in verse 24 as applying to all those followers, up to and including their own time, who face similar difficulties. Likewise verses 34–36, which describe the alienation from family that loyalty to Jesus can bring, also reach beyond the narrative context, especially in light of verses 37–39, which lay down the general principle that one must lose one's life to find it.

Rather clearly, then, the discourse presents suffering as inherent in the life of the follower of Jesus, and this emphasis is related to the eschatological tone of the speech. Verse 23 makes it clear that, just as the harvest has already begun, so the final consummation is expected in the not-too-distant future: "you will not have gone through all the towns of Israel before the Son of Man comes." The expected persecutions and family disruptions, then, are to be understood as part of the turmoil and chaos that belonged to the script of the eschatological drama.

If the full force of verse 23 is accepted, however, one must also conclude that the mission to Israel remains in progress even after the risen Jesus (28:16–20) lifts the limitation laid down in 10:6 and 15:24. And this insight has important implications with respect to the issue of how the reader is to interpret later passages that envision God's judgment against Israel (see especially 21:33—22:14). Although the end of the story looks primarily to the Gentile world as the future of the community of Jesus' followers, it is not as if (as many interpreters would have it) God has by this point pronounced a final sentence on the totality of the people (see pp. 156–57 and "The Crowds/The People," pp. 191–92).

The emphasis on suffering is to some extent mitigated by the words of comfort at the center of the discourse in verses 26–31. What these verses promise, however, is not physical deliverance but God's unfailing presence and care, and interspersed with the words of comfort are stringent warnings. The one "who can destroy both soul and body in hell" is neither Satan nor any of his agents but the God who alone has power over life and death.

Verse 32, moreover, warns that Jesus' advocacy before God can lead to condemnation, as well as acceptance.

In the end, however, the discourse speaks of reward rather than punishment. Verses 40–42 serve not only to provide a positive conclusion but also to broaden the focus of the speech from those who travel in Jesus' name to include those who offer them hospitality on their way. Here again the reader will easily transfer these injunctions from the situation of the Twelve to the later Matthean community and indeed beyond it.

Verse 11, however, does more than signal the reader, through the formulary ending, that a second discourse has been completed. It also brings the reader back into the story line, reintroducing the Twelve as the immediate recipients of Jesus' words and referring once again to Jesus' ministry of teaching and proclamation.

Thinking Today about Matthew 10:1—11:1

Christian Witness and Social Morality

The strong emphasis on suffering as inherent in Christian witness in chapter 10 raises an important issue. How does one capture the spirit of this theme without falling into an antiworldly masochism on the one hand or blunting the force of the sayings through an easy accommodation with a culture in which a nominal faith that costs nothing is a widespread model of church membership? Interpreters informed by progressive theological perspectives are likely to translate the call to witness into sociopolitical categories, thus challenging the idolatries of a consumption-based society and the arrogance of power in foreign affairs. Those with a stronger evangelical or orthodox bent would tend to focus on the phrase "because of my name" and emphasize the importance of asserting specifically Christian theological claims against a secularized mentality.

A more fruitful approach than either of these, in my estimation, would be one based on the perception that in the gospels Jesus' words and deeds convey a particular understanding of who *God* is (see "The Point of the Christological Claim," pp. 36–37). From such a starting point, the dichotomy between a narrow confessionalism and a generalized social morality could be bridged. If witness to Christ is understood not abstractly but as embracing the vision of God as expressed in the story's characterization of Jesus, then confession and social witness become inseparable. One cannot truly witness to Christ without embodying the specific values implicit in his messianic deeds (see pp. 61–70 on chaps. 8–9), so that one's potential suffering is not for a merely doctrinal stance but for an understanding of what God desires in terms of human relationships in the world.

The eschatological background of the discourse may seem to some to be in competition with this approach, but it can be valued as a sign of the ultimate significance of the stands human beings take in the affairs of the world. Likewise, the emphasis on the judgment of God in verse 28 need not be read as a crude appeal to fear of everlasting torment. Its rhetorical power can serve as a challenge to purely therapeutic understandings of divine-human relations that end in moral bankruptcy by denying human responsibility and the reality of sin. (See also "The Imaging of Evil," pp. 33–36.) It also reminds the reader that from a Christian perspective the only "opinion" that counts with respect to human obligation is that of God.

The brief words of comfort in verses 26–27 are as important for what they do not say as for what they do say. The promise of God's presence and care in the midst of suffering, as opposed to actual deliverance, provides the opportunity to think beyond a simplistic promise of future reward to more profound reflection on what the concept of "reward" might mean within a nonapocalyptic framework. It is implicit in the biblical logic of reward that one is in fact "rewarded" for obedience to God performed *for its own sake*! Images of reward and especially of deliverance have their place, but the alternative promise of God's presence in the midst of an *unredeemed* situation is one that Christians can find particularly meaningful in an age that is uneasy with some of the traditional language about divine interventions in the world (see also "Reward, Punishment, Judgment, and the Actions of God," pp. 181–84).

11:2—12:50 The Conflict Emerges

11:2–30 Contrasting Responses to Jesus

The reference to "the deeds of the Christ" in 11:2 reminds the reader of all that Jesus has done up to this point, especially the miraculous works in chapters 8—9. The doubt expressed in the question the disciples of John the Baptist bring from his prison cell is surprising in light of 3:11–17, but it places in sharp focus the question of Jesus' identity. Because the only discrepancy between Jesus' words and deeds and John's preaching in 3:7–12 is that Jesus has not yet exercised eschatological judgment, the reader must understand this as the root of John's question. Jesus' deeds have so far manifested mercy rather than judgment, and it is to such deeds, along with the proclamation of good news to the poor, that Jesus points as the basis for decision about him. Once again, the question of Jesus' identity proves inseparable from that of the understanding of God he represents. As becomes clear in 12:1–14, the issue is whether one is offended by Jesus' practice of mercy.

The reintroduction of John in connection with the question of Jesus' identity serves both to refine the reader's understanding of John and to make explicit the theme of conflict that has appeared only fragmentarily thus far. John's role is a complex one. Verse 11 subordinates him to Jesus by placing his ministry before the coming of the rule of heaven, but verse 12 declares that the attack on John was in fact a violent assault on that Rule. Then verse 14, by identifying John with the office (presumably not the actual person) of Elijah, suggests a way of reconciling the two perspectives. John, the precursor of the Messiah, stands at the point at which two periods of a history of salvation overlap. Founder of a movement prior to and separate from that of Jesus—as is evidenced by his having his own disciples—he is not, strictly speaking, a follower of Jesus. Yet the meaning of his ministry is precisely that he points to Jesus as the coming one.

In a sense, then, Jesus addresses the question of his own identity by clarifying that of John. And if, as is probable, first-century Israelites expected Elijah to return as harbinger of "the great and terrible day of the LORD" (Mal. 4:5) but not specifically as a predecessor of the Messiah, this merely illustrates that the early Christian community could not simply plug its emerging beliefs into a set of preconceived categories. It worked, rather, with a wide range of fluid notions that it reshaped. And this observation applies above all to the notion of Messiah, which was standardized among Jews only after the New Testament period. Both in Jesus' time and that of Matthew, Israelites were familiar with a range of broadly "messianic" expectations but not with a single, self-consistent notion of "the Messiah."

What is at work in Matthew 11, however, is a reflection of the clash between some of those expectations and the Matthean community's understanding of Jesus as Messiah. Many people awaited God's victory over evil in the specific form of Israel's triumph over its enemies, and opponents of both Jesus and the early church could legitimately point out that God's judgment against the wicked was not yet evident. A subtle note in the background of Matthew 11 is thus the discrepancy between Jesus' ministry of mercy and the expectation of judgment—expressed, indeed, in John's own doubts. The incorporation of John's witness in 3:12, however, means that the note of judgment is retained, because John did speak of Jesus as judge.

This note is reaffirmed in verses 16–24 in connection with the developing theme of conflict. At the beginning of chapter 11, the reader knows already of opposition from the scribes and Pharisees (9:3, 10–11, 34; see also 3:7–10; 5:20; 7:29), but has heard nothing of the general rejection of Jesus' call to repentance. The clarification of John's role in verses 2–15, however, sets the stage for 16–24, which make that rejection explicit. In 16–19, Jesus upbraids the contemporary generation with his comparison to petulant children refusing to respond to one another either in the game of "weddings" or in that of "funerals." The people have rejected John's ascetic lifestyle and proclamation of judgment on the one hand and Jesus' contrasting behavior and emphasis on God's mercy and inclusiveness on the other. Then, in 20–24, Jesus proclaims the negative fate of the Galilean cities in the eschatological judgment. Earlier passages have given the reader some knowledge of the nature of the opposition to Jesus, but chapter 12 will provide further concrete examples. In the meantime, the reader is clear that Jesus and John are united not only by a common message but also by their rejection from a majority of the people. Crowds still follow Jesus, but there is no general movement toward repentance.

Rejection, however, is not the only reaction. As some came to John for baptism (3:5–6), so others are following Jesus, but who are those who have responded positively? In verse 25, Jesus gives thanks that God has "hidden these things from the wise and the intelligent and…revealed them to infants." The reader will identify "these things" with the meaning of the events that have so far taken place in the narrative, especially Jesus' words and deeds in chapters 5–9, and will understand the contrasting terms "wise and intelligent" and "infants" in an ironical sense. It is specifically the scribes and Pharisees who have appeared as Jesus' opponents and whose failed leadership (5:20; 7:29; 9:36) accounts for the people's general intransigence; it is they also whom the majority of Israelites would identify with wisdom and authoritative teaching. By contrast, the identification of Peter, Andrew, James, and John as fishers (4:18–22) and of Matthew as a tax collector (9:9) suggests that those who respond positively are generally of lower social standing or in some way marginalized. This impression is strongly reinforced by such passages as 5:1–6; 8:1–13; and 9:10–13. The reader must thus recognize in the plot not only the emergence of two contrasting receptions of Jesus, utterly at odds with one another, but also the reversal of expectations. It is those least "qualified" by training and status who, ironically, understand what the supposedly learned and devout do not.

The contrasting responses to Jesus also confront the reader with the necessity of decision about him, and the strong christological claim in verses 25–28 clarifies the nature of the choice. Jesus addresses God as Father, refers to God as "my Father," and presents himself as recipient of God's authority. He also speaks of the exclusive knowledge Son and Father have of one another and asserts his power to reveal God to others. Scholars have often noted that this passage, with its exclusivistic language and emphasis on revelation, is more characteristic of the gospel of John than of the synoptics (see, e.g., John 14:6). But it performs a crucial function in Matthew, solidifying the reader's understanding of Jesus as Son of God and emphasizing that one's decision about Jesus is a decision about God as well.

It is important, however, to interpret the passage in its broad Matthean context. As strong as its christological claims are, it is not an assertion of Jesus' status in metaphysical terms that can be abstracted from the content of his words and deeds—that is to say, from the specific understanding of God he embodies. Immediately, in verses 28–30, Jesus presents himself as "gentle and humble in heart," reminding the reader of the words and deeds *of mercy* that have preceded in chapters 5—9 and pointing ahead to the healings in 12:1–14 that receive the scriptural sanction, "I desire mercy and not sacrifice" (12:7; Hos. 6:6; see also Mt. 12:7). In addition, as Elaine Wainwright observes, in verses 7–15, Jesus and John are linked specifically by their relationship to God's rule (*Shall We Look for Another?* p. 72) We could thus say that Jesus' identity is a function of his messianic deeds (vv. 4–11), rather than vice versa.

It is also important not to treat certain elements in 25–27 as if they were systematically formulated propositions intended to serve as the logical basis of further doctrinal statements. The language of verse 25 sounds deterministic, but in the biblical idiom, generally one can speak simultaneously of God's all-determining will *and* human freedom and responsibility. To find here a simplistic predestinarianism—as if God arbitrarily chose who would respond and who would not—is to miss the actual function of the paradoxical language. Even as it points to God's empowering action, it invites readers to *choose* the role of "infants" for themselves; for in verse 28, Jesus issues his invitation to "*all* you that are weary…"

Neither should one try to make tight logical projections from the statement that "no one knows the Father except the Son" to ground a christological exclusivism that denies knowledge of God to all but Jesus' followers. It would never have occurred to a first-century reader steeped in the Hebrew Scriptures to deny that the righteous characters in the biblical stories had such knowledge, nor would it make sense to think that in Matthew John the Baptist lacked it because he belonged to the earlier era. There are, moreover, a number of passages in Matthew that would seem actually to indicate a more general availability of God's mercy (see "The Judgment of God, Inclusivism, and Grace," pp. 177–81). In any case, the function of the passage is not to make a systematic statement on the abstract question of extra-christological (or extra-ecclesiological) salvation but to present Jesus as the one who both reveals God and shares God's authority. This claim speaks directly to the reader, but it also plays a crucial role in the plot. The presentation of Jesus' knowledge of God as exclusive is a way of making the characters' decisions about him the equivalent of a decision about God. The point is that because Jesus is in fact God's Messiah/Son one's response to him at this particular point in the history of salvation is either an acceptance or a denial of the good news of God's dawning rule.

A number of scholars find in verses 25–28, along with a few other passages in Matthew, an explicit Wisdom christology, that is, an identification of Jesus with the figure of personified Wisdom who appears in a strain of Israelite literature as a manifestation of God. This female figure (*sophia*, the Greek term for wisdom, is a feminine noun), is variously portrayed as created "before the beginning of the earth" (Prov. 8:22–23), with God at the creation (Wis. 9:9), and coming forth from God's mouth and covering the earth "like a mist" (Sir. 24:2). In the view of these scholars, just as in the gospel of John, Jesus appears as the incarnation of the pre-existent divine Word (*Logos,* a masculine noun), so in Matthew, he is the incarnation of Sophia/Wisdom.

However, this interpretation depends largely on an investigation of how the author of Matthew edited the document Q, which also stands in the background of Luke (see p. 4). Central to the argument are the changes the author of Matthew apparently made in various Q passages, attributing Wisdom's words and deeds to Jesus and thus identifying Jesus with her. It is difficult, however, to reconcile a theology of incarnation with Matthew's virgin birth motif, and it is unlikely that a literary reading of Matthew, without reference to the changes made in Q, would yield an actual identification of Jesus with Wisdom (see my article "The Wisdom Passages in Matthew's Story" and pp. 168–70 on 23:37–39).

The figure of personified Wisdom does play an important role in Matthew but in connection with the plot rather than in any notion of incarnation. The key wisdom passages occur in two clusters in Matthew (11:16–19, 28–30; 23:34,37–39), each at a turning point in the story. In chapter 11, the rejection of Jesus becomes explicit for the first time; and in chapter 23, his alienation from the contemporary Israelite leadership appears as complete: Their rejection of him is final, as is God's decision regarding them. Wisdom, who in Israelite speculation also suffers rejection, thus seems to serve as a model of Jesus' own career.

In 11:28–30, then, Jesus speaks in a way parallel to Wisdom but probably not as her incarnation. The force of 11:19—"wisdom is justified by her deeds (as over against Luke 7:35: "by all her children")—is not to identify Jesus as Wisdom but to present his *deeds* either as Wisdom's own (which is to say, as God's own) or simply as analogous to hers. Nevertheless, even the identification of Jesus' deeds with those of the female Sophia is, to use Elaine Wainwright's term, "transgressive"—which is to say, it "breaks open gender distinctions" (*Shall We Look for Another?* p. 77). Yet this note is partially muted by the Son-Father-Lord terminology in verses 25–27. In any case, the broad point of verses 28–30 is that Jesus' works of mercy and power in chapters 8—9 validate him as acting for God/Wisdom.

The net effect of the wisdom motif in chapter 11 is to emphasize what is at stake in a decision about Jesus, both for the characters in the story and for the reader. Because Jesus is so closely allied to God, to decide about one is to decide about the other. Again, however, it is clear that the decision is not one of merely formal acceptance of doctrine because Jesus' invitation in verses 28–30 to take his "yoke" draws on the rabbinic image of the Law as yoke. To embrace Jesus is thus not only to acknowledge his status but also to accept his teaching and embrace his lifestyle.

The reader must therefore think back to the Sermon on the Mount in order to understand what it means to follow Jesus. However, the reader will also understand that following Jesus entails the acceptance of God's grace and mercy, for verses 28–30 bring chapter 11 to a close with a promise of "rest" and an overwhelming statement of the "easiness" of his yoke. Balancing the rigorous call to a "higher righteousness" in the Sermon on the Mount, then (especially 5:1–48), is a proclamation of radical grace. The Jesus who calls his disciples to a new level of obedience calls them first to himself ("Come to *me*") and offers them relief. In 12:1–14 it will become clear that Jesus' "easy" yoke stands in explicit contrast to the rigid and burdensome teachings of the Pharisees (see also 23:4). Thus the paradox is that Jesus' demands are simultaneously "easier" and "harder" than those of his opponents. They entail a deeper commitment, but they are supported by Jesus' own manifestation of God's grace and mercy, and they lead ultimately to "rest"—God's eschatological acceptance.

The phrase "gentle and humble in heart" will open up a wide range of signification for the reader. Jesus' gentleness contrasts with the heartless attitude of the Pharisees as presented in Matthew, and the quotation from Isaiah in 12:18–21 implicitly plays off his nonviolence against a military triumphalism. The term *praüs* ("gentle"), however, seems in 5:5 to indicate not merely humble people but the humiliated, or oppressed, and this connotation is probably not absent from 11:29 (see pp. 45–46). To say that Jesus is "gentle and humble in heart" means not simply that he is nonviolent but also that he takes his stand in solidarity with all those of marginalized status in society.

12:1–50 The Opposition Becomes Explicit

Chapter 12 begins with the repetition of a phrase from 11:25, "[a]t that time," which reinforces the impression created by the transitions between the various scenes in chapters 11—12 that all the events and teachings in these two chapters take place on the same day. This invites the reader also to look for thematic links throughout the section as a whole.

The links are not hard to find. Jesus referred in 11:2–6 to his deeds and teachings as signs of his status and in 11:28–30 to his easy yoke and humble heart that stand in implicit contrast with the attitude of the Pharisees. Between these passages, he noted this generation's rejection of both John and himself and then pronounced woes upon the unrepentant cities of Galilee. Against this background, the stories and sayings in chapter 12 appear as illustrations of the hard-hearted attitude of Jesus' opponents, in contrast to his own humility and merciful deeds and teaching. They thus explain these opponents' rejection of Jesus and John. The entire section constitutes a turning point in the narrative, at which the opposition to Jesus becomes explicit and its specific nature becomes clear.

The themes of mercy and the rejection of Jesus are at the forefront in 12:1–14, the stories of Jesus' conflict with the Pharisees over the Sabbath. In each case, the issue is the circumstances under which human need overrides prescriptions against work; and in each case, Jesus appears on the "liberal" side, stressing compassion over legal stipulations. The Pharisees appear as not only utterly rigid but also possessed of evil intent, because their response to Jesus' interpretive triumph is neither reconsideration of their position nor further argument but an explicit conspiracy "to destroy him" (12:14). Their insincerity, moreover, is underscored by the illogic of their position as disclosed in verses 22–32, Jesus' condemnatory words in verses 33–37, and especially their request for a sign in verses 38–42.

The reader has been prepared in various ways for the turn of events in chapters 11—12. John the Baptist attacked both the Pharisees and Sadducees as insincere in 3:7–10, and in chapter 9, the scribes found his pronouncement of forgiveness blasphemous (9:3) and the Pharisees objected to his eating with tax collectors and sinners (9:11). Jesus' response in this latter instance provides a strong link to the story of the plucking of grain on the Sabbath at 12:1–7, because in both cases Jesus quotes Hosea 6:6, "I desire mercy and not sacrifice." The effect of this repetition is not only to underscore mercy/love as a prominent theme but also to place this theme at the center of the conflict that drives the entire plot. It emphasizes in the most explicit way so far that the question of who Jesus is entails something more than whether he is the expected Messiah. That is, it interprets that confessional question in terms of the more ethical and, in one sense, more concrete question of which specific understanding of God the Messiah should represent.

It is thus clear that Jesus' opponents reject him not really because he cannot produce a sufficient sign, for in the narrator's evaluation his works in chapters 8 and 9 are his messianic deeds. One must think of the request at 12:38 as the demand for the impossible and illogical—some type of incontrovertible proof that would negate the very character of faith. The scribes and Pharisees make this request ultimately because they reject the mercy he represents, which is to say they reject his representation of what God is like.

Matthew's uncompromisingly negative view of the Pharisees is now emerging in full force and will be reaffirmed more stridently later in the narrative (see especially chap. 23). It is therefore important to caution the interpreter against accepting the narrator's portrayal of this group as historically accurate. There were undoubtedly significant differences between the approaches to the Jewish law represented by the Matthean community and the emerging Pharisaic leadership, and most likely, also between Jesus himself and an earlier generation of Pharisees, but this should not be blown out of proportion.

Rabbinic texts exhibit a wide range of opinions on legal matters in general and Sabbath observance in particular, and the principle at work in Matthew 12:1–14—that human need should not be ignored in determining ritual obligations—was widely recognized. In fact, the more "liberal" traditions, such as that of the famous teacher Hillel, expressed sentiments closely akin those that appear here. And it seems to have been a hallmark of the Pharisaic movement to render the Law relevant to and bearable within the lives or ordinary people (see also "Powerful Texts, Dangerous Potential," pp. 88–92, "Religious Exclusivism and the Problem of Other Faiths," pp. 160–64, and "The Judgment of God, Inclusivism, and Grace," pp. 177–81).

In the context of Matthew's narrative, however, the Pharisees appear as loveless proponents of an oppressive tradition of interpretation, utterly without compassion for those whose lives might be made difficult by their regulations. If these stories exhibit a harsh denunciation of the Pharisees, though, they also reflect a positive attitude toward Jewish scripture itself. In 12:1–8, Jesus answers his opponents first with a precedent from 1 Samuel 21:1–6 involving David and then follows it (v. 5) with an allusion to Numbers 28:9–10, which he explicitly designates as "in the law." This latter element, lacking in the Marcan (2:23–28) and Lucan (6:1–5) parallels, places the entire story in the context of an inner-Jewish debate regarding the application of the Torah. This is particularly evident in the declaration that the priests who do their work on the Sabbath remain *guiltless*. (It is notable, also, that Matthew does not contain Mark's provocative declaration that "The sabbath was made for humankind, and not humankind for the sabbath" [2:27].) The Matthean narrative thus remains consistent with 5:17–20, Jesus' declaration of the continuing validity of the Law.

It should be remembered, however, that 5:17–20 opens into the antitheses in verses 21–48, in which it becomes clear that it is the law as interpreted by Jesus that remains operative. Moreover, Jesus issues a strong injunction to love in 5:43–48 and in 7:12 summarizes the entire teaching section of the discourse with the Golden Rule, which serves in Matthew as a functional equivalent of the love command. So, too, in 12:1–14, another equivalent of this command—the injunction to mercy—defines the true intention of the Law. The point is that Jesus' love-centered interpretation is a response to human need. The disciples pluck the grain specifically because they are hungry, and the man with the withered hand in verses 9–15 experiences genuine deprivation.

One might of course argue—and the objections of the Pharisees must be seen in this light—that the hunger was not life threatening and the man could have waited one more day for healing. At this point, though, the deeper logic of the accounts breaks the bounds of legal debate. The point is that it is pointless to split hairs when genuine human need is at stake. The man could wait for healing, and the disciples could presumably wait to eat; but why should they have to, when in the meantime suffering would continue?

It is important, in approaching the strong christological affirmation in 12:8 ("For the Son of Man is lord of the sabbath"), to keep the thematic texture of 12:1–14 in mind. The christological justification stands bracketed by the two stories that illustrate the themes of human need and merciful action, and each story contains defenses by Jesus that logically stand on their own. Thus the "[f]or" in 12:8 introduces an additional justification for Jesus' legal renderings—an appeal to his authority as Son of man—that in some measure stands in tension with his other arguments. Is the disciples' action permissible because hunger in itself overrides Sabbath restrictions, or because Jesus pronounces it so? The thematic development of the passages suggests that the scriptural injunction to mercy carries its own weight, but Jesus' authority is clearly a major Matthean theme, already seen clearly in 11:27: "All things have been handed over to me by my Father."

Once again, 5:17–48 is instructive, because it presents Jesus as the authoritative interpreter of the Law. The point of 12:8 is not that Jesus wields an arbitrary power of determining permissible action but that as

Messiah he has the authority to interpret the Law in order to make God's true intention clear, which is exactly what he does in 5:21–48. Jesus does not "make" it acceptable to meet human need on the Sabbath but shows authoritatively that God has already said through scripture that it is so. It is in that sense that he is "lord" of the Sabbath.

A more difficult question is how to understand the specific force of 12:6: "I tell you, something greater than the temple is here." Many commentators have understood the "something" as Jesus himself, although the neuter gender of the Greek adjective *meizon* has led others to suggest that it refers to the presence of God's rule. Ulrich Luz (*Matthew 8–20*, pp. 181–82), however, insists that the immediate context requires a different rendering: It is the injunction to mercy, mentioned in verse 7, that must be the "something greater." This point is well taken, because the christological affirmation does not come until verse 8.

The issue is complicated by the use of a parallel term in verses 41–42 in the "sign of Jonah" pericope. Here a different adjective (*pleion*) is employed to proclaim once again the presence of "something greater" than Jonah or Solomon, but in this latter case there is no reference to mercy and the issue is specifically Jesus' messianic status. *Pleion* is also neuter, however, which suggests that the reference in this instance is to the situation that Jesus' presence heralds—the dawning of God's rule—rather than Jesus himself.

What, then, about the "something greater" in verse 6? Is it likely that it means something different from the similar phrase in 41–42? A purely sequential reading supports Luz's reading of 12:8 as a reference to mercy. But 12:8 immediately undergirds the injunction to mercy with Jesus' authority, thus implicitly broadening the reference of *meizon*. Mercy, the equivalent of love, is now perceptible as the very core of God's desire and demand because Jesus has appeared on the cusp of God's reign as the definitive interpreter of the Law. From here it is only a short step to the phrase in 41–42, where the "something greater" signifies more directly the new, eschatological situation. Jesus' presence, his messianic deeds and his teaching, are in fact the very presence of God's rule. That is why no further sign need be given; it would be redundant.

The issue of Jesus' identity thus turns out to be synonymous with the question of the presence of God's rule on the one hand and the right understanding of the Law on the other. To know who Jesus is means also to know that God is characterized by mercy and therefore to experience the rule of God in one's very midst.

To know all this is also to experience the Spirit in one's midst, and vice versa. When in 12:22–32 the Pharisees attribute Jesus' power of exorcism to Beelzebul (a term of uncertain origin, associated with foreign deities, which here refers to Satan), they reveal their own opposition to the Holy Spirit and thus their evil intent, which Jesus identifies and condemns in verses 33–37. Just as good things (love and mercy, for example) come from within the heart, so does evil. Yet the condition of the heart manifests itself in words, and those words become the basis for eschatological judgment (vv. 36–37).

This principle of judgment is at work in the Beelzebul passage, because the issue there is defined in terms of speaking a word against Jesus or the Holy Spirit. Because the reference in verses 31–32 to the so-called unforgivable sin has caused such enormous anxiety among devout Christians through the centuries, it is important to give closer attention to it.

If chapters 11—12 make the conflict between Jesus and his opponents explicit, 12:22–45 constitute the very apex of the narrator's definition of the issue: Here the irreconcilable nature of the disagreement appears in graphic terms. The Pharisees accuse Jesus of collusion with Beelzebul, but Jesus' reply pronounces the generation they represent evil (v. 34) and unrepentant (38–42) and says that they are possessed of demons themselves (43–45). After dismantling the logic of the accusation in verses 25–27, in 28–30 he raises the issue of the work of the Spirit, introduces the image of plundering the "strong man's" house, and states emphatically that those who are not for him are against him.

The net effect of these latter verses is to couch the issue in stark either/or terms; there is no middle ground. Because the initial charge had to do with exorcism, it is clear that it is this practice that constitutes the plundering: By casting out demons, Jesus is plundering Satan's (the "strong man's") house, which is to say he is conquering Satan's rule and establishing God's in its place. This theme will become more explicit in chapter 13. At the moment, the issue is the consequence of this state of affairs for Jesus' opponents. And the force of verses 31–32 is to pronounce unforgivable their attribution of the Spirit's power, manifest in Jesus' deeds, to Satan. The point, however, is not to create a formal, abstract definition of a mysteriously unforgivable sin valid for all time, but to place the conflict between Jesus and his opponents in the sharpest, most uncompromising terms. Later in the story, the narrator will spell out more explicitly the consequences of Jesus' rejection for the generation that turned away from him (see also pp. 154–58, and "The Crowds"/"The People," pp. 191–92).

The broadening of the focus from the Pharisees to the generation itself is explicit not only in the "sign of Jonah" passage (12:41–42) but also in the return of the unclean spirit in verses 43–45. The point here is that even though Jesus is breaking Satan's power through his messianic deeds, the people as a whole (represented by their leadership) remain unrepentant and therefore subject to Satan's recolonization. The returning demon finds the house empty—which is to say, his presence has not been replaced by an alternative power—and hence is "ripe for the picking" again. The future tenses in Jesus' pronouncements about "this generation," moreover, give them a quality of prediction that focuses the reader's attention on the future. It is now becoming apparent that the people will in fact wreak havoc on themselves, precisely because they are missing the opportunity for repentance.

The reference to the sign of Jonah in 12:39–41 is another element that encourages the reader to anticipate future turns in the plot. The declaration in verse 40 that "for three days and three nights the Son of Man will be in the heart of the earth" is a clear allusion to Jesus' coming death, despite the discrepancy between this phraseology and the resurrection on the third day. The resurrection itself remains only vaguely implicit, however, and the weight of the passage is its condemnatory note. It is only in an ironical sense, moreover, that "sign of Jonah" constitutes a sign. It is by consigning the Son of man to burial in the earth that the generation seals its fate; the resurrection will for them signify not another opportunity to repent but God's final judgment.

The section ends with 12:46–50, Jesus' statement regarding his true family. Jesus distinguishes those who do God's will, identified as his disciples, from his biological family. Against the background of chapters 11—12, however, the reader will interpret the passage not in terms of Jesus' relation to his kindred (which is not an issue in the story) but in relation to the populace as a whole. The Pharisees and scribes have already taken their stance against Jesus and so cut themselves off from his circle and God's rule. In the background, however, there are still the crowds whose status remains ambiguous. (Note their presence at 11:7 and 12:46. In this latter passage, the RSV unfortunately renders the term "the people," but the NRSV has "crowds.") This passage thus serves both to invite the reader to identify with Jesus' true family, his coterie of followers, and to drive the plot forward. Having drawn so sharply the lines of conflict between Jesus and his opponents, the narrator can now supply an image of a community of believers that is emerging.

Thinking Today about Matthew 11:2—12:50

Powerful Texts, Dangerous Potential

This section, focused so intensely on the issue of Jesus' identity, presents yet another opportunity (see "The Point of the Christological Claim," pp. 36–37) to "unpack" the christological question by tying the decision about

Jesus to a decision about the nature of God. Indeed, it is this section more than any other that invites such reflection. In 12:1–14 the theme of Jesus as the arbiter of God's mercy receives its strongest concrete representation, and in 11:25–30 we find one of Matthew's most explicit proclamations of grace.

The turn in the plot that takes place in these chapters, however, raises the further possibility of connecting the call to decision with some other motifs. The Sabbath controversies are invaluable illustrations of the ways in which religious orthodoxies and formalisms can actually undermine a faith-based call to minister to human need. In addition, the passage about Jesus' true family (12:46–50) offers a classic opportunity for distinguishing radical faith from attachment to familial or cultural norms. The strong notes of judgment, moreover, are classic illustrations of the either/or dimension of Christian faith. They offer rich resources for reflection on how our contemporary society manifests an emptiness that invites "demonic" possession, ignores prophetic signs, and rejects manifestations of God's gentleness and mercy.

These very aspects of this section, however, are fraught with dangers. It is important to distinguish between the one-dimensional Pharisees in Matthew's plot, who are not only unbending and hypocritical but also genuinely evil, and the historical group that played such a crucial role in shaping the Judaism that survived the Roman destruction of the ancient Jewish nation, for the identification of the Pharisees with hypocrisy is still extremely widespread and feeds anti-Jewish sentiments in both overt and subtle ways.

One helpful interpretive move has long-standing precedent in Christian preaching, and that is to focus on the "Pharisees" in our own Christian communities and the "Pharisee" in each of us. This is a valid approach, but what is too often missing is a disavowal that the texts accurately describe either the historical Pharisees or Jews in general.

The potential for anti-Judaism haunts much of this section, but particularly 11:20–24 (the woes on the Galilean cities) and 12:38–40 (the sign of Jonah), because in the first case Jesus condemns the cities collectively and in the second indicts the entire generation. It is easier to employ the former passage in a critique of our own culture's insensitivity to signs than it is the latter, which emphasizes Jesus' death and resurrection as a confirmation of Israel's apostasy. Such a move is possible but is far more appropriate with respect to the Lucan parallel (11:29–32), which lacks the whole death/resurrection motif and treats Jonah's preaching as itself the sign.

The Matthean version of the sign of Jonah remains highly problematic because, as Ulrich Luz has noted, it treats Jesus' death and resurrection as a self-evident divine disclosure, rather than a paradoxical sign grasped only in faith and only as God's gift. The result in Christian history has been that the church has arrogantly appropriated it as a kind of possession and used it as a theological weapon for condemning the Jewish people as a whole. Thus Luz ends his reflection with a bit of ironical fancy:

> Here we must ask whether someday the Son of Man, in the light of this church that possesses the signs, will reverse the Christian expectation of judgment so that in the last judgment, for example, Jews will assume the role of the Ninevites, and the Christians, who so long possessed the Jonah sign of the resurrection, will be condemned on the basis of what they have done with this sign. (*Matthew 8–20*, p. 223)

I regard this comment not only as morally justified but also as containing a valid hermeneutical move. Far from a rejection of the text, it is an instance of turning a text against itself. In other words, the insensitivity to signs that Matthew attributes to the generation to which Jesus preached can also be identified in the church insofar as it has failed to purge itself of anti-Judaism and other forms of bigotry. In fact, one might also enlist Matthew's own insistence that the church itself will undergo judgment (see 13:36–43; 22:11–14) to support the point.

Another danger in the materials in this section is that the prophetic sense of either/or can lead to oversimplification and even distortion of issues. A clear case in point is 12:30: "Whoever is not with me is against me, and whoever does not gather with me scatters." The most obvious negative potential here is that of a religious exclusivism and imperialism that rejects all traditions other than the Christian one as simply invalid or even demonic. Such views are more likely to be found in the conservative churches than in the liberal, but there is a corresponding pitfall that lies in wait for the latter. Because the issue of Jesus' identity opens into that of his representation of the character of God, one meaningful way of interpreting 12:30 is to couch the issue not in terms of a formal confession of Jesus but in terms of taking one's stand for the social and existential possibilities he represents. But here again there is a danger of reducing complex issues to simplistic dichotomies.

My point is not that the either/or dimension of the Christian proclamation is invalid. Without a strong sense of the absolute as a starting point, there can be no gospel message or moral witness. Points on a spectrum are meaningless without a sense of the two contrasting end-points, and God cannot be reduced to one power merely parallel to others in the universe. Nor do I mean that debates on issues should generally be solved by finding a middle position. To the contrary, I value Matthew 12:30 precisely because it serves as an antidote both to weak compromise and the tendency in our culture to reduce all points of view to equally valid/invalid subjective opinion. Human rights abuses, the wanton exploitation of workers, the despoliation of nature, and the various forms of discrimination that plague our world need to be named as demonic, and the complicity of the ingrown lifestyles of many Americans in such horrors needs to be exposed.

In the end, however, most issues are complex, and one should not sacrifice either intellectual integrity or openness, even for the sake of prophetic witness. There are occasions that demand a bald, unqualified indictment of injustice and oppression. There are others, however, that call for approaches that wrestle with ambiguities without forfeiting a basic commitment to the justice and mercy Jesus represents.

Matthew 11:25–30 provides an important reminder of one important means toward that end. There is a double edge here, for on the one hand this passage serves further to contrast Jesus' demeanor to the harshness of the Pharisees, but its strongest note is one of grace. Although it is subject to misuse as a proclamation of "cheap" grace, it also provides a point of contact with persons whose complicity in injustice is a product more of weariness and lack of direction than of ill will or unconcern. In a way parallel to some elements in the Sermon on the Mount, it can provide an alternative to a direct attack on lifestyles: the assurance that people do not *need* to do the ultimately unproductive things they do—whether the rituals observed are those of misconceived religion or the debilitating cultural "rat race"—in order to have life.

Matthew 12:31–32, the statement on the "unforgivable sin," presents its own peculiar problems. The most puzzling aspect of the passage is the distinction between blasphemy against the Holy Spirit and blasphemy against the Son of man. There are many theories about the force of this distinction, but the most compelling is the view that the saying originated among Christian prophets in the postresurrection period. In that context the point was that persons who had rejected Jesus himself could now be forgiven. However, those who rejected the prophets' own spirit-inspired proclamation of Jesus could not, because this proclamation brought with it, in their minds, the force of the eschatological judgment (Boring, "The Gospel of Matthew," pp. 286–87, and *The Continuing Voice of Jesus*, pp. 218–21).

In light of this discussion, Ulrich Zwingli's classic statement on the passage seems unnecessary, because it assumes that there really is an unforgivable sin. Yet it is worth repeating, in light of the extreme anxiety the passage has caused: "If they have repentance, they have the Spirit" (quoted in Luz, *Matthew 8–20*, p. 209)—that is, anyone who is worried about having committed this sin and feels repentant could not possibly have committed it. But what Christians in our day ought in fact to worry about is the way the passage functions in Matthew's narrative, that is, as a condemnation of the Pharisees. In this context, its point is that the Pharisees have blasphemed the power of the Spirit working in Jesus by attributing his exorcisms to Beelzebul. Such identification of some people as hopelessly lost is precisely what has led to all the forms of fanatical confessionalism that constitute a grim side of Christian history.

Jesus, God, and Gender

Elaine Wainwright's sophisticated "feminist re-reading" of Matthew dovetails with the intention of this commentary to identify undercurrents that compete with dominant strains of meaning. She sees in chapter 11 a tension not only between the emphases on Jesus' identity on the one hand and his works on the other but also between "closed categories of comparison and open-ended processes of understanding" (*Shall We Look for Another?* p. 83).

On one level, Jesus stands alone as the exclusive revelation of God and recipient of divine power—a male figure, relating to God as Son to Father, who appoints twelve males to extend his work (10:1–4). This aspect of the text has played a fateful role in the ecclesiastical interpretation and use of Matthew through the centuries, but the Wisdom imagery for God and Jesus' sharing of his knowledge of God with others (11:27) runs counter to such emphasis, as does the fact that 11:28–30 shares motifs with prior texts concerning Wisdom and Moses (e.g., Deut. 34:10; Sir. 6:18–37). Wainwright thus concludes that "[j]ust as Moses and Sophia [Wisdom] were types for Jesus, so Jesus is a type for all who enter into a special relationship with the God of Jesus" (*Shall We Look for Another?* p. 83). Thus Jesus is important not because of what he is in himself but because of the human possibility and understanding of God he represents.

Also, the use of female imagery for God, together with the identification of Jesus' deeds with those of Sophia, not only breaks down traditional gender distinctions but also undercuts the tendency to treat language about either God or Jesus as one-dimensional. And the result is that the reader is invited to move beyond surface designations such as "Son" and "Father" into an open-ended process of reflecting on Matthew's witness to Jesus. On Wainwright's reading, undercurrents of meaning in a passage that on the surface presents Jesus as the exclusive representative of God in a male-defined hierarchy suggests ways contemporary readers may draw on their own experiences to find here a Jesus whose function is more democratic and independent of gender. In terms of the approach of this commentary, this does not mean outright rejection of the dominant strain of meaning in Matthew. It means rather that interpreters are free to revalue that strain as they bring it into a conversation involving both contemporary experience and submerged aspects of the text itself.

13:1–52 The Third Discourse

Parables and the Rule of Heaven

The narrator's comments in 13:1–3a set the stage once again for formal teaching as Jesus sits in a boat and begins to speak to the crowd on the shore "in parables." Later, in 13:53, the now familiar formula, "When Jesus had finished…" (see p. 10), marks off 13:1–52 as a third major discourse. In it Jesus not only teaches in parables but also explains his reason for doing so (vv. 10–17) and offers interpretations of two of them privately to the disciples (vv. 18–23, 36–42). The initial phrase in verse 1, however, links the teaching in this chapter to the preceding narrative, in which the conflict between Jesus and his opponents mounts and there are increasing signals that the people as a whole will eventually reject him. The reader will thus approach the present segment both in order to grasp Jesus' teachings directly and to understand their role in the developing drama.

The initial parable (vv. 2b–9) concerns the fate of seeds sown in a field, and it is followed by Jesus' statement on the reason for parables (vv. 10–17) and then his interpretation of the parable (vv. 18–23). In verses 10–17, Jesus answers the disciples' question about why he speaks in parables by referring to "mysteries" (NRSV: "secrets"; Gk. *mysteria*) of God's rule. The disciples, he explains, enjoy a privileged status. God has enabled them to understand these "mysteries" but has withheld understanding from those outside the privileged circle: "To you it has been given to know the secrets of the kingdom of heaven, but to them [the crowds] it has not been given." Verse 12 underscores the point: As in the raw world of economics, the "haves" will get even more, and the "have-nots" will lose what little they had!

The point is not to endorse economic exploitation but to lend vividness to the declaration of God's grace. But this very emphasis on grace seems to imply that as God gives to some, God also withholds from others. A close reading of verse 13, however, reveals a subtle qualification: "The reason I speak to them in parables is *that* [emphasis added, ="because" (RSV), not "so that," as in Mark] 'seeing they do not perceive, and hearing they do not listen.'" The people's failure to understand, that is to say, is not the *result* but the *cause* of Jesus' speaking in parables. He withholds the "secrets" or "mysteries" from the crowds *because* they do not understand, and the quotation from Isaiah 6:9–10 explains why they do not: "they have shut their eyes; / so that they might not look with their eyes, / and listen with their ears." The people's obtuseness is thus a result of their own choice, their hardening of their own hearts to God's revelation. But a certain paradox still remains. Those who reject Jesus do so of their own volition; but it is by God's grace that the disciples understand.

Verses 16–17, which conclude Jesus' explanation of the reason for parables, reemphasize God's grace, noting that what the disciples are experiencing is precisely what the prophets and righteous ones of earlier times awaited. The interpretation of the parable in verses 18–24, by contrast, further explains why some are rejecting Jesus. Although the explanation contains confusion about whether the seed symbolizes the preached word or persons receiving it (whereas the parable itself implies an identification of the receivers with the various soils), the point is clear enough. In some cases, "the evil one" (the devil) snatches away the word; in other cases the problem is lack of endurance in the face of persecution, and in yet others it is "the cares of the world and the lures of wealth"—matters that Jesus has addressed in the Sermon on the Mount.

Since earliest Christian times, interpreters have understood both the parable of the sower and its interpretation as addressing church members, exhorting them not to fall away after having heard the word. Some recent interpreters, however, argue that these verses should be read exclusively in the light of their place in the Matthean narrative, in which case they serve only to make the point I have already noted—that is, to explain Jesus' rejection. What such a reading fails to notice, however, is the way in which the great discourses in Matthew tend to stand out of the narrative to address the reader directly. The Sermon on the Mount plays on universal ethical themes, and the missionary discourse subtly shifts from a focus on the disciples' mission to Israel (10:5: "Go nowhere among the Gentiles") to the later community's witness in the Gentile world (10:18: "you will be dragged before governors and kings because of me, as a testimony to them and the Gentiles").

The reader will make the parables discourse do double duty also, applying it to the life of the church as well as to the narrative situation. One will almost inevitably hear in the descriptions of the judgment in verses 39–43 and 49–50 a warning to church members, and the mention of "persecution" in verse 21 is strongly suggestive of the postresurrection situation.

It is important, however, to define precisely how the church comes into play here. Because in the explanation of the parable of the weeds

(vv. 36–43) the sower stands for the Son of man, who will send angels to "collect out of his kingdom all causes of sin and all evildoers," some interpreters have identified the rule (kingdom) of the Son of man—clearly the equivalent of the rule of God/heaven—with the church. This would mean that it is *only* the judgment of the church that is in view. In 37b, however, we read, "the field is *the world*." This indicates that the scene of judgment, identified with the rule in verse 41, is the world at large. But how can the world be identified with the Son of man's rule? The apparent answer is that the rule, existing only in a hidden way in the present (vv. 31–33), will appear in its fullness at the end of the age and be superimposed on the world at large just before the judgment. Although it will temporarily include evildoers, the angels will "weed them out," just as—in a parallel image—they sort out the fish in the parable of the net (vv. 47–50), separating "the evil from the righteous."

On the one hand, then, one must think of a general judgment of the world in which good and bad persons are distinguished and sent to their respective fates. On the other, however, there is a specific judgment on the church itself, in which faithful and faithless members are identified as such. The judgment of the church, in other words, is one aspect of a more general judgment.

Christians are certainly accustomed to the notion that mere membership in the community does not automatically ensure righteousness. What is surprising, however, is the identification of the field as the world. For if the world as such is the scene of a judgment that separates the good from the evil, and if the church stands as a subset within that world, which itself contains both good and evil, the implication is that the distinction between good and evil cuts across the church and the world. That is to say, as both good and evil are found within the church, so the world itself contains both good and evil. If this implication is allowed its full weight, we would then have an indication of the possibility of salvation apart from the Christian community and apparently apart from Christ. (See Pregeant, *Christology Beyond Dogma*, pp. 107–113.)

Such a reading seems to violate another aspect of the logic of the parable/interpretation, however. Because it is the Son of man who sows the good seed, the implication is that they are to be identified specifically with those who have responded to Jesus. Alternatively, as some interpreters have argued based on a particular reading of 25:31–46 (see pp. 174–76), the good seed are primarily Jesus' followers but include among their number those non-Christians who have treated Christian missionaries kindly. In either case, according to this point of view, they are in some sense products of the Christian mission.

The problem with such readings, however, is that they make the parable/ interpretation view all evil in the world as opposition to the Christian mission, as if there had been none in the world before that mission. It would thus appear that there are two competing lines of logic at work, one focused specifically on the Christian mission and its opposition and another pointing more broadly to the universal conflict between good and evil, now exemplified in the interaction between Jesus and his followers and the world at large. And to the extent that one honors the latter, the broader conflict between good and evil, it becomes necessary to recognize the fragments of a universalistic perspective that stands in tension with Matthew's christological focus.

Both lines of logic issue from a single concern that is deeply entrenched in the Matthean narrative. The phrase "causes of sin and...evildoers" in verse 41 recalls the pervasive emphasis on ethical action and the continuing validity of the Law (5:17–20), as does the image of bearing fruit in the first parable/interpretation complex. It is totally consistent with Matthew's emphases to understand the judgment that is symbolized in various ways in this chapter to be carried out specifically on the basis of ethical/unethical action.

The implications of this material for the church should not be allowed to obscure its narrative role. Not only does it attempt to explain Jesus' rejection but it also keeps alive the interaction between Jesus and the larger public. Although the reader sees that the tide is turning against Jesus, that interaction will continue; thus one must imagine Jesus still seeking to communicate with the crowds, even in the face of a disappointing response. If Jesus acknowledges in verses 10–15 that the people have hardened their hearts, this does not mean that he ceases to call them to repentance. In contrast to Mark, Matthew gives no indication that the parables are intended to confound, and verses 34–35 in fact suggest the opposite. Jesus tells "the crowds all these things in parables" in order to "proclaim what has been hidden from the foundation of the world."

Apparently, then, Jesus is still trying to make disciples of the crowds in order to reveal to them something formerly hidden. And what has been hidden must be what is disclosed in the parables that he tells to the people at large—that is, in Daniel Patte's words, "the hidden existence and origin of evil since the beginning, the hidden character of the kingdom which, in the beginning, is like the smallest of the seeds or like a small lump of leaven hidden in a great amount of flour but which will surely triumph..." (Patte, *The Gospel According to Matthew*, p. 195).

These very themes, of course, will also have special significance for the reader reflecting on the life of the church, for the message the crowds seem to be rejecting is that which nurtures the community. The community can understand their own conflicts with the outside world in light of the ongoing cosmic battle between good and evil, and they can take heart that the inauspicious state of Jesus' own followers, as well as their present community, will eventually give way to vindication in the rule of God. The tiny mustard seed will become so big one can call it, hyperbolically, a tree (vv. 31–32). So also the church! And the "subversive" images (v. 33) of a woman and leaven (both signifying impurity in rabbinic literature) assure them that the word they bear will eventually "infect" the world as leaven does with an enormous amount of meal (which is enough for a great banquet).

The reader will understand these points as basics, potentially available to the crowds, surely at work in the life of those who follow Jesus, but what of the "mysteries"? These must be identified with the points Jesus makes in his private interpretations for the disciples. In addition to depicting the judgment of the wicked and fainthearted, these verses also for the first time in Matthew use the term Son of man to apply to Jesus in his specific role as judge of the world. According to Patte, then, "the mysteries of the kingdom as expressed in 13:36–43 are primarily revelations that Jesus is not merely the meek and merciful Son of man during his ministry but also the eschatological Son of man, the wrathful judge at the end of time (cf. 10:32–33; 11:20–24), and that this judgment will be based on what people do" (Patte, *The Gospel According to Matthew*, p. 198).

Combining the mysteries and the public teaching, then, the reader will conclude that although God's rule is currently present in the world only in hidden or nascent form, the word that Jesus has sown will in time be visibly triumphant. Jesus' followers will be vindicated at the day of judgment, on which those who do good are separated from those who do evil. In the meantime, those who follow Jesus must be aware that they are caught up in the cosmic conflict between two competing rules, that of the devil and that of God.

In that situation, they must exercise both patience and restraint. Like the slaves of the householder in the parable of the weeds, they will be tempted to think that it is their job to pull up the weeds—to purge their own community of all evildoers. Perhaps they will be discouraged that they cannot rid society itself of wickedness and injustice. However, just as the householder told the slaves to wait until the harvest (13:29–30), so they must leave it to God to do the judging in God's own time. Some interpreters argue that the parable cannot apply to internal church discipline, because Matthew 18:15–18 (see also 16:18–19) grants the power of excommunication to the community. Such a judgment, however, stems from too rigid a standard of consistency. The combined force of the two passages is to recognize the two dangers—utterly laxity on the one hand and stifling severity on the other—that religious communities always face when confronted with behavior that violates their standards.

The discourse closes with a short scene (vv. 51–52) in which Jesus asks his disciples whether they have "understood all this." Here again the applicability of the discourse to the life of the church is manifest, and here again typical Matthean emphases assert themselves. Jesus' response to the disciples' "yes" is clearly positive. Because they do in fact understand, they apparently qualify as "scribes" in the new community, persons who can interpret the traditions, but which traditions, specifically? The new and the old—which is to say, Jesus' own teaching on the one hand and the whole body of Hebraic witness to God's revelation on the other. Just as in the Sermon on the Mount Jesus affirmed the Law but gave it his own interpretation (5:17–48), so now the community does the same, aided by interpreters "trained [more literally, "discipled"] for the kingdom of heaven"—that is, Christian interpreters who have heard and understood Jesus' proclamation. In later passages, it will become clearer that the community's practice of interpretation is an ongoing process (16:19; 18:18–20).

These closing verses probably presuppose a specific scribal office within the Matthean community, but insofar as the reader will naturally identify with the disciples in the narrative, the question-answer sequence also conveys something about the Matthean understanding of the nature of discipleship: It involves *understanding*. This can hardly mean a merely intellectual grasp of abstract truths, however, for in the closely related passage 11:28–30, Jesus' injunction to "learn from" him is followed by a testimony to his gentleness and humility and a promise of "rest." And throughout the gospel, Jesus' teaching is defined by ethical demands rooted in the ideals of love and mercy. The understanding Jesus seeks is thus a deep immersion in God, mediated by Jesus himself, that transforms one's being and produces the fruit of just action.

Thinking Today about Matthew 13:1–52

Interpreting the Parables

Modern scholarship has created a problem for the informed reader when it comes to the parables, for most scholars distinguish between parables and allegories, and many are convinced that only the former are to be attributed to the historical Jesus. Further, it is almost universally recognized that in the New Testament Jesus' original parables have often been made into allegories or given allegorical interpretations.

In an allegory, each element in the story points outside the story to realities with which the hearers will already be familiar. Thus one interprets an allegory by decoding it, that is, figuring out what each of its individual elements stands for. A genuine parable, however, signifies as a totality; its individual parts do not refer to specifics beyond the story itself. Its meaning, moreover, is intentionally indefinite, forcing the reader to enter into its world and make an interpretive leap. A parable, in C.H. Dodd's apt description, is designed "to tease [the mind] into active thought" (*The Parables of the Kingdom*, p. 5). Whereas an allegory merely reminds people of what they already know (how else could they do the "decoding"?), a parable creates new knowledge. By engaging the imagination, it calls for new insights, encourages the hearer to view things in a different way, and often challenges or even inverts conventional wisdom.

Some gospel commentators chide parables specialists for drawing the distinction too sharply and for merely assuming that Jesus did not tell allegories. The distinction is not absolute, but I remain convinced that the full-blown allegories in the New Testament emanate from the early church, not the historical Jesus. We can find important meaning in both "levels" of a parable (the form in which Jesus actually told it and the form it takes in the gospel narrative), but to avoid confusion the reader needs to make a distinction between the two.

The present chapter affords a good opportunity for reflection on the issue, because it contains prime examples of both parables and allegories. Scholars usually recognize the stories of the mustard seed, the yeast (more properly, leaven), the treasure, and the pearl as parables told by the historical Jesus, perhaps now slightly modified. Many scholars, however, regard 13:47–50 (the net) as Matthew's own composition; it is in any case an allegory of the last judgment. The sower (vv. 1–9) is usually considered an authentic parable of Jesus, somewhat modified by tradition, but it takes on allegorical meaning in its gospel setting. The explanation of this parable in verses 18–23, like the explanation of the parable of the weeds in verses 36–43, is clearly allegorical and the product of later tradition. The "parable" of the weeds itself (vv. 24–30) is often attributed to later tradition, because it is difficult to assign a nonallegorical meaning to it and the theme (don't purge the community) seems more appropriate to the postresurrection situation.

The three shortest parables in chapter 13—of the leaven, the treasure, and the pearl—carry dramatic meaning wholly apart from the Matthean context. The treasure and the pearl are commanding in their presentation of God's rule as a gift and surprise, which motivates one to give up all else for its sake. It is crucial to understand that the demand of God's rule follows from its quality as grace and a source of joy, not vice versa. The most salient aspect of these stories is that in each case the person's routine way of life is, as John Dominic Crossan put it, "rudely but happily shattered" (*In Parables,* p. 34).

Much energy has gone into the debate about whether the action of the person who finds the treasure is moral or even legal. One school of thought holds that the treasure employs an amoral mode in order to drive home its point; it is irrelevant whether the action is just or not. Another view (Scott, *Hear Then the Parable*, pp. 397–401) is that the "shadiness" of the action is actually part of the meaning, as is apparently the case with the parable of the unjust steward (Lk. 16:1–7). If this is so, then it has something in common with the parable of the leaven in verse 33, which makes use of images of impurity (a woman, leaven) in order to make its point. Far from a simple parable of "growth," this latter story presents God's rule as something that is actually subversive of standard religiosity and cultural norms. It is also something that is hidden from normal perception, because the verb weakly translated as "mixed" in the *New Revised Standard Version* actually means "hid" (RSV).

The parable of the mustard seed also invites abstraction from the Matthean context, but the Marcan version (4:30–32) is probably closer to the original. There the seed (with biological correctness) grows into a shrub, not a bush, and the birds nest in its shade, not its branches. In any case, the point is not natural development but, once again, surprise and gift. It is the contrast between the seemingly insignificant beginning and the dramatic ending that mirrors God's rule, not the process of gradual growth. Thus Crossan classifies the mustard seed along with the pearl and the treasure as a parable of "advent" (*In Parables*, pp. 45–52). And it should be noted that the Matthean version's very absurdity—the confusion of a shrub with a tree—actually increases the shock of the contrast.

In playing on the theme of small beginnings versus dramatic conclusion, it is important to remember the radical differences between both the Jesus movement and the early church on the one hand and the situation of North American churches of the majority culture in our own time. Expressions of hope for eventual vindication by beleaguered and oppressed communities in the ancient world become arrogant, imperialistic, and triumphalist when appropriated uncritically by those who are in many ways at ease in the world. There is truth in the contention that authentic Christianity is indeed ridiculed and rejected in our culture, but what many Christians experience is probably being ignored rather than being taken seriously enough for persecution. Thus the question arises about whether and to what extent many of our church communities can claim to manifest authentic Christianity in any meaningful sense. The parables of advent in Matthew 13 (the mustard seed, the pearl, and the treasure) have potential for raising that question, but it may be that the only way we can legitimately lay claim to these parables of advent and contrast is to take a visible and risky stand in solidarity with those in our world who are in more evident ways oppressed.

The parable of the weeds and its interpretation seem irreducibly allegorical, whether they are applied specifically to the church or to its interaction with the world. Commentators often identify "tolerance" as a theme here; the point, however, is not really respect for others' opinions but assurance that God will eventually deal with troublemakers. Davies and Allison thus find here a thematic unity with the parable of the sower: Both image God's eventual triumph over evil (*The Gospel According to Saint Matthew*, II, p. 408). Patience and dependence on God, then, are perhaps better descriptions of the point. This material does lend itself to counsel against "witch hunts" in the church or community, but it should be remembered that the presupposition is that there are in fact some weeds— that is, disciples of "the enemy."

Another aspect of the explanation of the parable in verses 36–43, the implicit inclusivism, or extra-ecclesiastical/christological salvation created by verse 38 ("the field is the world"), raises an important question, both in terms of Matthew's christology and in terms of the relationship of Christians to those outside the church. Because the issue appears more clearly in 25:31– 46, I will delay the discussion until that point (see pp. 174–76).

The hope of a literal future judgment that runs throughout this chapter raises questions from the perspective of a progressive theological stance (see "The Judgment of God, Inclusivism, and Grace," pp. 177–81). Equally problematic is the absoluteness with which Matthew 13, in company with much biblical writing, draws a distinction between good and evil (see "The Imaging of Evil," pp. 33–36). We are much more inclined today to think in terms of ambiguities and gradations, and with good reason: We have witnessed horrendous atrocities committed by persons fervently committed to their version of some truth. Our judgment against such atrocities, however, itself depends on a fundamental good/evil distinction, however little this point may be recognized by society at large and respected thinkers of our day.

It thus becomes important to find ways of thinking about good and evil that take into account both the ancient, classical insistence on absolutes and our modern/postmodern experience of ambiguity. Although it is necessary, from any perspective that is in any sense biblically rooted, to preserve the good/evil distinction, it is possible to do so while recognizing two points. First, it is necessary to recognize degrees of good and evil; life just does not come to us, for the most part, in terms of absolute either/or choices. Second, what is in fact good, in the sense of beneficial, to one group of persons might well be evil, in the sense of destructive, for another. There are competing interests in the world, and legitimate interests often come into conflict with one another. Thus it is no easy matter to define either the common good or what is right in individual ethical action.

We therefore need to learn how to draw on the power of the biblical rhetoric of good/evil and either/or in order to portray the seriousness of decision and also to take the complexity of life into account. By way of example, it is important to name as evil the exploitation of workers in sweatshops and to expose its roots in economic dogmas that have ruled moral questions out of court. It is equally important, though, to draw contemporary Christians into a creative process of seeking practical solutions and exploring viable options rather than simply pronouncing condemnation.

It is with good reason that since early times interpreters have applied the parable of the sower to the life of the church, and there is no reason to reject that practice. This material remains a rich and valuable resource for encouraging Christian self-examination. But it also plays a specific role in the Matthean narrative: It helps explain Jesus' rejection, and this means that it can foster a judgmental attitude toward non-Christians and Jews more specifically. However, one reading strategy to avoid such a consequence might be to place oneself in the position of the person confronting Jesus for the first time, in recognition of the sense in which an "unbeliever" dwells perpetually in each of us.

Reading this material as a parable of the historical Jesus holds an even greater potential, but it involves a more complex task than is the case with the shorter parables in chapter 13. Scholars generally think that the original version of the sower has been extensively modified in all the New Testament versions, and there is some variation among the proposed reconstructions of that original. In general, though, the thought is that the parable did not intend to allegorize specific types of failure among hearers of the word and was not concerned with "growth." Rather, it drew a sharp distinction between (three instances of) loss and gain in order to dramatize the "miraculous" sprouting of God's rule against all odds. Important treatments of this parable are found in Crossan (*In Parables*, pp. 39–52) and Scott (*Hear Then the Parable*, pp. 343–62), but particularly interesting from the perspective of this commentary is Theodore J. Weeden Sr.'s interpretation from the perspective of process thought in his article, "Recovering the Parabolic Intent in the Parable of the Sower."

13:53—16:20 Crisis of Identity

Further Responses to Jesus and Intimations of a New Community

13:53—14:36 A Spectrum of Responses: Jesus' Identity as the Focus

The third great discourse, 13:1–52, is bracketed by two stories concerning Jesus' family. In neither case does the family appear as negative in itself. Nor does Matthew contain a parallel to Mark 3:21, in which Jesus' relatives try to restrain him because people think he is mad. However, the theme of family works together with that of rejection in the following way.

The first of the stories, 12:46–50, ends with Jesus' pronouncement that those who do the will of God are his "brother and sister and mother." In the second, 13:53–58, when Jesus teaches in the synagogue in his own hometown (presumably Nazareth), the people are skeptical and offended, precisely because they know his origins: "Is not this the carpenter's son? Is not his mother called Mary?…Where then did this man get all this?" As we have seen, the discourse itself interprets the varying responses to Jesus in 11:2—12:50 in light of the cosmic conflict between good and evil, between God's rule and that of Satan. The effect of the bracketing is thus to allow the themes of cosmic conflict and Jesus' family/hometown to interpret one another. Taking Jesus' side in the conflict—opting for the rule of God he proclaims—means placing the will of God above community loyalty and, indeed, even family.

Jesus' comment in 13:57 adds another note to the narrator's explanation of his rejection by his people: "Prophets are not without honor except in their own country and in their own house." It is not so surprising that Jesus is rejected by his own, for that is the classical fate of the prophets. Just as Jesus earlier identified John as a prophet (11:7–15), so now he implies that one must view his own ministry against the background of the prophetic tradition, marked as it is with confrontation and tragedy.

The distinction between Jesus' biological family and hometown on the one hand and his true family on the other also prepares the reader for the founding of the new community, the church (*ekklesia*), in 16:13–20, the passage that will close out the second major section of the narrative. Thus from 13:53 to that point, the reader gets several hints about life in that new community.

Crucial for understanding the section beginning at 13:53 is Peter's acknowledgment of Jesus at 16:16, which prompts the founding of the church. The varying attitudes to Jesus that appear in this sequence revolve around the increasingly explicit issue of who he is.

The question of Jesus' identity is linked to the question of faith, and the construction of the narrative defines the two basic possibilities with another instance of bracketing. At the beginning of this section, the story of Jesus' rejection in his hometown ends with an explanation (13:58): "And he did not do many deeds of power there, because of their unbelief." Then in 14:34–36, the narrator marks off a subsection with a contrasting account. At Gennesaret, people from the surrounding region bring their sick for healing. Their faith is so great that, like the woman in 9:18–25, they believe that even touching the fringe of his cloak will give them what they need.

Between the brackets, in 14:1–33, the reader has an opportunity to observe the faith status of the disciples, and the result is ambiguous. To their credit, they make the proper response to Jesus at the conclusion of the story of his walking on the water; they worship him, "saying, 'Truly you are the Son of God.'" In various ways, however, they show that their faith, though real, is still only partial. Peter's wavering confidence as he attempts to join Jesus on the water prompts Jesus to address him as "you of little faith" (see also 6:30; 8:26; 16:8; 17:20). Before that, in the account of the feeding of the five thousand (vv. 13–21), the disciples are ready to dismiss the crowds to go buy food before Jesus tells them otherwise; and when he commands them to feed the people, they can see only the limitations of the provisions they have. From a mundane perspective, their hesitations are understandable; but from the point of view of the narrative, the disciples are ignoring the possibilities inherent in Jesus' presence with them.

If the stories in 14:13–36 contrast the disciples' partial faith to the deeper faith of the people of Gennesaret, the account of John's execution (14:1–12) begins the whole sequence by depicting sheer opposition to God's rule. In this flashback scene, Herod the tetrarch (NRSV: ruler)—Herod Antipas, son of Herod the Great, now ruling over Galilee and Peraea—appears as completely malevolent. Verses 3–5 indicate that he wants John dead because of John's criticism of his marriage to his brother's divorced wife, considered incestuous in Leviticus 20:21. It is only fear of the reaction of the people that has prevented him from acting—just as similar fear will be at work in 26:3–5 as the chief priests and elders plot Jesus' death. So although it is his wife Herodias's scheming that actually sets the murder in motion, Herod appears as fully guilty. His grief in verse 9 should be understood in relation to verse 5: He has no concern for John's life, only a continuing fear of what the people will think.

The beginning of this story also serves to focus on the question of Jesus' identity, because Herod speculates that he must be John the Baptist come back from the dead. The issue is kept before the reader not only by the miracles in 14:13–33 but also by specific phraseology. On the water,

Jesus uses the formula that God utters in the Septuagint version of Exodus 3:14: *ego eimi*—"It is I," or, simply, "I am." Especially in the context of walking on the water—a feat attributed to God in such texts as Job 9:8 and Psalm 77:19—the reader will hear this as an indication of Jesus' divine status. And the confession of faith in verse 33 gives specificity to it. He is, as the narrator made clear early in the story (3:17), the Son of God.

The question of Jesus' identity dovetails with the theme of the nascent community. In the story of the feeding of the five thousand, the Christian reader can scarcely miss echoes of the eucharist. Jesus' words and actions in verse 19 closely parallel those at the Last Supper (26:26–29). The notation that "all ate and were filled" combines with the emphasis on the vastness of the crowd in verse 21 to suggest symbolic significance: Jesus the Son of God provides sustenance to the people in a prefiguration of the eschatological messianic banquet.

However, Jesus' action is not the only intimation of the later Christian community. Employing an emphatic construction ("*you* give…"), Jesus tells the disciples themselves to feed the people; it is they, drawing on the meager five loaves and two fishes they already have, who perform the actual distribution. Jesus' divine power makes their action possible, but their service to the hungry crowd will naturally suggest the ministrations of later church leaders who stand in continuity with them.

The mysterious scene on the water also encourages the reader to think of the church. The crisis in the story occurs when the disciples are alone in a boat, while Jesus is off by himself on a mountain praying. Having struggled all night, they are far from shore but unable to reach their destination because of the wind. Once again, the specifics are telling. As David Garland notes, the wind ceases precisely when Jesus and Peter enter the boat, and it is in the boat that the disciples worship Jesus as the Son of God. It is the boat itself, moreover, that is "battered," and the Greek verb (*basanizo*) can also be translated "tortured" or "harassed." Verse 24 is thus, Garland remarks, "a fitting description of the persecution of the church" (*Reading Matthew*, p. 158). And the image of the disciples in the boat, worshiping the one who has saved them from the sea (symbol of chaos), combines with that of the disciples feeding the crowds by Jesus' power to create subtle overtones of the postresurrection community.

The boat motif also plays into the narrator's characterization of the disciples as works still in progress, and attention to it can illumine an ambiguity in the story: the nature of Peter's failure. On the one hand, Peter's venture onto the water seems commendable; he asks, and receives, Jesus' bidding before he takes a step. On the other hand, it is not at all clear that it is an act of trust rather than mistrust—an attempt to verify that the figure on the water is in fact Jesus. Not only do the disciples take the figure on the water for a ghost, but Peter's lack of confidence is revealed in the phrasing of his question: "Lord, *if* it is you..." (emphasis added). Furthermore, if the boat symbolizes the church, it would appear that it is there, in the boat, not out on the water, that Peter belongs—especially because the crisis has not been resolved. (See Garland, *Reading Matthew*, p. 158.) From this point of view, the problem is not that Peter lacks the faith to accomplish a legitimate mission but that in this instance he has in fact misunderstood his role. What, after all, would be the *point* of joining Jesus on the water?

Both this story and the subsection as a whole, however, end on positive notes. Despite the flaws of both Peter and the other disciples, they all worship Jesus. The scene in the boat is followed by the account of the less ambiguous faith of the people of Gennesaret. Yet the reader remembers also the conflicts in the preceding chapters and the ominous note sounded in the story of Herod's execution of John.

In summary, the subsection 13:54—14:36 draws together the themes of the continuing cosmic conflict, Jesus' identity, varying responses to him, the real but imperfect faith of the disciples, and the postresurrection community. At this point, the question of Jesus' status as Son of God predominates over that of the specific divine traits he represents. This latter issue, however, is never far from the surface, for Jesus' role as God's Son is to nourish the hungry crowds and save the hapless boat and crew from the destructive forces that harass them.

15:1—16:12 A Spectrum of Responses: God's Requirements as the Focus

The preceding subsection was bracketed by stories of contrasting responses to Jesus: rejection in his hometown in 13:53–58 and the faith of the people of Gennesaret in 14:34–35. Now a new subsection is marked off by somewhat more complex accounts of responses. In 15:1–2, a group of Pharisees and scribes come from Jerusalem to challenge him because his disciples fail to honor the "tradition of the elders" regarding hand washing before meals. Jesus answers them in 15:3–9 with a devastating critique of their own hypocritical use of tradition and then in verses 10–20 addresses the crowds on the broad issue of what defiles a person. The end of the subsection is delineated by 16:1–12. In 16:1, the Pharisees and Sadducees test (or "tempt") Jesus by asking for a sign from heaven. He answers them and departs from them in verses 2–4, but in verses 5–12 the Pharisees and Sadducees are still at issue as he warns his disciples against their "yeast" and is finally able to get the point across that "yeast" is a metaphor for "teaching."

Both the beginning and ending segments, then, focus on the negative responses of the Jewish leadership to Jesus. Pharisees, scribes, and Sadducees—all are utterly opposed to Jesus, seeking only to trip him up without ever giving him a real hearing. In partial contrast, however, stand the disciples. On the one hand, Jesus again applies to them the term "little faith" because they miss the point of his metaphor. Nevertheless, "little faith" still contrasts with no faith, and in any case, here again in 16:12 as in 13:51 the reader learns that they do in fact come to understand his point.

The disciples' understanding is more than intellectual acumen, as verses 9–10 make clear, but what is the link between understanding the metaphor of yeast and grasping the significance of the feedings of the five thousand (14:13–21) and the four thousand? Some interpreters see allegorical significance in the numbers of baskets collected. Such a reading is credible for the Marcan parallel (Mk. 8:14–21), because in that account the disciples explicitly say "seven" and "twelve." These statements are missing in Matthew, however, so the meaning must be of a broader nature. And it must have something to do with faith, because that is precisely the issue that the term "little faith" raises.

In both feeding accounts, Jesus is compassionate toward the crowds (14:14; 15:32), and in both instances, the people eat and are filled (14:20; 15:37). We noted above the overtones of the eucharist in the first story, and the same applies to the second. Thus one function of the stories is to enhance the reader's image of Jesus as the compassionate Messiah/Son of God who meets the needs of the people in both spiritual and material ways—a point that is further underscored in the account of Jesus' healings in 15:29–31. In the first feeding story, however, the disciples show not only misunderstanding as they do in Mark, but also a lack of trust in Jesus' ability to provide. When Jesus tells them to feed the people, their reply is, "We have nothing here but five loaves and two fish" (14:17). Then again, despite his miraculous action at this point, in the second story they show a continuing lack of confidence: "Where are we to get enough bread in the desert…?" (15:33).

In the Marcan account, there is no explanation of the meaning of "leaven," and the emphasis is apparently on the disciples' failure to grasp the significance of the numbers seven and twelve. In Matthew, however, Jesus responds to the disciples' proposal that his warning deals with their neglect to bring bread by addressing them as "[y]ou of little faith." The effect is to link their misunderstanding here with their earlier lack of trust in Jesus' ability to provide bread. Faith and understanding thus go together.

The same lack of faith that prevented the disciples from understanding what Jesus was about to do in the feedings lies at the basis of their inability to grasp the metaphor of leaven. The real issue is whether they are able to trust Jesus to provide for human need. That is why Jesus can ask them, "Do you not remember the five loaves for the five thousand…?" (16:9).

The disciples do come to understand, just as they show proper understanding when they worship Jesus as Son of God in 14:33. Yet their "little" faith still sets them apart from the Canaanite woman in 15:21–26, whose faith Jesus terms "great."

This latter story also ties into the theme of Jesus' specific ministry to Israel, in contrast to the Gentile mission that he will inaugurate at the end of the gospel. It is important to remember that immediately following the next subsection (16:13–20), we have the beginning of the third major part of the gospel. At 16:21, Jesus begins to teach his disciples that he must die, and from that point until the entry into Jerusalem in chapter 21, the narrative is dominated by the dual motifs of the journey toward Jerusalem and Jesus' continued instruction to the disciples about his coming death and resurrection (David R. Bauer, *The Structure of Matthew's Gospel*, pp. 96–104). Jesus will cast out one more demon (17:14–19) and engage the collectors of the temple tax (17:24–28) before leaving Galilee, and additional encounters and opportunities for teaching await him in Judea and Jerusalem, but a decisive turn occurs at 16:21; the emphasis is no longer on Jesus' proclamation and ministry to Israel but on his coming death. Thus the present subsection, 15:1—16:12, which leads to Peter's climactic acknowledgment of Jesus, effectively closes out Jesus' attempt in Galilee to gather the "lost sheep of the house of Israel" to him (15:24).

This phrase, which concludes the story of Jesus' healing of the Canaanite woman's daughter, echoes his limitation of the disciples' present mission to Israel in 10:6. It thus reminds the reader that Jesus' mission has so far been limited to Israel—a point underscored by the notation in 15:31 that the people Jesus healed "praised the God of Israel" (contra some interpreters who think this means they were Gentiles). On the other hand, the phrase actually functions as a kind of foil because the healing constitutes an exception to the limitation of the mission, as did the earlier healing of the centurion's servant (8:5–13). The narrator thus reinforces the impression that the mission will eventually extend to Gentiles as well as Jews.

The story of Jesus' encounter with the Canaanite woman raises some perplexing questions for the contemporary interpreter, however, for Jesus not only refuses the woman's request at first but also uses an uncomplimentary epithet for Gentiles. Moreover, it is the woman who brings Jesus to a more inclusive perspective, rather than vice versa. Reflection on these points can uncover some important undercurrents of meaning in the narrative, and I have provided some reflections along these lines later ("Jesus, Gentiles, and Gender," pp. 122–24). Such questions, however, do not seem to be a concern of the narrator.

Several clues both at the beginning and the end of the subsection indicate that a fundamental turn in the plot is developing. At 15:1, the narrator notes that the Pharisees and scribes come from Jerusalem, thus directing attention to the power base of the Jewish leadership. Then in 16:1–4 the unlikely coalition of Pharisees and Sadducees creates the impression that the opposition to Jesus is taking on a more unified and "official" character. And, finally, verse 24 has a climactic ring about it. When Jesus repeats his statement from 12:38–42 regarding the "sign of Jonah" (this time without the veiled reference to his death and resurrection), the reader will remember that this is the second time Jesus' opponents have asked for a sign. They have thus learned nothing from the earlier encounter and have in fact made their demand even more ridiculous by specifying a "sign from heaven," by which they apparently mean some cosmic demonstration in contrast to the earthly deeds of exorcisms and healings Jesus has performed. The notation in verse 4 that Jesus "left them and went away" will thus suggest something more than the end of this particular conversation.

If 13:53—14:36 elevated the issue of Jesus' identity over that of the specific content of his character and teaching, the situation is reversed in the present material. The controversy with the Pharisees and scribes in 15:1–9 and Jesus' subsequent teaching in verses 10–19 focus on the question of what God truly requires of human beings, but the character of both Jesus and his opponents also becomes an issue because their respective teachings reveal who they are and how they relate to God. The issue here is not the Jewish law as such, not even the validity of the rules of ritual purity it contains, because Mark's provocative statement (Mk. 7:19) that Jesus "declared all foods clean" is missing from Matthew's version. Without that statement, the emphasis falls on the validity of the Pharisaic tradition itself—that is, the oral law that the Pharisees propagated alongside the written Torah. The hand-washing requirement comes not directly from Torah but from the Pharisees' application of the requirements for priests (Ex. 30:17–21) to laypersons as well. In Matthew, it is this alone that Jesus rejects.

The debate, however, transcends both a merely technical reading of the Law and the issue of Pharisaic tradition, for Jesus rejects that tradition precisely because it is being used for purposes that contradict God's will. The charge in verse 5 is that the Pharisees allow people to dedicate some of their material resources for the temple in order to make it unavailable in case their parents should fall into need and lay claim to it. In verses 3–4,

Jesus says this practice violates the commandment to honor one's father and mother. Consistent with 5:17–20, then, Jesus upholds the Law, but consistent with Matthew's emphasis on the love commandment as the principle for interpreting the Law (22:40), in verses 10–20 he takes the discussion in an explicitly moral direction. Denying that unwashed hands defile, in verse 19 he names the things that do defile with a list that focuses on human beings' treatment of one another. The Pharisees are hypocritical (v. 7) because they overturn God's commandments with their human tradition; what God has commanded is not a set of narrowly "religious" requirements but justice in human relationships.

Once again, then, Jesus appears as the proponent of justice and mercy, whereas his opponents represent hard-heartedness, even though none of these qualities are named in this instance. Thus when the subsection ends in 16:5–12 with the discussion of the "leaven" of the Pharisees and Sadducees, one must think in these terms. Jesus' opponents reject him because they do not accept who he is; but they do not accept who he is because they reject what he stands for. It is specifically because of their teaching that Jesus pronounces that God has not "planted" them and will therefore root them up (15:13). However, it is the Jesus who here stands for justice in human relations who can speak of God as "*my* heavenly Father" (emphasis added). It is essential to grasp this point when interpreting the dramatic scene that follows in 16:13–20.

The contrast between Jesus and his opponents serves primarily to advance the plot, sharpening the conflict and preparing for the foundation of the community. At the same time, elements in this subsection also apply rather directly to the life of that community in the postresurrection situation. Most particularly, the initial encounter with the Pharisees and scribes justifies its apparent rejection of Pharisaic teaching on ritual purity, as is seen in the way the narrator closes the subsection in 16:12: the disciples understand that Jesus is warning them specifically against "the teaching of the Pharisees and Sadducees."

16:13–20 Peter's Acknowledgment of Jesus and Jesus' Founding of the Church

In the final subsection, Jesus and his disciples come to the district of Caesarea Philippi, where Jesus confronts those who follow him with the issue of his identity. The first question, regarding the opinions of others, builds toward the second, with its emphatic use of the second person plural (discernible in Greek) pronoun: "But who do *you* say that I am?" The reader has known Jesus' identity since the beginning of the narrative, and the disciples have already worshiped him explicitly as Son of God in 14:33 in spontaneous response to his miraculous actions on the sea. Now, however, Jesus himself raises the issue as a matter of formal acknowledgment. Thus the theme of identity, woven into the preceding narrative in various ways, comes to a head.

The passage abounds with difficulties, as the varied interpretations of numerous points show. Does Peter answer as an individual person, or on behalf of the others? Does Jesus give an unrepeatable role to Peter, or does he institute an office that Peter holds but will be passed on to others? What is "this rock" on which the church is built—Peter himself, or something else? What is meant by the "keys of the kingdom of heaven" and the power to "bind and loose"? And, finally, what does it mean that "the gates of Hades will not prevail against" the church?

Recent interpreters, fortunately, have largely left behind the rancorous debates surrounding the traditional Roman Catholic reading of the passage as depicting the founding of the papacy. Thus the various interpretations no longer follow strict denominational lines as they tended to do for so long, and fairly wide agreement has emerged on two key points. First, it is Peter himself who is the "rock," not his faith as in the classical Protestant reading, which means that Peter is in fact given a special role. Second, however, this role cannot be equated with the formal and continuing office of the papacy.

A study by Chrys Caragounis (*Peter and the Rock*), however, has challenged the consensus on the first point, and David Garland (*Reading Matthew*, pp. 170–71) has endorsed his reading. The issue turns in part on the significance of the Greek term for Peter, *petros*, which is different from that for "rock," *petra*. *Petros*, a masculine noun, classically meant "stone," a small, movable object, whereas *petra*, feminine, meant "rock" in the sense of a geological configuration. The reigning interpretation is based on two theories. The first is that behind verses 17–19, which appear only in Matthew, there is a tradition going back to the early church (and some would say Jesus himself) that appeared originally in Aramaic, the primary language in first-century Jewish Palestine. The second is that behind the two Greek terms lies a single word in Aramaic, which was probably the primary language of Jesus and the earliest Jewish Christians. That word was *kepha*, which appears in the New Testament as Peter's Aramaic name, Cephas. Thus the meaning of verse 18 is, "you are 'Rock,' and on this rock I will build my church." When the verse was translated in Greek, however, the masculine *Petros* was naturally used to designate Peter, whereas the feminine *petra* was chosen for the second half of the verse because it had the specific meaning of "rock" as opposed to "stone." Thus the wordplay was somewhat distorted.

As Caragounis shows, however, by New Testament times the two Greek words had become interchangeable, so that one could easily have preserved the supposed original wordplay simply by translating the second part of the verse as "on this *petros.*" The whole issue of an Aramaic original thus becomes largely irrelevant, and the difference between the two terms in the Greek text, *petros* and *petra*, takes on significance. They must have different meanings in this context, which means that "this rock" cannot be a reference to Peter himself. This conclusion should in no way be surprising. To speak of Peter as "this rock" in a direct address to him would be extremely odd to begin with, and there is nothing else in the gospel of Matthew (or the New Testament generally) to suggest that Peter himself was understood as in any sense the foundation of the church.

According to Caragounis, then, *"[t]he [petra] is the content of Peter's insight, i.e. that Jesus is the Messiah"* (*Peter and the Rock*, p. 107, italics original). The wordplay is based not on the identity of the two words, as those who look back to an original Aramaic often contend, but on their similarity in form and meaning—actually, a more usual way for a wordplay to work. And Caragounis suggests this as a paraphrase of its intended force: *"As sure as you are [called] Petros, on this rock [i.e. of what you have just said…] I shall build my church"* (p. 113).

To say that in Matthew, Peter is not the foundation of the church is not to deny his strong leadership role, but the preceding interpretation is consistent with two important facts. First, although Peter alone makes the confession and it is Peter as an individual person that Jesus pronounces blessed, the question was posed to the disciples collectively: The "you" in verse 15 is plural. Second, verse 19—in which Jesus gives Peter the "keys of the kingdom" and the power to bind and loose to Peter alone (here the "you" is singular)—is partially paralleled in 18:18, where Jesus gives the latter power to the disciples collectively. It would seem, then, that Peter's acknowledgment is made on behalf of all the disciples and his leadership role is representative rather than strictly hierarchical and authoritarian.

Matthew 16:13–20 has thematic connections not only with chapter 18, the church discourse, but also with 11:25–27 and 28:16–20. In the latter passage, the very end of the gospel, Jesus implicitly passes his own authority, given by God, to the disciples, in order that they may carry out their mission to the world. The phraseology, "All authority in heaven and on earth has been given to me," is highly reminiscent of the first half of 11:27: "All things have been handed over to me by my Father." The second half of that verse has strong links to the present passage. In 11:27, Jesus states that "no one knows the Father except the Son and anyone to whom the Son chooses to reveal him"; and in 16:17, Jesus pronounces Peter blessed because his acknowledgment of Jesus is a specific result of God's revelation to him. It is thus clear that in Matthew, Jesus founds the church and passes on to it the very authority God has given him; it is not incidental that he refers to it in verse 18 as "*my* church."

Because of the "church" theme, this passage, like few others in the gospels, brings together the two functions we have so often seen at work in Matthew. It advances the plot and at the same time speaks directly to the postresurrection church. In terms of plot, it caps off the theme of opposition to Jesus; because the Jewish leadership is rejecting him, he founds an alternative community. This point will become clearer as Jesus begins to teach explicitly about his death and resurrection in the following chapters. But from the perspective of the postresurrection community of Jesus' followers, the passage will also legitimate this community, over against the competing Jewish leadership, and will empower its members with the confidence that Jesus has promised perseverance against "the gates of Hades."

The general force of this latter phrase is clear enough—the church will in fact prevail—but its specific meaning is a matter of dispute. The first point to make is that Hades does not mean hell. It is the term for the realm of the dead in Greek mythology and corresponds to Sheol in the Hebrew thought, not to Gehenna. The latter was the name of a ravine near Jerusalem that in the first century B.C.E. took on the metaphorical meaning of a place to which the wicked were assigned after death. Sheol, however, was not a place of punishment but simply the abode of all the dead, who continued a kind of shadowy existence quite unlike the later notion of a true everlasting life.

More difficult is the meaning of "gates," and it is linked to the question of whether the verb translated "prevail" in the NRSV, *katischyein*, should be understood as meaning "withstand" or "overcome." The issue, in other words, is who (church/Hades) is attacking whom? Because gates generally function to defend a city, some interpreters think the point is that the church will storm the gates of death and overcome it. Thus "prevail" would mean "withstand." Alternatively, one could take "gates" as synecdoche, a literary device in which the part stands for the whole, and understand *katischyein* in an active rather than a passive sense. That is to say, death cannot overcome the church because, as Davies and Allison note (*The Gospel According to Saint Matthew*, p. 633), in the Septuagint the Greek verb in question "is always active when followed by the genitive." The latter would seem to be the better interpretation, because it also fits well with the understanding of the boat in 14:22–32 as a symbol of the persecuted church.

The phrase "keys of the kingdom" is traditionally interpreted in conjunction with particular understanding of the nature of Peter's leadership role and the phrase "bind and loose." According to this view, possession of the keys makes Peter the gatekeeper of heaven who by "binding" and "loosing" determines who is in and out of the church and thus ultimately heaven. Neither of these interpretations is necessarily correct, however.

In the first place, in Matthew "'the kingdom of heaven' is not equated with the heavenly world" (Davies and Allison, *The Gospel According to Saint Matthew*, II, p. 634). Nor is it equated with the church (see pp. 94–97, on 13:36–43). In 23:13, Jesus accuses the Pharisees of preventing people from entering it, and the keys image is best understand in a parallel way. Peter holds the power to open the gates of God's rule to persons in the here and now. How, specifically, does he do so? By "binding" and "loosing." But what do these terms mean? A wide range of scholars agree that they must be understood as equivalents of parallel terms in rabbinic literature, where they have to do with legal interpretation. This would mean that Jesus is speaking of the power to interpret what the law permits and forbids. This reading is almost certainly correct; it fits well not only with the immediate context, Jesus' criticism of the teaching of the Pharisees in 15:1–20 and the narrator's comment at 16:12, but also with the strong Matthean emphasis on the Jewish law and its interpretation.

The immediate context of the parallel in 18:18, however, suggests that the power to interpret what is permitted or forbidden includes the authority to exclude persons from the community because the preceding verse (18:17) says with respect to anyone who ultimately refuses to accept the authority of the church community in a dispute, "let such a one be to you as a Gentile and a tax collector." (See "The Problem of Forgiveness," pp. 139–40, for a discussion of the tension between this verse and the implication of unlimited forgiveness in 18:21–22.) The parallel in chapter 18, as we have already seen, also places the authority given to Peter in the context of the authority given the disciples collectively. Thus in the present passage Jesus not only founds the church but also empowers its leadership to make decisions about how the Jewish law, which in Matthew remains valid (5:17–20), is in practice to be interpreted. This means that faithfulness to the law is defined not in terms of a rigid literalism but as a dynamic and ongoing process of discovery—analogous to that which was at work in rabbinic Judaism itself, despite the caricature of the Pharisees and scribes in Matthew.

The section closes with Jesus' warning to the disciples "not to tell anyone that he was the Messiah." The parallel verse in Mark (8:30) follows immediately on Peter's acknowledgment of Jesus and constitutes at least a partial rebuke of Peter. It thus plays into the pervasive theme of the "messianic secret," which is linked to the Marcan notion that the disciples did not truly understood Jesus in the preresurrection situation. Such a view of the disciples is foreign to Matthew, however, which makes a point of noting the disciples' understanding. The secrecy theme is muted in Matthew, though not entirely absent. Because 16:20 comes after Jesus' blessing of Peter, it is in no sense a rebuke. It is in fact somewhat puzzling. This means that, like the ending of many a chapter in a well-constructed novel, it encourages the reader to read on for further explanation.

That explanation will not be long in coming, for in the verses that begin the final section of the narrative, Jesus will start to focus on the disciples and to teach them about his coming death and resurrection. Thus the secrecy commanded in verse 20 would seem to be related to the fact that the teaching about his death is for the disciples alone, those who are capable of understanding it. Yet it will immediately become apparent that even they do not take easily to the notion, which will result in the rebuke of Peter after all.

Thinking Today about Matthew 13:53—16:20

Professing Faith in Jesus

What does it *mean* to acknowledge Jesus as the Messiah? The concluding passage of this section, Peter's dramatic acknowledgment of Jesus at Caesarea Philippi, is a classic portrayal of a Christian profession of faith. But it can also foster an approach to faith that is purely abstract and otherworldly, void of any existential content—content, that is, that reflects and speaks to the concrete lives that human beings live. In order to determine what it means to acknowledge Jesus, we also have to ask *why* anyone *should* make such an acknowledgment. And in order to do so, we must first note some fundamental differences between the presuppositions that underlie the gospel of Matthew and those that underlie our own worldview.

In the context in which the gospel of Matthew appeared, questions regarding the reality of God or the spiritual dimension were not at issue. Both the Matthean community and the rival Jewish teachers assumed the notion of a deity who had chosen Israel and was working with it through the historical process for the salvation of the world. The only question was who truly *represented* God, and the Matthean narrative is structured in order to show that it was Jesus who did so. Beyond the world of Judaism and nascent Christianity, of course, these specific presuppositions did not function. Yet the vast majority of people in the ancient world assumed a spiritual order of some nature, and the issue at that point would not be pure unbelief versus the gospel message but rival conceptions of the divine.

In our world, by contrast, those who believe in God and/or a spiritual dimension are on the defensive. Although the vast majority of Americans profess belief in God, the purely secular consciousness is strong enough to make it incumbent on religious people to deal seriously with the question of whether there is anything to the universe other than matter in motion. Belief is thus an issue not only in the church's interaction with the world but in its internal life as well. The skepticism of the age is subtly present even in the minds of the strongest believers. This is a point paradoxically attested by the ferocity with which the various religious fundamentalisms pit themselves against the wider culture.

What does it mean to acknowledge Jesus as the Christ, and why should anyone do so? Before approaching those questions for our time, it is important to see how the structure of the Matthean narrative implies some answers from the perspective of first-century Christian readers.

The gospel of Matthew assumes at the outset the reader's faith, or at least disposition toward faith, by naming Jesus as Messiah, son of David and son of Abraham, in the very first verse. Then, throughout the story, the narrator assures the reader that the events in his life are direct fulfillments of passages from the Hebrew Scriptures. The weight of the story, however, falls on Jesus' words and deeds: He teaches, casts out demons, heals the sick, raises the dead, accepts sinners into his fellowship, and prepares his followers for the time after his death. In all of this, there is a correspondence between his teaching and his deeds. Making mercy and love the central components of his teaching, he manifests these attributes in the works he performs. Totally unlike the "sign from heaven" his opponents demand, these works meet concrete human need on the one hand and convey symbolic value on the other. Although he affirms the continuing validity of the Jewish law, Jesus cuts through the tangle of his opponents' rules and regulations to identify what God wants most from human beings—the love and mercy that is manifest in his own words and deeds.

The result is that through the course of the narrative the reader is encouraged to compare God as represented by the Jewish leaders and God as represented by Jesus. Thus a narrative reading of 16:13–20 necessarily reaches far beyond that passage—primarily backward into the concrete details of Jesus' ministry to Israel in Galilee—to find both the existential content of Peter's acknowledgment and the reasons for it.

When we come to the question of faith in Jesus in our own context, it should be immediately apparent that some aspects of Matthew's construction of the issue offer more potential than others. Neither scriptural "proof-texts" nor literal readings of miracle-stories will be ultimately satisfying, even if at some stages of faith development they might provide some measure of support. Attention to the specific contents of Jesus' ministry, however—the meaning of his deeds and the contents of his teaching—can provide a way of "unpacking" the question, "Who do you say that I am?" Approached in such a way, this question can take a form in our time that is not tied to the specific presuppositions of the ancient world.

The starting point will not be whether Jesus fulfills scripture or fits the category "Messiah," but whether the stories of his words and deeds resonate with our experience in the world. The question, in other words, is whether these stories encourage us to believe something that in some sense we already know to be true: that our lives are pervaded and empowered by a reality beyond ourselves, characterized by infinite love and mercy on the one hand and a demand for justice on the other.

This is only the starting point, however, for the meaning of Jesus' life cannot be grasped apart from the whole Hebrew tradition in which he stands. To acknowledge him as Messiah/Christ or as "Son of the living God" is to interpret his life as a way of drawing together various strands of Hebrew tradition in order to present as definitive a specific understanding of humanity before God. This much seems indisputable, but a major theological problem for our generation remains: how to maintain our affirmation of Jesus as the Jewish Messiah without denying the continuing validity of the Jewish religion. We will return to this issue at a later point. (See "The Judgment of God, Inclusivism, and Grace," pp. 177–81.)

The stories of healings and feedings in this section provide good material for fleshing out faith in Jesus with specific content, whether or not one connects them directly to Peter's acknowledgment of Jesus in 16:13–20. There are traps here, too, of course, and not all on the side of a naïve attitude toward claims regarding the miraculous. Early liberalism's rationalistic explanations of the feedings—for example, the people really had lunches with them all along but kept them hidden so they wouldn't have to share—have little to do with the meaning of the stories as presented in the narrative. What these stories do present is the image of Jesus as nurturing humanity, and their eucharistic overtones invite metaphorical readings that take the food as spiritual sustenance provided in the Christian community. It would be tragic, however, in light of the vast world hunger and poverty in our day, to ignore their more "materialist" implications. Jesus' injunction in 14:16, "*you* give them something to eat" (emphasis added), provides an obvious opening for calls to Christian service on both levels—that of political activism and ministry to the spiritual needs of individual persons.

The story of Jesus' rejection in his hometown (13:54–48) had a particular significance for the Matthean community that for us is both less meaningful and fraught with problems. Insofar as we view it in a literal way as reflecting Israel's hard-heartedness, it plays into the anti-Judaism that many Christians in our day are seeking so hard to overcome. As a component in the Matthean narrative, however, it has important implications for contemporary U.S. society. For one thing, it raises a question similar to that which emerges in the Beelzebul controversy (12:22–32): What is the basis of Jesus' actions? The people deny neither Jesus' works nor his wisdom, but they reject him—not in this case because they attribute these to Satan but simply because they think they know who he is. The underlying assumption is that a true representative of God would have to produce some sort of credentials, and Jesus' familiarity to them prevents them from seeing in his deeds the activity of God. In a broad sense, the problem is their inability to discern the divine within the earthly sphere—even in cases where it virtually explodes on the scene! Readers in our day should have no trouble identifying contemporary examples of those who *will not* open themselves to intimations of transcendence in their own experience. One thinks immediately, for example, of persons who persistently focus on the negative aspects of life to the exclusion of moments of redemption. Other examples might be of persons who insist on reducing all acts of human kindness to biological or social causes alone, or of those who assume without question that scientific explanations of the origin of life rule out any meaning or purpose in the process that brings life forth.

Matthew 13:54–58 is also an endorsement of voices of dissent, especially when read in conjunction with 12:46–50 ("Who is my mother, and who are my brothers?"). In the context of the narrative, Jesus represents a new possibility emerging within the old, a new direction through which the ancient promises of God are being fulfilled. The rejection of Jesus thus represents an inappropriate clinging to the past, a refusal to let God build on it in order to create a future. A central issue in both 13:54–58 and 12:46–50 is a kind of idolatry: the choice of a particular traditional understanding of God over the God who is at work in the events of the present time. Traditional images of what the church should be, a narrow focus on one's family or group, and an uncritical nationalism linked to half-truths about an idyllic American past—all are contemporary versions of a similar mind-set.

Jesus' identification of himself as a prophet in 13:57 is significant, because one of the strains in the Hebrew Bible most important for New Testament interpretation is the prophetic. In Matthew, prophecy tends to be reduced to prediction, but in this passage, the more profound meaning breaks through. Here Jesus is parallel to the great prophets who challenged kings and priests on the issue of what God wants of the people at a particular point in history.

The story of Herod's murder of John the Baptist plays into this theme also, for not only does the narrator say at 14:5 that the people considered

John a prophet, but in 11:7–15, Jesus himself has already affirmed John's prophetic office and further proclaimed him "more than a prophet" and "Elijah who is to come." When Herod has John put to death, he repeats a typical pattern in Hebrew history: Prophets challenge the powers-that-be, and those powers react with violence (see Mt. 5:12; 23:29–39). In the context of the Matthean narrative, John's death foreshadows that of Jesus himself, who also falls victim to the official violence of the state. Neither the obscure issue of the illegitimacy of Herod's marriage nor voyeuristic speculation about the nature of Herodias's daughter's dance should be allowed to get in the way of the profound issue of prophetic witness that is raised in this story. On the other hand, the exploitation of a young woman by her mother, within the context of the intrigues of a corrupt ruling class, calls up equally tragic parallels in our own troubled society.

The story of Jesus' walking on the water (14:22–33), as we have seen, is symbolic of Jesus' presence with the persecuted church. Persecution is hardly the concern of the average Christian in our society if we think only of the early church's experience of suffering simply for claiming the name of Christ. If, however, we think what happens to people in our world who stand for the concrete values embraced by Jesus, then the matter is rather different. Certainly Christian communities in Latin America who engage in praxis based on liberation theology know what it means to suffer for Christ's sake, as do many North American activists for social justice.

When Matthew 14:22–33 is viewed from this perspective, the theme of the disciples' fear begins to stand out; and when the phrase "little faith" is interpreted in light of that theme, it begins to take on deeper meaning. As we have seen, this section of Matthew provides images of varying degrees of faith. A meaningful way to approach this material, therefore, is to focus on the presentation of faith as a reality in process. It is an inherently comforting thought that the disciples themselves—most particularly Peter—are presented as works-in-progress. When we add persecution and fear to the equation, however, the issue becomes more complex. How can we maintain faith in the face of the unimaginable suffering that the last century, into which we entered at the height of human optimism, has brought?

The Power of God Revisited

There is no simple answer to the question raised above, but here is another point at which dialogue between the ancient world and our own can be particularly fruitful. In the biblical world of thought, God for the most part appears as capable of unilateral action in the world. That is to say, God holds all the power in the relationship between God and the world. There is thus a tendency to ascribe to the divine will all that happens. On the other hand, there is a pervasive assumption of human free will and responsibility. If we take all these passages at face value, we will find that a grand paradox runs through the scriptures: God controls everything, but human beings are responsible for their deeds. It is not clear, however, that the biblical writers always intended that their deterministic language—language suggesting that God literally controls everything—should be taken literally. Certainly there are many passages, in any case, in which God appears as more interactive, responding to events in the world rather than controlling them. Glaring examples, in fact, are found in the first chapters of Genesis. In Genesis 3, the sin of Adam and Eve clearly disrupts God's plan, and the expulsion from the garden is clearly a response to this unexpected turn of events. And even more revealing is Genesis 6:6, in which God expresses regret for having made humanity—a clear indication of the contingency of events in the world.

There is nevertheless a great deal of tension between the biblical passages that suggest God's total control and the contemporary way of thinking. Aside from scientific determinists, who attribute all happening to strict, mechanical causes, most people in our world are thoroughly committed to a belief in human free will. Yet many Christians remain tied to a literal reading of the biblical assertions of God's absolute and unilateral power, believing that it is an indispensable part of the biblical faith. And indeed many find such a belief necessary precisely in order to cope with the tragedies of personal life and human history.

Because ancient writers tended to equate divine power with absolute and unilateral control does not, however, mean that such an equation is necessary. It is logically possible to assert that God has the greatest power in the universe without claiming that God has all the power. Some recent theologians argue that some aspects of the biblical tradition—most particularly, God's loving relation to the world—are best preserved when God's power is *not* conceived in this way. From their point of view, God's power is persuasive rather than coercive, which is to say it is the power of love as demonstrated in the central Christian symbol, the cross.

Another way to deal with the problem of evil that is raised by stark tragedy, then, is to revalue biblical assertions of God's power in a way that honors some strong biblical teachings on the one hand and our own experience of freedom on the other. Although it remains fundamental to Christian faith to assert that God is the sovereign power of the universe, this need not mean that God controls either the forces of nature or human activity in a direct and simplistic way. For some Christians, it seems that the best way to cope with tragedy is to believe that God will literally deliver us from it. An alternative way, however, is to make a very different affirmation involving three components: (1) God is present with us in the midst of suffering, as the symbol of the cross indicates; (2) God is the fundamental power of the universe who can make a future of any situation, no matter how tragic; (3) because God is eternal, nothing of worth in human experience is ever lost.

In the story of Peter's acknowledgment of Jesus, a very different type of tension appears—one that has more immediate practical consequences. From one point of view, the investiture of Peter with "the keys of the kingdom" and the authority to bind and loose is an endorsement of official power within the church. It is not surprising that the passage was used in later times to support a hierarchical and authoritarian approach to ecclesiastical decision-making. The parallel passage at 18:18, which grants the power to bind and loose to the disciples collectively, mitigates the hierarchical element more clearly than it does the authoritarian one. One can appeal to both passages in support of the right of church leadership to enforce a particular judgment.

The other side of the matter, however, is that by granting the power of binding and loosing, both passages clearly affirm the right of the continuing community to *re*-interpret tradition. It is a recognition, in other words, of the ongoing character of tradition and thus a rejection of the notion that scripture stands alone and immutable, bearing self-evident meaning that can be determined through simple reading. Just as Jesus himself affirmed the continuing validity of the Law but reinterpreted it (5:17–48), so now the community receives the authority to do the same. It is very likely, moreover, that it is not only the Hebrew Scriptures that the community must reinterpret but Jesus' own teachings as well, for at 13:52, Jesus describes the "scribe who has been trained for the kingdom of heaven" as one who brings out of the treasure "what is new and what is old." The interpreter, apparently, is commissioned to draw on both the Hebrew Scriptures and the Jesus-tradition in order to render it meaningful and effective in the present. However, there would be no need for such activity if either element were understood in a static, simplistic way. The interpreter must engage in a creative process. As 18:20 suggests, however, that process takes place in the context of a community in the midst of which the risen Jesus dwells.

Some scholars have accused the gospel of Matthew of fostering fundamentalist tendencies by a relentless emphasis on the fulfillment of scripture and an insistence on the continuing validity of every "stroke of a letter" in the Law (5:18). There is some truth in this charge, but Jesus' reinterpretation of the Law in 5:21–48 and the affirmation of the ongoing nature of tradition show another dimension in Matthew that seems actually to predominate. This is hardly surprising, because rabbinic Judaism itself engaged self-consciously in the process of reinterpretation.

In any case, the tension between these two perspectives is once again an invitation to bring Matthew into conversation with our contemporary world. If 5:18 ("not one letter…will pass from the law") is a reminder that the Christian community is constituted on the basis of God's revelation to Israel, and by implication also that it owes allegiance to Jesus' own teaching, Jesus' conferral of the power to bind and loose is a recognition of the absolute necessity of fostering a creative engagement between those traditions and the experiences that belong specifically to our own day and age. Fundamentalism, in the end, is a notoriously unbiblical approach to the Bible, precisely because it ignores the freedom of interpretation and expansion on tradition that the Bible itself in many ways encourages. (For further reflections on the problem of divine power, see "The Power of God as Problem," pp. 24–26.)

Jesus, Gentiles, and Gender

Matthew 15:21–28, the story of Jesus' encounter with the Canaanite woman, is paralleled by Mark 7:24–30. The stories differ in that Mark identifies the woman as Syrophoenician and lacks Matthew's account of Jesus' initial refusal of her request on the grounds that his mission was only to "the lost sheep of the house of Israel." In both, however, Jesus speaks of Gentiles as dogs. Also in both, it is the woman who leads Jesus to a more inclusive view, rather than vice versa.

The unflattering portrayal of Jesus in this story has given rise to many attempts to find an acceptable interpretation. Perhaps the most common understanding has been that Jesus' initial refusal of the woman was simply a way of testing her faith. But there is little indication of such a motive in the story itself, and it is difficult to read the remark about Gentiles in such a light. Consequently, the story remains highly problematic for many contemporary readers.

In a now-classic feminist treatment of this story, Sharon Ringe speculates that a historical incident lies behind the Marcan version, a memory of a moment in which Jesus was caught with his compassion down and was in fact brought up by a woman's bold challenge ("A Gentile Woman's Story"). From a sociological perspective, Gerd Theissen has proposed a reading of the Marcan version that focuses on the fact that the woman comes specifically from the economically affluent region of Tyre and Sidon. As Garland summarizes Theissen's argument,

> Rich Tyre was perceived as posing a threat against Galilee as a permanent aggrandizer. Economically, Tyre took bread away from Galilee. Jesus may have shared the prejudice of the underprivileged

against the privileged. What he might be saying is: "Let the poor people in the hinterland be satisfied first for once. It is not good to take the bread of the poor people and throw it to the rich heathens in the city." (*Garland, Reading Matthew*, p. 165, citing Theissen, "Lokal—und Sozialkolorit in der Geschichte von der syrophönikischen Frau (Mk 7.24–30).")

Both these approaches offer important insights, but they relate more to the pre-Matthean levels of the story than to its role and meaning within Matthew itself. In this latter setting, the story serves two primary functions, the first of which is to contrast the woman's great faith with the "little faith" of the disciples. This contrast is severely ironical, because the woman is doubly marginalized as both female and Gentile—and not simply Gentile, but Canaanite and thus representative of Israel's archetypal enemy.

The second function is to serve as a bridge between Jesus' own mission, exclusively to Israel, and the mission to the world at large, including Gentiles, which he will commission after his resurrection (28:16–20). By having Jesus first assert the priority of Israel in God's plan of salvation and then make an exception to his usual restriction, the narrator addresses readers who might have problems with Gentile inclusion. It is thus the reader's prejudices, not Jesus', that the story seeks to expose and overturn (see Boring, "The Gospel of Matthew," pp. 337–38).

As in so many points in Matthew, however, the dominant role that this story plays in the Matthean narrative by no means exhausts its potential for meaning. Elaine Wainwright has approached the stories in Matthew in an innovative way, asking how the different house churches that made up the Matthean community as a whole might have understood the various elements in the gospel. Her efforts along these lines parallel my own interest in identifying undercurrents of meaning that stand in tension with the more evident strains.

As Wainwright notes, in the usual reading of the story, Jesus himself, as sovereign Lord, is in full control and remains unchanged by the encounter. Taken by itself, however, the story really does seem to read otherwise. Thus building on Elisabeth Schüssler Fiorenza's critique of what she calls "kyriarchy"—focus of the authority of an elite male figure in a hierarchy of power—Wainwright suggests that some groups of original readers might well have taken the story more at face value and cherished it as signifying the empowerment of the community of believers itself (*Shall We Look for Another*, pp. 84–92; see also Schüssler Fiorenza, *But She Said*, pp. 8, 122–25). She thus finds a place for Ringe's feminist insights even on the level of the Matthean narrative itself, not just on that of the pregospel tradition.

In any case, to the extent that we take the woman's double marginalization seriously, the story holds the potential to mediate a subtle tension in the gospel as a whole. On the one hand, there is a genuine emphasis on inclusion of the outcast and on the power of the community. On the other, however, the inclusive Jesus is the middle term in a line of patriarchal authority, passing on to the male disciples (with one male, Peter, playing a central role) what his Father has delivered to him. The result is that the inclusiveness is implicitly bounded by a rather traditional system of authority. When a passage like 15:21–28 is allowed to challenge that dominant strain, however, new possibilities for reading and valuing the story of Jesus arise. More specifically, it becomes possible to understand the processes of interpreting the Torah and decision making as much more open-ended and inclusive of the varied voices within the community that would otherwise be the case.

Even such a positive valuation of the story of the Canaanite woman, however, still leaves us with a Matthean Jesus who expresses an attitude that from our contemporary perspective seems prejudiced. Neither the rhetorical advantage of describing the woman in negative terms before praising her faith nor a sense of Israel's priority in God's plan of salvation can from our perspective justify the use of a term of abuse to describe Gentiles. Yet the contemporary reader needs also to understand the broad frame of reference—ancient Israel's struggle to maintain its distinctive faith—out of which such language issues. It thus becomes important, as at so many points in Matthew, to bring this troublesome element of the narrative into conversation with other aspects that stand in tension with it.

16:21—28:20

Death and Resurrection

16:21—17:28 Preparing the Disciples

The phrase at 16:21, "[f]rom that time…Jesus began…," repeats the grammatical construction of 4:17, which signaled the beginning of Jesus' ministry to Israel. Here it introduces the third major section of the story in which Jesus prepares his disciples for his coming death, enters Jerusalem and teaches there until his arrest and execution, and is ultimately raised from the dead. The preceding section ended, immediately following Peter's climactic acknowledgment of Jesus as "the Messiah, the Son of the living God" (16:16), with Jesus' stern warning to the disciples "not to tell anyone that he was the Messiah" (16:20). Although 16:21 constitutes a major turn in the plot, the material in the present section is closely linked to what has immediately preceded, making the injunction to silence intelligible.

The link, however, is not a smooth transition but a jarring juxtaposition of opposites. In 16:13–20, Peter (along with the reader) basks in the glow of Jesus' unqualified acceptance of his statement and his subsequent conferral of authority. In verses 21–23, by contrast, Jesus' announcement of his coming death and resurrection provokes a strong objection from Peter that results in a severe rebuke: "Get behind me, Satan! You are a stumbling block to me; for you are setting your mind not on divine things but on human things." Then, in verses 24–28, Jesus complements his interpretation of his messianic mission by defining discipleship in a corresponding way: Those who would follow him must take up their own crosses.

The question of Jesus' identity is thus transmuted into that of the nature of both messiahship and discipleship. And it becomes clear that the command for secrecy has to do with its belonging not to the public sphere of Jesus' teaching but to his private instruction to his disciples; it is one of the "secrets/mysteries of the kingdom of heaven" to which Jesus referred in 13:11. The disciples' failure to understand, moreover, suggests why that must be so: It is not a notion that is easily grasped—not, in any case, in the categories of "normal" thinking.

Jesus' response to Peter's objection poses the issue of the nature of his role as a sharp dichotomy: To try to divert him from his divinely appointed destiny is to side against God in the cosmic conflict. Thus he even calls Peter "Satan" in a phrase strongly reminiscent of his rebuke of the devil in the temptation story (4:1–11). And in a biting parody of the positive wordplay in the preceding scene that compared Peter to a rock on which the church is founded, he now calls him a "stumbling block" or "stone of stumbling."

Against the background of 16:13–20, verses 21–23 force the reader to come to terms with complexity, both in the plot and in the characterization of the disciples. The Peter in whom Jesus has just placed his confidence is suddenly accused of serving the enemy's cause, and the high moment of Jesus' recognition as Messiah/Son of God takes on an ominous tone as the nature of his actual role is revealed.

Verses 24–28 go one step further and demand reflection on the nature of discipleship itself, and at that point the text reaches beyond the plot and addresses believers in the postresurrection community. It is ultimately to them that Jesus says, "If any want to become my followers, let them deny themselves and take up their cross and follow me." He elaborates on this demand through reference to a broad principle, but the point remains specifically tied to Christian discipleship. The presupposition of verse 25 is that one's life itself is in a fundamental sense the ultimate value, because without it nothing else can be gained. However, the paradoxical declaration that one must lose one's life to find it exposes an ambiguity in the very notion of "life" itself: What *is* it, in the deepest sense? The broad point is that sheer physical existence, survival, and the accumulation of worldly commodities do not in fact constitute *true* life; that, to the contrary, is something found only when one transcends them for a greater good.

Verse 24 makes clear that this greater good is found by following Jesus, and verse 27 places the issue in the context of his eventual return as the Son of man who will judge the world. In that time, nothing a person has gained in this world will be valuable enough to buy back a life that has been thrown away through a false understanding of what life is. Verse 28 is somewhat problematic for the reader, because it states that some of those who actually heard Jesus will still be alive when the end comes. It is conceivable that there would in fact be such persons at the time of the writing of Matthew, but to focus on this question is to miss the real force of verses 27–28 in this context. These verses support Jesus' radical call to discipleship by declaring, first, that at the end of the age those who follow him will be vindicated and, second, that the end is not far off. It is thus primarily to the later reader that the theme of nearness of the end applies, and we will see more nuanced reflection on the time of the end in chapter 24.

Read in this way, verses 27–28 are for the postresurrection community a promise rather than a threat. This means that verses 22–28 as a whole convey an ultimately positive message. Jesus corrects Peter, but he does not reject him; he uses Peter's moment of faithlessness in order to instruct his followers in the meaning of discipleship and give them a word of assurance that the way of the cross is the way to life. And one may even read Jesus' command to Peter, "Get behind me," as a call to "get in step."

The narrator does not comment on why Peter could not accept Jesus' announcement, but a theological approach to this question is more fruitful than a psychological one. What Peter cannot accept is the notion that the Messiah should suffer, not only because this would ultimately involve his own suffering but also because it would seem to make no sense. If one expects a messiah to bring worldly deliverance, then death on a cross hardly seems a means toward that end. Nor, despite the explanation in verses 24–28, do the disciples appear to get beyond such thinking at this point, because following Jesus' second announcement of his death and resurrection they are described as "greatly distressed" (17:23).

Between the two announcements comes the dramatic story of Jesus' transfiguration on the mountain (17:1–13) and the disciples' failure to heal a boy possessed by a demon (vv. 14–20). We thus have the repetition of the pattern found in 16:13–28: a "high" moment followed by a "low." On the mountain, Peter, James, and John see Jesus in a form that suggests his eventual heavenly glory, and they even hear the voice of God confirming Jesus as God's Son. When they all descend, however, they find that the other disciples have been unable to make use of the authority over demons Jesus gave them at 10:1 because of their "little faith" (17:20). This incident intensifies a duality that has run through the characterization of the disciples: On the one hand, they show both faith and understanding; on the other, their faith is indeed "little," and at points their understanding is lacking as well.

The scene on the mountain is finely nuanced. The very fact of the vision expresses Jesus' confidence in those he has brought with him, and in verse 8, the notation that "they saw no one except Jesus himself alone" suggests an appropriate focus on him. But Peter's suggestion of constructing three dwellings, or tents, is passed over as irrelevant, as the voice of God interrupts him and enjoins the disciples to listen to Jesus. A mild rebuke is implied, presumably because Peter seems to place Moses and Elijah on a par with Jesus and, by suggesting the tents, to allow a moment of present ecstasy to obscure the divine plan that Jesus is working out. And God's injunction to listen to Jesus, although in a broad sense applying to all his teaching, must in context refer primarily to his announcements of his death and resurrection.

The incompleteness of the disciples' understanding is also evident in the conversation as they descend the mountain in 17:9–13. Jesus now commands the disciples to "[t]ell no one about the vision until after the Son of Man has been raised from the dead." For the reader, this injunction adds further explanation for the secrecy: Jesus' messiahship is such that its nature cannot be grasped apart from the resurrection; that event alone will make it intelligible. As for Peter, James, and John, however, the fragmentary character of their understanding appears in their question: "Why, then, do the scribes say that Elijah must come first?" (17:10).

This question is based on Malachi 4:5–6, which states that Elijah, who according to 2 Kings 2:11 had not died but had been carried to heaven, would return "before the great and terrible day of the LORD comes." It is unclear whether Jewish tradition had linked Elijah's return specifically to the coming of the Messiah, but that issue has little effect on an understanding of the present passage. The disciples' question apparently stems from Jesus' mention of the resurrection. Not yet clear on what Jesus means in verse 9, they apparently leap from the term *resurrection* to the notion of the general resurrection associated with the end of the age. Thus it becomes relevant to ask how this can take place if Elijah has not yet appeared.

Jesus has already identified John with Elijah at 11:14, so we must imagine that the disciples' understanding in this matter has been incomplete. Now, however, Jesus is able to complete that understanding. Elijah has in fact already come, but "they"—those who oppose God's rule—have done to him "whatever they pleased." The sense in which his role is to "restore all things" remains unclear: among the possibilities are purifying or reconstituting Israel, presiding over the resurrection of the dead, or initiating a restoration of the cosmos itself. In any case, the disciples now understand that John in fact played the role of Elijah, and Jesus is able to make a connection between John's death and his own. But the narrator does not say whether they grasp the latter point or not.

It is important to note that the story reveals a process of growing understanding. The disciples "see no one except Jesus...alone"—implying that they understand his superiority to both Elijah and Moses—only after they have been taught by the voice of God from heaven. Moreover, they understand who John was only after Jesus makes this clear to them.

The specific significance of the two figures, Moses and Elijah, is another widely debated point. A long-standing interpretation is that they represent the law and the prophets. The context, however, supports a rather different notion. The explicit association of Elijah with the end-time suggests that Moses is here valued for his own eschatological significance: for Jewish eschatological expectations, based on Deuteronomy 18:15, 18 (see Acts 3:22–26), also included the hope for a "prophet like Moses." And if John corresponds to Elijah, it is likely that Jesus here in some sense corresponds to Moses. A major point of the story, however, is that Jesus is superior to both Moses and Elijah.

Jesus' two announcements of his coming death and resurrection, 16:24–26 and 17:22–23, bracket all but the last segment of the material in this section. Against the background of the hints regarding the emergence of a new community in 13:53—16:15 and the actual founding of that community in 16:13–20, the material now under consideration appears as explicit preparation of the disciples for the postresurrection situation. That is why it stands out of its narrative context and speaks so directly to the later reader. However, part of its power is that the narrative agenda is so artfully woven together with the teaching agenda. Jesus' teaching his disciples the meaning of discipleship on his way to his death makes that instruction all the more authoritative for the later community.

The final segment of this section, 17:24–27, has puzzled many commentators. Part of the problem is that the phrase *temple tax* seems most likely to refer to the annual half-shekel tax that supported the sacrificial cult. If that is so, the story makes sense as an incident in the life of Jesus but would seemingly have little value after the destruction of the temple in 70 C.E., the period in which the gospel of Matthew was written. Also, the relevance of the story to its narrative context has not always been apparent to interpreters. Coming between Jesus' lengthy preparation of his disciples for his death and resurrection and the discourse on church life in chapter 18, it has often seemed out of place.

A careful consideration of the context, however, suggests a solution to the problem. David Garland understands the passage as a "theological object lesson" the purpose of which is to teach that harmonious relations with others sometimes necessitate relinquishing one's rights and avoiding causing offense to others ("Matthew's Understanding of the Temple Tax," p. 90). In the story, Jesus first proclaims that it is unnecessary to pay the tax, but then he sends Peter off to do so anyway—by admittedly unusual means—in order to avoid offending others. The passage thus forms an appropriate transition from Jesus' preparation of his disciples in the preceding material to the discourse in chapter 18, in which Jesus not only deals with specifics of relations within the new community but also warns against causing others to stumble.

The logic of the analogy in verses 25–26 is that because kings tax their subjects, not their own families, the children of God are free from taxation. But who, specifically, are "the children"? One suggestion is Israelites in general, which would make sense if we were thinking of an actual incident in the life of Jesus. The point would be that all Jews are free from the tax, but Jesus' followers will pay it anyway out of deference for those who think it necessary. In a post–70 C.E. situation, however—after the destruction of the Temple—the tax itself can no longer be an issue. Therefore the advice is best understood as directed specifically to the Christian community. This tiny minority, standing in some measure at odds with the larger Jewish society, understands itself to be God's true children.

Thinking Today about Matthew 16:21—17:28

Interpreting Creative Tensions

The passage that opens this section, 16:21–28, contains some of the most powerful images in the New Testament, and much of the power comes from tensions either that are within the material itself or that emerge as the reader tries to render it meaningful in the present. One point of tension is between the broad principle applied to discipleship in verse 25 (that one must lose one's life to save it) and the eschatological sanction that is given in the verses that follow, particularly verse 27 (the Son of man will return and "repay everyone for what has been done"). Understood in its most profound sense, the proclamation that one must lose one's life to find it needs no secondary justification and is even perhaps distorted by attempts to provide such. If the point is that we find our true selves only by giving way to something beyond ourselves, the Son of man's "repayment" of persons for their deeds is in danger of reducing a genuinely moral/spiritual point to the level of practicality. Follow Jesus, because if you don't, he will judge you in the end!

By recognizing the tension, however, the contemporary reader gains a perspective from which to allow the text to speak to the present. The principle of losing one's life to find it has both a universalistic and an intuitive thrust: One either "gets it" or does not "get it" when confronted with such a notion. The idea of an eschatological "payback" has a kind of moral symmetry about it, but it involves some very specific beliefs that are in no way self-validating. Rewards and punishments at the end of time are simply not part of our everyday experience!

If the job of the interpreter is to bring both these elements in the text into conversation with the present, the more immediate, self-validating aspect—the intuitively grasped rightness of the principle of losing one's life to find it—would seem to offer the better starting point. Thus the force of verse 27 would not necessarily depend on belief in a literal end of history in which Jesus hands out rewards and punishments. This motif might rather serve as a poetic way of highlighting the ultimacy of the decisions we make.

Another point of tension within the passage itself is that between the universal principle and its specific application to the life of the Christian. A universalistic reading holds a legitimate appeal: There are many outside the bounds of Christianity who find their lives by giving them over to broader understandings of existence. However, in tying the principle specifically to Christian discipleship, the gospel of Matthew also ties it to the specific way of life that Jesus represents in this story—the way of love and justice. Verse 27 is particularly important in this respect, because the phrase "for what has been done" serves as a good reminder that in Matthew following Jesus entails concrete actions such as those enjoined in the Sermon on the Mount.

A different sort of tension is created when persons in our contemporary world confront the concepts of messiahship/discipleship as defined by suffering, with questions arising out of marginalization, oppression, and abuse. Arthur Miller has provided a powerful image expressing the legitimate objection to the call for self-sacrifice in his play *After the Fall*. The lead character, Quentin, is plagued with guilt about the suicide of his former wife, Maggie, whom he left after a long period of struggling with her self-destructive behavior. As the play draws to a climax, his ruminations reach a crescendo, as he asks himself how he could justify having left her. Agonizingly, he begins to formulate the question:

> But in whose name do you turn your back?...I saw it clear—in whose name you turn your back! I saw it once, I saw the name!...In whose name, in whose blood-covered name do you look into a face you have loved, and say, Now you are found wanting, and now in your extremity you die. It had a name.

Then, near the very end, after numerous "conversations" with Maggie and other characters living and dead, he is able finally to articulate his answer:

> And the name—yes, the name! In whose name do you ever turn your back—but in your own? In Quentin's name. Always in your own blood-covered name you turn your back!

Any person who suffered abuse in childhood or in an adult relationship, any person who has been subjected to violence and intimidation because of race or political expression, knows the importance of this kind of affirmation of the individual person's right to self-realization. And anyone who has had her or his legitimate attempts at self-realization stifled in the name of religious values knows that passages such as Matthew 16:24–26 have played key roles in the justification of innumerable forms of oppression. They have provided convenient authorization for convincing those without power to remain without power and those oppressed and abused to submit to the coercive power of others in the name of Christ. Women, minorities, political activists, and any who have suffered disempowerment or persecution are clearly justified in raising serious questions about this and similar biblical materials.

We need not, however, simply negate this text. For despite its historical misuse, it continues to make an important witness. Aside from relationships of abuse and oppression, our society manifests a strong tendency to exalt the rights of the individual person to such an extent that all sense of wider responsibility or the common good is erased. We have in fact entered a period in which the very notion of giving up any desire whatsoever out of deference for another is simply unintelligible. Thus a creative reading of these texts will seek to bring the two points of view into dialogue.

Such a dialogue will, in the end, have to place a qualification on Quentin's statement. From a Christian perspective, it is never simply one's own individual interests that justify any given action, but the effect that this action has on the whole. It is ultimately in the name of God as revealed in Jesus that one may assert one's individual worth against illegitimate claims of others. Quentin's self-justification should probably remain an open question, because in such a case it is impossible to make absolute judgments. But that very point also sets Quentin's situation apart from some of those situations of abuse and oppression with which we are all too familiar, in which there is no ambiguity at all. Quentin speaks of his own name as "blood-covered," but that is a designation that does not apply to genuine victims.

Discernment is all-important in the use of the call to self-denial, because different persons and different congregations will have different experiences and backgrounds. It is not for everyone in every situation. Even so, there are subtle ways to channel its impact. It is possible to argue, for example, that abused persons who have clung to the role of victim do in fact need to "give up their lives," by abandoning their destructive self-images and opening themselves to empowerment.

The ambiguities involved in Quentin's case are indications of an irreducible tension that resides within the very notion of losing one's life to find it. For the truth is that the interests of the individual person can never be simplistically identified with the whole, whether one defines the latter in social or in cosmic terms. Recent theological developments, however, can mitigate that tension and put it in a different perspective. According to some progressive theologians, God should be understood not as a being "outside" the world but as the inclusive self of the world—that is, as in a sense the mind of the universe, which constitutes God's body. Within such a frame of reference, the individual person's own ultimate good is in one sense identical to that of the whole, or God, for what is valuable about the individual person is that individual person's contribution to the whole. This particular concept of God is most often associated with, but is not limited to, the "process" or "process-relational" theology growing out of the philosophical ideas of Alfred North Whitehead and Charles Hartshorne (see bibliography on process thought, as well as chapter 3, "God and the World," in Sallie McFague, *Models of God*).

Of course, traditional theology also traces the individual person's worth to God, but because God and the beings in the world are separate entities, that worth is conferred from outside the person. This means, paradoxically, that the person's value is weakened at the same time that the person appears to maintain a certain independence from God. In process thought, however, because individual persons are in fact parts of God, they have value both in themselves and as parts of the whole, and it becomes easier to explain how giving oneself to something beyond oneself results in the most profound form of self-realization.

The conversation about the temple tax, when read as an object lesson in foregoing one's rights for the sake of others, involves many of the same tensions as the other material. It has far less rhetorical power, however, although the bald declaration that "the children are free" offers a good starting point for just the kind of dialogue discussed above. And explicit reflection on the notion of freedom can be very important for a society that confuses freedom with unrestrained individualism.

Viewed in themselves, the announcements of Jesus' death, often termed the "passion predictions," also present problems. They seem not only to imply a divine determinism but also to raise in a different way the question of victimization. When the narrator says at 16:21 that Jesus "must go to Jerusalem...and be killed," the implication is that the necessity issues from God's own will. And when at 17:22 Jesus himself announces his coming death he uses the verb *paradidonai*, which is better translated as "delivered" (as in the RSV) rather than "betrayed" (as in the NRSV). In addition, although Judas' action (10:4; 26:14–16, 20–25, 47–50) may also be in view, the ultimate agency is in all probability that of God.

The issue of determinism has far-reaching ramifications, for attributing Jesus' death directly to God's will weakens its sociopolitical force by obscuring its roots in the oppressive use of power and the contingent decisions of human beings. At just this point, however, it is important to pay attention to the complexity of the thought patterns at work in the narrative.

From 4:17 to 16:20, Jesus carries out a ministry to Israel, proclaiming God's rule, teaching, casting out demons, and healing. By chapter 11 it has become apparent that although he has gathered disciples and crowds still follow him, the people as a whole are not responding. The Jewish leadership forms the core of outright opposition, but passages such as 11:16–24 indict the entire generation for failure to repent. The indictment, however, rests on the assumption that Jesus actually expects a positive response. That is why the Sermon on the Mount ends at 7:28 with a reference to the crowds, who have apparently overheard the teaching he has directed toward his followers: These very crowds are potential disciples. Likewise, Jesus' severe indictment in chapter 11 leads into an invitation in verses 28–30: "Come to me...Take my yoke upon you..." It thus appears that one aspect of the logic that holds the narrative together is the assumption of contingency: Jesus preaches to the people of Israel because *they could choose to follow him*.

This note of contingency stands in opposition to the deterministic strain according to which it was necessary for Jesus to die, and it is obvious that one cannot take both strains literally. On one level, the interpreter must recognize the typical biblical paradox of necessity and contingency: In Exodus, God hardens Pharaoh's heart, but Pharaoh is still responsible for his evil actions. This is not an ultimately satisfying explanation, however, because in the minds of many Christians, either one side or the other actually wins out. That is, Jesus' death is either seen as God's preordained plan or a willfully pursued act of injustice. If the latter view is common in contemporary liberal Protestantism, the former has been the choice of the overwhelming majority of Christians through the ages.

The most creative approaches to this problem will seek to preserve both elements in a way that goes beyond the mere assertion of the paradox. From a strictly logical point of view, the note of contingency, the faith that the future is truly open, is absolutely necessary, for the story makes no real sense apart from it. From a theological perspective, it is equally necessary to affirm that God is at work in the story of Jesus; but such an affirmation need not depend on a divine determinism. Thus if the reader has some leeway in interpreting the story from a contemporary perspective, it is possible to see Jesus' death not as God's preordained plan but as a response to a particular situation. It is, in fact, only after Jesus has failed to persuade the people that his full-scale teaching about his coming death and resurrection begins. (The crucifixion is anticipated earlier in the notation regarding Judas' betrayal at 10:4, but this takes the form of a retrospective comment by the narrator.) If the story is read in such a way, the sociopolitical aspect is recovered and the reason for Jesus' death and resurrection actually becomes more intelligible. Through Jesus' death, God allows the forces of evil to play out their hand; but through the resurrection God triumphs over them.

This solution, admittedly, still leaves God in the position of in some sense sending Jesus to his death, so that the victimization of Jesus is still at issue. This problem, however, arises in part from a failure to grasp a point noted in the Introduction (p. 2; see also "The Point of the Christological Claim," pp. 36–37). Throughout the story, Jesus stands squarely on the divine side of the divine-human relationship. The force of the image of God allowing Jesus' death is not God's willingness to sacrifice *someone else*; it is rather the redemption of the world through God's *own* suffering (see also "Competing Currents in a Perfect Ending," pp. 195–200).

The transfiguration account is among the more difficult texts to approach from a progressive point of view; it is not easily transmuted into inner-worldly terms. For this reason, however, it can serve the important function of pointing to the transcendence that must undergird any adequate call for justice or ethical action. There is not much power to such calls if they are based solely on human preference and if they are not in some way supported by a strong doctrine of grace. To present Jesus, in this imaginative way, as manifesting the glory of God's ultimate rule, however, is to make the boldest and most engaging of claims: that the understanding of life Jesus represents is a reflection of God's own understanding and supported by God's own power.

Demand and grace come together in the story in the presentation of the human Jesus as filled with the glory of God. Moreover, grace continues to operate in Jesus' words of comfort in verse 7 and in the exorcism he eventually performs in the story that follows. What it will ultimately take for the postresurrection community to grow beyond their "little faith" is to draw on the power of Jesus himself, who (as the reader will learn in chap. 18) is present in their midst. And a hint of this point appears in 17:8: "they saw no one except Jesus…alone."

18:1–35 The Fourth Discourse

Life in the New Community

In 18:1–5 the disciples ask Jesus, "Who is the greatest in the kingdom of heaven?" They have apparently not been squabbling as they have in Mark 9:33–37 about which *of them* is greatest. They simply want to know who will have first rank, or perhaps simply what the criteria for ranking will be. Nor does the story carry the sharp irony it does in Mark, where it comes immediately after the second passion prediction. Nevertheless, the general context of teaching that defines messiahship and discipleship as suffering and humility combines with Jesus' answer to preserve a measure of the irony: greatness in God's rule is defined in a way that inverts ordinary values, which the disciples still manifest in some degree by asking the question at all.

Jesus makes the point by standing a child among them as a model of the humility that makes for greatness in God's rule. In fact, he proclaims, the prerequisite for entering that Rule at all is to "change and become like children." The verb rendered "change" in the *New Revised Standard Version* is *straphein*, which would more literally be translated "turn." Although *metanoein* is the more common New Testament word for "repent," *straphein* can carry a similar weight and clearly does so here (Hagner, *Matthew 14– 28*, p. 517). The point is that one must repudiate the typical values of society—power, glory, wealth—in favor of humility. And the image of the child would not suggest to the ancient mind the sentimental qualities it does for us: The child's humility is that of the powerlessness and marginalized. Truly to repent, therefore, means to relinquish the attempt to control others and gain something for oneself in favor of a role defined by service and deference to others.

The role of the child in verses 1–4 is clearly analogical: Jesus' followers should be *like* children. However, it is unclear whether the reference in verse 5 is to such a child-*like* follower or to an actual child. In any case, reception of the powerless constitutes acceptance of Christ, and in verses 6–7 the child-image is transmuted into that of "little ones," which once again signifies those who follow Jesus. The only question is whether the reference is to followers in general or to a specific group among them, that is, those who are in some way the weakest and most vulnerable. The latter seems more likely because verses 6–7 take the form of warnings to the community. The point is that those with recognized standing in the community should not be disdainful of the "little ones" or in any way risk putting them in danger of losing their faith. Most likely, then, we should think of such persons as new members, those who have shown a propensity for giving in to temptations, and those less schooled in the teaching of the community.

Some interpreters think the "little ones" are specifically Christian missionaries, because the same term is applied to this group in 10:42. Such an interpretation makes little sense in chapter 18, however. What the two groups would seem to have in common is not a specific function or status but vulnerability.

In context, verses 8–9 should probably be interpreted as reinforcing 6–7. That is to say, one must purge oneself of one's own sins in order to avoid causing others to stumble (Davies and Allison, *The Gospel According to Saint Matthew*, II, p. 765). In any case, the parable of the lost sheep in verses 10–14 draws verses 6–14 under the theme of caring for the "little ones." In Luke 15:3–7, Jesus tells this parable to justify to the Pharisees and scribes his eating with sinners; thus the lost sheep stands for the lost people in Israel at large, to whom Jesus has a special ministry. In Matthew, however, the lost sheep is the wayward member of the church; and the force of the parable is to try to win such a person back. Verse 14 summarizes the concern at work since verse 6: "So it is not the will of your Father in heaven that one of these little ones should be lost."

At verse 15, the issue shifts to a difficult question of church discipline. The specific concern is not disruption of the church itself but instances in which one member claims to have been wronged by another. Verses 15–17 outline a specific procedure involving three steps. First, the claimant should attempt to settle the matter privately with the other person. If that approach fails, the issue is raised before one or two witnesses. This practice reflects Deuteronomy 19:15, although the witnesses in this case are not those who are eyewitnesses of the wrongful act itself but persons who can confirm what is said in the "hearing." Should this second-level attempt fail, the wronged party can bring the matter to the church community for a judgment. And it is apparent from verse 17 that the community as a whole has the power of exclusion, a kind of excommunication.

Jesus delivers the entire discourse to the disciples so that when in verse 18 he repeats the words on "binding and loosing" he said to Peter in 16:19, he is, in the context of the narrative, speaking to them. But the explicit mention of the church in the preceding verses shows that the authority Jesus gives applies more properly to the later community. And this impression is increased by verses 19–20, which presuppose Jesus' physical absence. Jesus' spiritual presence is indicated in verse 20, as is evident in the last verse of the gospel (28:20): "And remember, I am with you always, to the end of the age."

In this latter passage, Jesus' presence is related to the worldwide mission he at that point commissions. In chapter 18, however, coming immediately after verses 18–19, it constitutes specific empowerment for the church's deliberations. "Bind" and "loose" in verse 18 indicate judgments on legal matters—what is permitted and what forbidden—and, in light of verse 17, extend to include the power of exclusion from the community (see also pp. 113–15 on 16:19). Verse 19 then gives the assurance that God accepts and ratifies the judgments that are made. (It can hardly mean that God will give anything two or three people pray for, because different groups might pray for different things.) And verse 20, finally, links God's ratification to Jesus' presence, which means that Jesus here plays the role of the Shechinah—the presence of God in the world—in Jewish thought. This understanding of Jesus as manifesting God's presence prevents verses 18–19 from signifying a simplistic ratification on God's part of whatever is yielded by church deliberations. The presupposition is that those who make judgments do so with Christ's guidance.

Taken as a whole, verses 15–20 present a model for dealing with a specific matter of church discipline that leads to a broad assertion of the church's power to exercise such discipline through a process of discernment and judgment in the presence of Christ. Care is taken to make excommunication the last resort and to place the judgments of the community in the context of the guidance of Christ, and the procedure seems to be communitarian rather than hierarchical and authoritarian in nature. Nevertheless, the verses make a strong statement on power of the community to make disciplinary judgments.

Against that background, verses 21–22 appear as an important word of caution that is reinforced in graphic terms by the parable of the unmerciful servant that closes the discourse in verses 23–35. If exclusion is a possibility, it must always be viewed as an extreme solution, never entered into hastily. What should most characterize the internal life of the community in the end is forgiveness, which is complementary to the calls to humility and care for the "little ones" in the earlier parts of the discourse.

The point is underscored by the extravagant terms in which Jesus describes forgiveness. Peter's suggestion that he should forgive as many as seven times is gracious by most standards, but Jesus' answer is outrageous: either seventy-seven or seventy-times-seven (the Greek will allow either interpretation). In the parable, the slave's debt is astronomical: According to Josephus, the yearly Judean tax revenue was six hundred talents. Thus the king's forgiveness of the debt is monumental, going far beyond the slave's (rather preposterous) request that he be allowed time to repay it. In addition, the force of the image of ten thousand talents would be rather like our playful term *zillion,* just as Jesus' answer to Peter is a dramatic way of saying that forgiveness should be limitless.

In context, the parable clearly takes on an allegorical meaning. The king's forgiveness of an outrageous debt mirrors God's own outrageous forgiveness (made concrete in Jesus' own ministry), and the slave's refusal of forgiveness of a debt owed him by a peer stands for the unforgiving community member. The point, made explicit in verse 35, is that those forgiven by God must forgive one another. The discourse on church life ends with that injunction, cast in the form of a warning.

Thinking Today about Matthew 18:1–35

The Problem of Forgiveness

There is much in this chapter that will strike the reader as completely straightforward, easily applicable to Christian existence in our time: the themes of humility, care for the "little ones," and radical forgiveness. There are, however, both tensions and problematic aspects in this material.

Issues surrounding the use of calls to humility and sacrifice to keep the powerless from becoming empowered were discussed earlier ("Interpreting Creative Tensions," pp. 130–35). Beyond this, many commentators find an uneasy relationship between the extravagant images of forgiveness in verses 21–35 and the provision for exclusion from the community in verse 17. There is not necessarily a contradiction here, because one could say that the limitless forgiveness in verses 21–22 depends on repentance. Significantly, however, this is not mentioned. And in any case, the greatest value of the juxtaposition of material in the latter part of the chapter may lie in the tension that is created. There are in fact no easy answers, once one enters the world of the concrete interactions of life in human communities. In the end, the way in which verses 15–20 are surrounded by calls to humility and care for all on the one hand and to radical forgiveness on the other is a recognition that deeply prayerful discernment is always the indispensable element in such cases. That is why even the affirmation of the church's judicial function cannot end without the statement of Jesus' role in the process in verse 20.

A more difficult question is raised by the parable about the king and the servant who fails to forgive. It ends on a note not of forgiveness and reconciliation but of God's condemnation, creating for some interpreters an unintended irony: God refuses to forgive those who do not forgive. The punishment of the slave in verse 34 is similar to the scene in 22:12 in which the ill-clad guest is cast into outer darkness. Along with 18:9, which threatens the "hell (*gehenna*) of fire," it points to a final, eschatological judgment and thus seems to place a limit on the grace of God. If, however, we value Matthew's references to a final judgment not as literal pointers to a future event but for their metaphorical value in underscoring the moral seriousness of human decision, the problem is mitigated (see "The Coming Rule of Heaven," pp. 41–44).

19:1—20:34 From Galilee to Jerusalem

The formulary statement in 19:1, "[w]hen Jesus had finished…," marks off the preceding material, chapter 18, as a major discourse. The notation, then, that Jesus leaves Galilee signals a significant moment in the plot. Jesus' work in that region is done, and by entering Judea he is moving toward Jerusalem, which he has already identified as the scene of his coming suffering and death. The fact that the territory beyond the Jordan was not technically part of Judea is beside the point; the narrator wants to show movement from Galilee, where Jesus has carried out a ministry of teaching, healing, and exorcism, back to the general region where the story began with his birth (2:1), and finally to Jerusalem where the climactic events will occur.

In 19:2, the narrator notes that Jesus performs healings among the crowds, but he does not mention teaching. Jesus' ministry is thus continuing, but the teaching material in chapters 19—20, consistent with the pattern initiated in 16:21, is directed not toward the people at large but toward his inner circle. We have already seen that this emphasis is consistent with the fact that Jesus has by now been continually rejected by Jewish leaders as well as much of the Galilean populace, has twice announced his coming death and resurrection, and has founded the community that will live on after his death. Here, in other words, Jesus continues to address the concerns of the postresurrection community through the disciples.

Although characters from outside this circle play into the narrative, they serve primarily as foils that allow Jesus to address issues that pertain to the postresurrection community. The material in these chapters thus continues the broad interests of chapter 18, the discourse on church life, but the specific concern is now domestic issues relating to community members rather than interactions among the membership.

Outsiders come on stage first, as the Pharisees come to Jesus with a question in 19:3. They have not appeared in the narrative since 16:1–4 and have not been mentioned since 16:12, just before Jesus founds the church and begins to teach about his coming death. Their reentry into the narrative will therefore remind the reader of the conflict that has been building. Although this theme has been less visible as Jesus has focused on his inner circle, it has come to the surface in his two announcements of his death and resurrection (16:21; 17:22) and will do so again in his third announcement in 20:17–19 and once more in an interpretation of the meaning of his death in 20:28. Thus the material in chapters 19—20 serves the narrative function not only of getting Jesus into the vicinity of Jerusalem but also of preparing for the final stages of the conflict that will be played out there.

The narrator adds to the element of conflict by noting at the outset that the Pharisees are seeking to "test" or "tempt" Jesus. As always, they are seeking only to undermine him, never to engage him in honest discussion. The issue they raise is that of the valid grounds for divorce. The meaning of the phrase "for any cause" is disputed, and its interpretation affects the entire sentence. It is thus uncertain whether the Pharisees are asking if divorce is ever permitted or if just any grounds will suffice. The latter is more likely, in light of the dispute between the rabbinic schools of Hillel and Shammai, which focused on a phrase from Deuteronomy 24:1–4.

The primary intention of this latter passage is to forbid a man to remarry a woman he has divorced, who has subsequently been married and divorced again. However, the rabbinic debate centered on Deuteronomy 24:1, which sets up the situation by positing that a man has divorced a woman "because he finds some indecency in her" [RSV; NRSV: "something objectionable about her"]. Because the verse clearly presupposes the man's right to divorce a wife, the question was what grounds were indicated by "some indecency" or "something objectionable." Hillel's group took the lax position that anything that displeased the husband was sufficient. Shammai's took a strict interpretation of "indecency," but whether they meant adultery exclusively or a wider range of improprieties is unclear. If the former, then in Matthew 19:9 (and 5:32) Jesus apparently sides with them. If the latter, then Jesus takes an even more rigorous stand, because the Greek term *porneia* in all probability refers here to sexual unfaithfulness.

Either way, Jesus transcends the bounds of the rabbinic debate. He does base his argument on scripture by citing Genesis 1:27 and 2:24. This is consistent with Matthew's view that Jesus did not abolish but rather fulfilled the Law (5:17–20). But in making this move, Jesus also deflects attention from the Deuteronomy passage to God's original intention in creation. Thus when his opponents ask why Moses commanded that one give a certificate of divorce (Deut. 24:1), he can say that "from the beginning it was not so" and view the provision for divorce as a concession to the people's hardness of heart. He actually says "your" hardness of heart, reinforcing the earlier portrayal of the Pharisees and also making them the "incarnation" of the obstinacy of the people that is thematic not only in Matthew but in the Hebrew Scriptures as well.

Jesus' answer, a prohibition of all divorce except in cases of adultery, comes in the context of a debate with the Pharisees. In the context of a continuing focus on the disciples, however, it serves to answer a question for the postresurrection community, and the interest in the community becomes evident immediately. In verse 10, the disciples comment, "If such is the case of a man with his wife, it is better not to marry." In other words, if the valid grounds of divorce are so narrow, perhaps it is better not to take the risk.

Jesus' reply has caused interpretive difficulties, because it is not immediately apparent what he means in verse 11 by "this teaching" that not everyone can accept. The most likely solution is that the phrase does not refer to the teaching on divorce in verse 9 but points forward to the statement about "eunuchs" in verse 12. He thus leaves the disciples' rather cynical statement aside and focuses solely on the question of celibacy, for which the phrase "eunuchs for the…kingdom of heaven" is surely a metaphor. The force of the statement is that there is in fact a reason to forego marriage, but it is not the one the disciples propose; and it is a possibility only for some: The celibate life allows one to devote one's total attention to the demands of the inbreaking rule of God. Although the gospels never make the point explicitly, one gets the impression that Jesus himself is a model of such as lifestyle.

The passage has caused much dispute through the centuries. One reason is that a few Christians have taken the metaphor of "eunuch" literally, which is understandable because the term is in fact meant literally in the first two instances—those "who have been so from birth" and those "who have been made eunuchs by others." But more energy has gone into the debate, largely between Catholic and Protestant interpreters of an earlier period, over whether these verses present the celibate state as superior. They can be read either way, but certainly there is no hint of a sharp distinction between distinct "classes" of Christians, such as developed in medieval Christianity.

Community concerns are evident again in 19:13–15 as Jesus blesses the little children brought to him after proclaiming that "it is to such as these that the kingdom of heaven belongs." These verses resume a theme present in 18:2–5, but now the metaphorical weight of the image of the child is balanced with a more literal concern. The command to let the children come to him signals that children are to be highly valued in the community, an attitude that stood in contrast to the attitudes prevailing at the time. The phrase "to such as these," however, broadens the point metaphorically: The community welcomes all who are outcast, vulnerable, less valued by society in general.

In 19:16, another outsider enters the story, but as in the preceding material, the conversation eventually turns back to matters internal to Jesus' band of followers. A rich young man asks Jesus, "Teacher, what good deed must I do to have eternal life?" The question is apparently sincere, but there are signs that the man has an inadequate understanding from the beginning. First, he addresses Jesus as "teacher," rather than as "lord" or "Son of David," in contrast to the blind men in 20:29. Likewise, Jesus' answer begins with a question that implies a broader deficiency. Because it is only God who is truly good, knowledge of what constitutes the good comes only from God—that is, from the commandments. Something is wrong at the outset if the man must inquire about what is required of him.

When asked to specify the commandments, Jesus quotes from the second table of the Decalogue, which has to do with interhuman relations, and then he adds the command from Leviticus 19:18 to love one's neighbor. When the inquirer claims to have met this standard, Jesus then issues his devastating answer to the original question: "If you wish to be perfect, go, sell your possessions, and give the money to the poor…"

Like verses 10–12, this passage has given rise to the question of a superior class of those who seek not only salvation but also "perfection." The Greek word translated here as "perfect," however, is best understood in the sense of "wholeness," or "completeness." And in any case, because the man asks specifically about eternal life, his departure signals the refusal of the rule of God itself, not merely a set of special requirements for the elite. If his sorrow indicates a level of sincerity in his quest, his actual response is a choice of worldly wealth over the life God offers through Jesus.

If the relevance of the story for the community is not already clear, Jesus' interchange with the disciples in verses 23–26 makes it so. The saying in verse 23 ("it will be hard for a rich person to enter the kingdom"), together with the image of the camel and the needle's eye in verse 24, interprets the incident as illustrating the extreme difficulty of rich persons' accepting God's rule. To get the force of verse 24 one must reject all attempts to soften its meaning. A long-standing legend, for example, has it that the "needle's eye" was a small gate in Jerusalem, through which a camel could barely squeeze if unpacked of its load. Thus Jesus' metaphor supposedly does not condemn wealth but only counsels humility on the part of those who have it. There never was such a gate, however, and this approach in any case completely misunderstands the language in which verse 24 is cast.

The statement is intentionally extreme—absolute and uncompromising. As such, it functions as hyperbole, an overstatement, designed to challenge the "normal" way of thinking at its roots. This means, on the one hand, that it should not be interpreted literally, as actually excluding every rich person from God's rule. But neither should one try to specify abstractly the conditions under which the rich might be included. The Christian community must always wrestle with the problem, acknowledging on the one hand that there are responsible uses of wealth but aware also of the corruption, self-deception, and injustice that almost inevitably come with it. In this respect, it is very much like some statements in the Sermon on the Mount (see "Struggling with Radical Demands," pp. 59–61).

The disciples' despair in verse 26 apparently reflects the notion, which represents one strain of Jewish thinking, that having wealth is a sign of God's favor. Their logic is, "If the rich can't make it, how can anyone?" Rather than challenging this logic directly, however, Jesus gives an answer that reflects back on the previous story: "for God all things are possible." Whereas the rich man had depended on his own ability to keep the commandments, and failed in the end, those who depend rather on God will be able to do so. In a gospel focused heavily on the Law, grace shines through once again. Riches lure, temptations lurk; but God is available. God is available, however, not to provide an alternative to the radical demands of the gospel but to empower persons to meet them.

That those demands are in no way relaxed is evident in Peter's question in 19:27: What reward will the disciples have if they have in fact left everything to follow Jesus? The answer in no way negates the question: "at the renewal of all things" the disciples will "sit on twelve thrones, judging the twelve tribes of Israel" and all followers will receive a hundredfold of all that they have left behind.

The "renewal" probably refers to a cosmic reconstitution in the eschatological age. To say that the disciples will "judge" the twelve tribes of Israel most likely entails a process of making judgments rather than merely "condemning" on the one hand or "ruling" in a neutral sense on the other. Those who understand the verb as the equivalent of "condemn" assume that "Israel" refers to an entity completely separate and distinct from church. This assumption is unnecessary, however, and it is unlikely in light of the constant effort in Matthew to affirm the connection of the new community to the Law (also, see pp. 156–58 on 21:43).

If one understands the church itself as still in some sense part of Israel, then the process of judgment means sorting out the faithful and unfaithful in Israel as a whole, not simply pronouncing condemnation on those who do not belong to the new community.

The statement with which this passage ends in verse 30 is at first glance puzzling, however. Many commentators find its repetition (in reverse) in 20:16 to be inappropriate to the context and a sign of rather simpleminded construction on the author's part. Davies and Allison (*The Gospel According to Saint Matthew*, III, pp. 61, 67–68), however, offer a credible explanation of the thought development from 19:27 to 20:16. The conjunction *de* in verse 30 should, as in the *New Revised Standard Version*, be translated "but," rather than "and," as some would have it; and the sentence must be understood as pointing forward, with the "for" in 20:1 indicating that an explanation will follow. Verse 30 would thus introduce a cautionary note after Jesus' affirmation of the disciples' important roles in verses 28–29. The meaning would be roughly, "Yes, you will be playing an important part in the new age, but remember: 'many who are first will be last.'" And then the parable of the workers in the vineyard (20:1–4) illustrates that point.

It is true that the parable does not really illustrate reversal, but rather a kind of equalizing. The workers who come late in the day get the same wages as the early workers, not more. But in a broad sense, it can be taken in such a way as to make the important point for the community that no one, no matter of how high a rank or how long a member, has priority over any other. Thus understood as a caution to community members, the parable will not appear as a condemnation of self-righteous Pharisees. And it undoubtedly has a broader sense than, for example, a warning to Jewish Christians not to think themselves better than Gentile members.

This interpretation brings the parable into close connection with 20:20–28, the passage in which the mother of James and John requests that her sons sit on Jesus' right and left hands in his kingdom. Jesus' answer is followed by a word to the remaining ten, who are indignant about the request, that serves yet again as specific advice for the community. Their community is not to be hierarchical and authoritarian, following the pattern of Gentile leadership; for greatness paradoxically expresses itself in servanthood, and those who would be first must act as servants.

Between the parable and the passage 20:20–28, Jesus makes his third announcement of his coming death and resurrection (20:17–19), which provides a theological foundation for both what precedes and what follows: Jesus himself will be "last" in the specific sense that he will be delivered up to the Gentiles—Romans—to "be mocked and flogged and crucified." In addition, 20:27–28 makes it explicit that his fate is a model for discipleship: "whoever wishes to be first among you must be [last];just as the Son of Man came not to be served but to serve, and to give his life a ransom for many."

The term "ransom" in this verse is likely to conjure up later theological debates about the "mechanics" of the atonement and raise the question as to whom the ransom was paid. But there is nothing whatsoever in the gospel of Matthew to suggest that this question—let alone an answer to it—is at all in view. Thus Davies and Allison (*The Gospel According to Saint Matthew,* Vol. III, p. 100) rightly conclude that "[e]ven when 1:21 and 2:26–29 are taken into account, it is impossible to construct a Matthean theory of atonement. We have in the gospel only an unexplained affirmation" (see also, "Competing Currents in a Perfect Ending," pp. 195–200).

Significantly, then, the narrative sequence in which Jesus focuses on his private teaching of his disciples (16:21—20:28) begins and ends by drawing parallels between his coming death and the demands of discipleship. Although one story remains before Jesus enters Jerusalem—that of the healing of the two blind men (20:29–34)—it serves as a transition to the entrance account. When the blind men address Jesus as "Son of David" and ask for mercy, they do what the rich young man failed to do: They not only address Jesus correctly but also confess their dependence on God's/ Jesus' mercy. They also follow him, and in context, this not only signifies discipleship but also creates a lead-in to the next scene: At 20:18 Jesus announces that "we are going up to Jerusalem," and the blind men are in Jericho, the last stop before the environs of the Holy City.

The act of following sets this account in partial contrast to an earlier story in which Jesus healed two blind men—9:27–30. These men, too, address Jesus properly and manifest faith, but as the narrator leaves them, they are spreading the news about Jesus in the district where they live, in direct contradiction to Jesus' command for silence. With this earlier story in the background, the one in 20:29–34 serves all the more as a paradigm for discipleship. As Jesus makes his way toward his death, it is time for decision.

The story also closes out Jesus' ministry before Jerusalem on a note of mercy, so characteristic of all that he has done so far. It not only models discipleship but serves a symbolic function as well. The newly gained sight of the two men who have called out for Jesus' mercy stands metaphorically for religious understanding, which the twelve disciples are still struggling to achieve. And that continuing struggle is evident from the request of the mother of James and John (20:20–28), the disciples' attempt to keep the children away from Jesus (19:13), and their cynical remark at 19:10 that it might be better not to marry (19:10). Jesus does not say so explicitly at this point, but the disciples are still persons of "little faith."

The reader will also find here a subtle turn in Jesus' relationship to the crowds that have followed him. They have remained with him all this time and have thus appeared as potential disciples. At 20:31, however, for the first time they do something that, although not explicitly criticized, is an indication of inadequate understanding and faith: They rebuke the blind men. The point is made only in passing; but the reader will hear more about the crowds, both good and bad.

Thinking Today about Matthew 19:1—20:34

The Teaching of Jesus Revisited

The content of Jesus' teaching in 19:1—20:34, which continues his concentration on the disciples and the life of the postresurrection community, contributes a symmetry to the narrative as a whole, for much of the material here recalls the Sermon on the Mount, the first of the great discourses, at the very beginning of Jesus' ministry. At that point, the teaching was for both disciples and potential disciples (see 5:1 and 7:28–29) and covered a wide range of topics. Here fewer topics are treated, and the teaching is more clearly directed to a distinct body of believers, expected to continue after his death. The themes of divorce (19:3–9; 5:31–32) and wealth (19:23–30; 5:19–21, 25–33) provide major links, and 19:16–30 exhibits numerous thematic similarities (Davies and Allison, *The Gospel According to Saint Matthew,* pp. 62–63; note the following: 19:17–18//5:20, 7:14; 19:18//5.21; 19:18//5:27; 19:19//7:11; 19:21//5:48; 19:21//6:20; 19:22//6:24; 19:30//5:1–12.) It should also be noted that the theme of forgiveness, central to the discourse on church life in chapter 18, is also strong in the Sermon (6:9–14).

In the end as at the beginning, then, a major aspect of Jesus' ministry is teaching with a decidedly ethical content, focused on human relationships. By recalling themes from the Sermon at this late point in the story, when Jesus is nearing the city where he will die, the narrator reminds the reader of the earlier teaching and solidifies the image of Jesus as the one who stands up for certain values at the cost of his very life.

As the links with the Sermon on the Mount suggest, there is much in this material that relates to issues of human relationships and justice. The themes of attachment to wealth versus leaving all and following Jesus stand out when juxtaposed against our consumer society, and the hyperbole in verse 19:24 ("it is easier for a camel to go through the eye of a needle") offers an arresting image that cries out for creative elaboration. Likewise, the passage on children suggests a severe indictment of a social system that exalts youth but allows so many children to live in poverty while wealth is wasted on ventures that are at worst destructive and at best stupid. The request of the mother of James and John invites reflection on power and privilege not only in society but also in the church, especially when viewed against the background of the third announcement of Jesus' death.

Application of the teaching on divorce in our contemporary world raises fundamental questions that have been discussed in some detail in relation to the Sermon on the Mount (see p. 49). An interesting footnote to that discussion is that despite the greater detail in the present passage, a fundamental question remains unanswered: whether a man who divorces his wife because of adultery is free to marry again. Neither passage addresses the question from a woman's perspective. So, even though the prohibition of divorce seems to function more literally than some of the commands in the Sermon on the Mount, the practice of application necessarily entails the kind of negotiation between worldviews discussed in relation to that material (see "Struggling with Radical Demands," pp. 59–61).

I have so far treated the parable in 20:1–16 only in very general terms and in relation to its Matthean context. It would be unfortunate, however, to miss the forceful and vivid imagery with which the parable speaks. In addition, it is helpful in exploring that imagery to disconnect the story from its present setting—that is, to seek to recover the form in which Jesus originally told it.

We have already seen that verse 16 is problematic, because the theme of the reversal of first and last does not really describe what happens in the story. Found also in Matthew 19:30; Mark 10:31; and Luke 13:30, the saying probably circulated without a context as a piece of oral tradition until the gospel writers incorporated it into their works. According to some scholars, verses 14 and 15 are also secondary, but very few deny the originality of the first part of verse 14: "Take what belongs to you and go." It is difficult to judge whether the remainder of 14 and 15 belongs to the original; they do not change the meaning fundamentally, but they do add a note of interpretation by emphasizing the householder's generosity ("I choose to give to this last the same as I give to you. Am I not allowed to do what I choose…?"). Because they are so highly interpretive, the likelihood is that they are not in fact part of the original. With or without them, the parable ends with a confrontation that calls the all-day workers' attitude into question in a dramatic way.

It is important to see how the dramatic element works. When the householder hires the original workers early in the morning for a denarius a day, he does what would be expected; the wages are standard. At the hiring of the second crew, about 9:00 a.m., when the householder promises to pay "whatever is right," the reader/hearer may wonder what this means but will almost automatically assume it will be less than the denarius. As the third and fourth crews come on board around noon and 3:00 p.m., however—and especially when a last group appears around 5:00—the expectation of a differentiation builds considerably.

The extreme discrepancy between early in the morning and 5:00 p.m. contributes much to the power of the parable. Although the householder fulfilled the bargain he had made, the hearer/reader can scarcely help but take the side of the early workers when they complain. Although he is in a strict sense just, the householder is skillfully made to appear unjust (Scott, *Hear Then the Parable*, p. 297), so bizarre is his method of remuneration. And it is the appearance of injustice in his action on which the parable turns. For in negating the natural tendency to side with the grumbling workers, and in pointing to the irrefutable fact that nothing wrong befell the early workers, the story forces the hearer/reader to reexamine the premises on which the original reaction was based.

If the parable as a whole is a metaphor for the way things are in the rule of God, the grumbling workers come to signify a human attitude that stands in opposition to that rule. In the original version, the householder should not be viewed as a direct allegorical signifier of God; the wages are at best only barely adequate. However, the hearer/reader will naturally find in his outrageous action at the end a symbol of God's radical grace. Similarly, the grumblers need not be allegorized into the Pharisees, despite the claims of many scholars, nor does the parable oppose the notion of reward; all the workers are hired based on reward.

The crucial point is that the householder's radical method of payment completely overturns the rules that normally apply to a relationship of work for pay. That his payment is technically just does not obviate that the last group has received about twelve times as much *per hour* than has the first! There is clearly a basis for the charge of unfairness, but the ending of the parable insists that the hearer/reader reject that charge. What kind of transformation must one undergo in order to approve the householder's action?

To answer this question, we must ask what was wrong with the grumblers' attitude. Nothing at all, except the basis that gave rise to it—the assumption that work in the vineyard was like any other work, that the reward to be received could be calculated based on the amount of work done. Although the householder's act did not question the relationship between work and pay, it did shatter completely the notion of calculation—the notion that some workers could, by virtue of longer hours or higher productivity, earn higher pay. That notion of course represents the way things are in the world of work, which suggests that to grasp the parable the hearer/reader must understand that things are not in fact thus with respect to the rule of God.

How so, specifically? It is not that there are no rewards; it is that in God's rule, reward is not something calculable so that some people can set themselves above others in a hierarchical relationship. The attitude of the early workers stands for any of the ways in which people try to claim special status before God, over against others. Moreover, the all-important point is that their attitude toward their fellow workers is the root of their failure to grasp the nature of God's rule. Thus, Luise Schottroff argues that "the parable has two focuses: the goodness of God and—as a consequence of this goodness—the solidarity of human beings" (Schottroff and Stegemann, *God of the Lowly*, p. 138).

The goodness of God becomes evident only at the end of the parable, because it is only here that the householder acts outrageously, foregoing what is technically "just" in favor of what is gracious and merciful. Yet once the hearer/reader can understand the reward as based on the latter, rather than as a calculable payment, it becomes clear that the call to the vineyard is itself an act of grace (Scott, *Hear Then the Parable*, pp. 296–98).

The force of the parable in its original setting—the mission of the historical Jesus—is considerably greater than that which it acquires in its Matthean setting. Nevertheless, the Matthean application of the story specifically to the church—as a warning against putting oneself first (Davies and Allison, *The Gospel According to Saint Matthew*, III, pp. 61, 67–68)— has its own usefulness, and it need not negate the radical way in which it calls into question the human tendency to calculate religious standing.

21:1—22:46 Jesus in Jerusalem

The Final Debates

The reader has long known what is about to happen in Jerusalem, because Jesus has on several occasions predicted his rejection, death, and resurrection. There is still an element of suspense, though, because the reader will naturally "hope against hope" for an alternative outcome; and in any case, the specific unfolding of events remains undisclosed. But it will come as no surprise that Jesus' days in Jerusalem will be marked by intensified conflict.

Because Jesus enters Jerusalem amid the adulation of the crowds who hail him as Son of David, this conflict does not appear immediately. It follows quickly, however, as he goes directly into the temple, disrupting the commerce related to the sacrificial system, and provokes the criticism of the chief priests and scribes. And the theme of conflict prevails as Jesus argues with the chief priests and elders over his authority, tells three allegories that condemn the religious leaders, and enters into a series of disputes that end with the notation in 22:46 that no one dared ask him a question after that.

Throughout this sequence, the narrator lumps all of Israel's religious leaders together as completely insincere, engaging Jesus only to trip him up. Moreover, the allegories show that the die is cast: Jesus' opponents have already rejected him, and the consequences are inevitable. The statement in 22:46 is therefore climactic: The interchange between Jesus and his opponents is at an end, and the drama will have to play itself out as Jesus has predicted.

21:1–27 Jesus in Jerusalem: The Initial Events

A subtle tension has been at work throughout the story. On the one hand, the narrator has linked Jesus closely with the title "Son of David" (1:1; 9:27; 15:22; 20:31), which calls up notions of military triumph and victory over Israel's enemies. On the other hand, Jesus' words and deeds suggest a different image: He has spoken of himself as "gentle and humble in heart" (11:29), and his "deeds of power" (11:23) have been directed toward the alleviation of individual suffering but not national liberation. The two images are not mutually exclusive, and we have seen that Jewish piety stressed David's own humble origins and spiritual qualities (see pp. 20–21 on 2:1–23). Yet tension remains, and the accounts in the first part of Matthew 21 play on it in order to enrich the reader's understanding of Jesus' messiahship.

Tradition has named the first story Jesus' "triumphal entry," but the title is appropriate only in an ironical sense. Jesus clearly takes on the role of a messianic king, and his comment to the temple leaders in the ensuing story (21:16) implies his acceptance of the title "Son of David" when the children repeat it. However, the processional bears few of the trappings of a celebration of military victory, and the quotation from Zechariah 9:9, found only in Matthew's version, explicitly stresses humility. The reader must therefore modify traditional expectations regarding the Messiah Son of David in light of the image of the nonviolent Jesus, the one who (reflecting Isa. 42:3) would not so much as "break a bruised reed" or "quench a smoldering wick" (12:20).

Aside from its specific content, the Zechariah quotation combines with verses 6–7 to reinforce the ongoing agenda of presenting the events of Jesus' life as fulfillment of scripture. Many commentators note that in the Matthean version Jesus seems to be seated on two animals at once—the donkey and its foal. Some have accused the author of ignorance of the device of synonymous parallelism in Hebrew poetry. (One line repeats the meaning of the preceding one in slightly different words; the original readers of Zechariah would have understood the colt and the donkey to be the same.) But the point of introducing a second animal is to link the event in the closest possible way to the specific words of scripture.

Scriptural fulfillment comes into play again in the story of Jesus' assault on those selling and buying in the temple, as Jesus defends both his action and the children's adulation with additional quotations. This account also contributes to the complexity of the reader's task in understanding the nature of Jesus' messiahship. To begin with, there is a degree of violence in his action, yet his compassionate nature appears in his healing of the lame and the blind. In addition, this healing conflicts with 2 Samuel 5:8, which indicates a prohibition of the blind and lame from the temple area and links that prohibition with David himself. Here again, the reader must bring together tensive elements to understand Jesus' role.

It is difficult to determine the specific meaning that Jesus' action in 21:12–13 (overturning the tables of the moneychangers and driving out those who were buying and selling) has in the Matthean framework. Here again tradition has provided a misleading label—the "cleansing" of the temple. Because Jesus will foretell the destruction of the temple in 24:1–2, he cannot be clearing out the corruption to reinstitute its proper function. Indeed, the original readers of Matthew in the late first century would have known that the temple was destroyed in 70 C.E. Also, it is important to remember that the commercial activity Jesus disrupts was essential to the sacrificial system that lay at the heart of the temple's religious function; and that system is itself sanctioned by the Torah that Jesus has clearly endorsed in 5:17–20. So this activity in itself is not the problem.

To grasp the full significance of the incident, we need to notice the subtle way in which matters related to the temple are woven into the gospel of Matthew as a whole. On two prior occasions (9:13; 12:7), Jesus has quoted Hosea 6:6: "I desire mercy and not sacrifice." In 12:7, however, Jesus uses the activity of the temple priests as a precedent for his own action, and in 21:13, his composite quotation (Isa. 56:7; Jer. 7:11) implies a positive function for the temple. It is not easy to piece together a coherent attitude toward the temple out of all this, but 23:23 may serve as a helpful analogy. Here Jesus condemns the scribes and Pharisees for neglecting the "weightier matters of the law" through their focus on minute details, but he ends by declaring, "It is these you ought to have practiced *without neglecting the others*" (emphasis added). If a similar attitude is at work in 21:12–14, it would appear that Jesus attacks neither the sacrificial system nor the financial activities as such, but he condemns the current operation of the temple as the locus of the corrupt religious leadership. These leaders have used God's good gifts of temple and law not to foster the obedience God truly wants— "justice and mercy and faith"—but in fact to subvert them to their own advantage. The commerce is only a convenient symbol of the essential corruption that is Jesus' true target. But, as we will see, that corruption has in fact rendered the temple obsolete.

If part of the reader's task in this section is to reflect on the nature of Jesus' messiahship, another aspect is to follow the plot of the larger story. Jesus' dramatic actions constitute a challenge to take sides regarding him. As he enters Jerusalem, the crowds (and vv. 9–10 suggest that these are people who have been following him, not the Jerusalem populace) hail him as Son of David and "the prophet Jesus from Nazareth in Galilee." Within the Matthean framework, this combination will appear as correct but inadequate. Jesus is in fact Messiah Son of David, but the term *prophet* is an insufficient complement: As the reader has long known by now, he is also Son of God.

The residents of Jerusalem appear one step further removed from the full truth as the narrator reports only that they are thrown into turmoil by the event. As things proceed, however, the reader finds that there are those who react in a negative way. The religious leaders meet his challenge with counterchallenges. They object to the children's use of the Davidic title, and they ask by what authority Jesus is doing "these things"—referring, presumably, both to his teachings and the actions just recounted. But Jesus meets their challenges with yet others of his own. He prefaces the scripture quotation in verse 16 with a rhetorical question ("have you never read…?") and with another question escapes the trap they try to lay for him in verses 23–37.

The net effect of the verbal contest is to expose the insincerity of Jesus' opponents and present Jesus as completely victorious in his reading of scripture and thus in his claim to represent God. In 21:23–27, the chief priests and elders reveal their lack of integrity through their deliberations: They are crowd-pleasers motivated by fear. In 21:14–17, the chief priests and scribes appear insensitive to the suffering of the lame and blind, and the reader will easily get the force of Jesus' question in verse 16. Of course these guardians of tradition have read the scriptures; but they refuse to understand them!

In all of this interchange, Jesus never gives a direct answer to the question of his authority (21:23). However, he demonstrates it as he defeats all his opponents in debate. The reader, of course, already knows the source of Jesus' authority: Jesus has made that explicit at 11:27, and the very voice of God has endorsed him at 3:17 and 17:5. The silence of Jesus on the issue now is another sign of the utter intransigence of the religious leaders: It is useless to make claims in the presence of those who will not listen.

It is against the background of intransigence that we must interpret the strange incident of Jesus' cursing of the fig tree in 21:18–22. Coming in the middle of Jesus' debates in the temple, just after his dramatic action there, the episode reinforces the symbolic weight of that action. Both the disruption of the commerce and the curse are modeled after the ancient Hebrew tradition of prophetic actions—symbolic deeds that enact God's decisions or intentions. Taken together, the two incidents signal God's irrevocable judgment against Israel's current leadership. Both the temple itself and the leaders who have corrupted it now stand under condemnation; they must wither under the judgment of God. In fact, the disciples' focus on the immediate withering (v. 19) shows that the process has already begun. Together with the debates in the temple, then, these incidents prepare the reader for the condemnatory allegories in 21:28—22:46.

Interestingly, however, the story of the cursing of the fig tree also issues a challenge to readers in the postresurrection community of Jesus' followers. Rather than simply marvel at Jesus' manifestation of power, they should realize that this same power is available to them as well, as they too struggle to deal with the forces that oppose them, if they will but have faith. Viewed from this perspective, the suddenness of the withering is a sign of the availability of divine power. Thus although the main focus of this section is on the plot, and more specifically on Jesus' condemnation of the religious leadership, the narrator slips in a lesson for the church. And this is hardly accidental, because we will observe a parallel move, with much greater weight, in 22:11–14—right in the midst of the condemnatory allegories.

21:28—22:14 Jesus' Condemnation of the Religious Leaders: Three Allegories

Jesus' demonstration of the insincerity of the chief priests and elders in 21:23–27 leads immediately into a series of allegories. Not only does Jesus make it clear that these apply specifically to his opponents, but the narrator also notes that these opponents recognize the point themselves, thus ironically reinforcing their own condemnation: "they realized that he was speaking about them" (21:45). It is yet another sign of their incorrigibility that even so their sole thought is to try to arrest him; they hold off only because of their fear of the crowds. Their cowardly manner is the other side of their hardened hearts.

The three allegories, which the text names "parables" (see "Interpreting the Parables," pp. 99–102, on the difference between parable and allegories) play up slightly different aspects of one overarching theme. They all refer to God's ongoing relationship to the chosen people of Israel and its leaders, and they all pronounce a negative judgment on the current generation of leaders.

The story of the two sons (21:28–33) is simple and straightforward, setting the context for the next two. The first son refuses to work in the father's vineyard, but later changes his mind and goes, whereas the second promises to go but does not. Matthew's Jesus provides an interpretation that not only coaches the reader in how to read what follows but also, by linking Jesus' mission to that of John the Baptist, helps gather the strands from the whole narrative (see 3:7–12). It is obvious that the second son represents the leaders of Israel who by virtue of their offices made a promise to produce the fruits of righteousness God expects. And their failure is multiplied because even after the "tax collectors and prostitutes"—the most unlikely of all candidates for God's rule, symbolized here by the first son— responded to John by repenting, these leaders do not get the point and make their own repentance. In a context dominated by denunciation, Jesus' pronouncement that the tax collectors and prostitutes "are going into the kingdom of God ahead of you" must mean that the leaders are not going at all.

The next two stories add specific details to the scenario. The vineyard of 20:1–16 reappears in 21:33–45, now as the property of a landowner who planted it and leased it to tenants. The reader will easily identify the landowner with God and the vineyard as a standard, scriptural image representing Israel; thus the tenants will naturally appear as ciphers for Israel's leaders. As the plot proceeds, the reader will identify the two sets of slaves with the various prophets God sent the chosen people through its long history and, of course, the landowner's son, murdered "outside the vineyard," with Jesus the Son of God who was put to death outside Jerusalem.

The story of the wedding banquet in 22:1–14 draws on different imagery and adds still further details to the drama. The reader will know that the rule of God is often associated with a great feast and will naturally identify God as the king and Jesus as the son for whom the feast is given. The slaves who issue the invitation but are rebuffed by the intended guests will again call to mind God's prophetic emissaries who are rejected by the people. In this case, however, the second group (v. 4) will suggest the church's own prophets who sought to draw the larger community of Israel into their fold following the resurrection (see 23:34), for it is the rejection of this second group that leads to the bizarre reaction of the king in verse 7: the sending of troops to destroy the city—a plot element missing from the other canonical version of the story (Lk. 14:16–24). Readers in the late first century would certainly see here a reference to the destruction of Jerusalem in 70 C.E. and interpret that event as God's retribution for both the crucifixion of Jesus and the refusal to accept the early Christian proclamation.

As in the story of the cursing of the fig tree (21:18–22), the narrator interrupts a sequence devoted largely to the condemnation of those who opposed Jesus (and, here, the Christian mission) to address the postresurrection followers of Jesus themselves. But here the point is negative, not positive. In verses 11–14, when the king enters the banquet hall, he notices a guest without a wedding garment and he has the hapless person cast out. Both the oddity of the king's expectation (someone summoned at the last minute would have no chance to get properly attired) and the dramatic content of verse 13 show that the scene (also missing from Luke's version) symbolizes final judgment. In the context of the larger allegory, the guest—having been called after the earlier refusals and destruction of the city—will logically have to refer to members of the Christian community. Here again, as in 13:29–30, the reader must reckon with God's intention to judge the church itself. Thus the warning at the end of the Sermon on the Mount remains valid for followers of Jesus: "And everyone who hears these words of mine and does not act on them will be like a foolish man" (7:26).

The judgment of the church is thus a theme in this section, but it is subordinate to the theme of judgment passed on those who initially rejected Jesus and the early mission. At this point, it becomes important to consider who the narrator has in mind when proclaiming that earlier judgment.

A great deal hinges on how one interprets two verses in the story of the vineyard tenants—21:41 and 43. In verse 41, Jesus' opponents fall into his trap by unwittingly pronouncing judgment on themselves when they draw the logical conclusion about how the king will respond to those who have murdered his slave and his sons: "He will put those wretches to a miserable death, and lease the vineyard to other tenants." Jesus confirms their answer in verse 43 in which he interprets the allegory by telling the leaders that God's kingdom will be taken from them and given to others, who will produce fruits. But the question is who these others are.

The Greek texts says that the kingdom will be given to an *ethnos*, a term that most frequently means a people or a nation, although in the plural it often takes on the specialized meaning of Gentiles. Whichever of these terms interpreters have preferred, they have generally understood the verse to mean that because of the Jewish people's rejection of Jesus, God has taken the kingdom away from them and given it to the church, which constitutes a new people. Many have argued that the church is thus, from the perspective of Matthean theology, either the *new* Israel (replacing the old) or the *true* Israel (faithful remnant of the old).

This line of interpretation fits with the view that the gospel of Matthew is written within a Christian community that now stands completely separate from Judaism, so that the church and the synagogue are utterly distinct entities. Some recent interpreters, however, view the matter differently (see, e.g., Saldarini, *Matthew's Christian-Jewish Community;* Harrington, *The Gospel of Matthew;* and Overman, *Church and Community in Crisis*). They believe that the Matthean community constitutes a marginalized group still within the Jewish community, vying for the loyalty of the people as a whole.

These interpreters read Matthew 21:41, 43 in a rather different way. Understanding *ethnos* not as "nation" or "people" but as "group" (a meaning the term did carry), they argue that Matthew's Jesus speaks not of the rejection of the Jewish people as a whole but only of the transfer of leadership from one group to another. The kingdom is thus taken from those who opposed Jesus and given to the community of his followers.

In favor of this latter interpretation, we may note that in 21:43–44 Jesus is in fact speaking directly to the chief priests and elders (see v. 23), and in verse 45, it is specifically the chief priests and Pharisees who "realized that he was speaking about them." The fact remains, however, that "people" and "nation" are the more usual meanings of ethnos in the New Testament. There are, moreover, reasons to think that the gospel of Matthew reflects a greater degree of separation than the proponents of this interpretation allow. At 16:18, Jesus founds an *ekklesia*, a church, not an alternative synagogue. This makes it difficult to believe that the recurrent phrase "their synagogues" (4:23; 10:17; 12:9; 13:54) simply distinguishes those led by the Pharisees from those populated by followers of Jesus. The synagogue as such seems in the Matthean vocabulary to be the gathering place of a group to which the readers of the gospel no longer belong.

This does not mean, however, that the Matthean Christians understand themselves as an utterly new entity replacing Israel—a "third race," to use a phrase from early Christian literature. We can imagine that they have recently separated from the synagogues but not, in their minds, from the people of Israel. In some sense, they think of themselves simply as (the faithful) Israel, still obedient to the Torah (as interpreted by Jesus), yet standing in a new situation after the destruction of the temple. In such a context, 21:43 would indeed call them to some sense of distinct peoplehood, but not in such a way as to set themselves over against "Israel" or "Judaism" or the "Jewish people" as aliens.

To be sure, the gospel of Matthew depicts God as rejecting a generation of Israel's leadership and sealing this judgment with the destruction of Jerusalem. However, this need not be seen as a final judgment against the entire Jewish people for all time (see "The Crowds"/"The People," pp. 191–92).

If this description remains vague and rife with tension, that is perhaps because neither the community nor the author of the gospel had developed a clear theological perspective on the issue. Nor should this be surprising, because the process by which any new community grows out of another and achieves self-definition is necessarily lengthy, difficult, and filled with ambiguities.

22:15–40 The Religious Leaders Question Jesus

In 21:15–40, the religious leaders pose a series of three questions to Jesus, and the narrator ensures that the reader will understand that their intention is not to have a genuine discussion with Jesus but either to discredit him or to trick him into making a self-incriminating statement. Thus in reporting that the Pharisees join with a group called the Herodians (the nature of which historians cannot with confidence identify) to inquire about paying the Roman tax, the narrator states explicitly that the intention is to "entrap him in what he said." In addition, the Sadducees' scenario regarding the seven brothers serially married to the same woman is designed not only to reduce the notion of the resurrection of the dead to an absurdity but also, perhaps, to embroil Jesus in the dispute between the Pharisees and Sadducees on this issue, for the Pharisees believed in the resurrection of the dead but the Sadducees did not. However, the narrator's interest is not in distinguishing the Pharisees and Sadducees from each other but to show that Israel's leadership as a whole rejected Jesus. As the chief priests, scribes, and elders questioned Jesus' authority in chapter 21, so now the two major "parties," together with the Herodians, unite in their utter refusal to hear what Jesus says.

The final question, which a Pharisee versed in the Law brings up, is this: "which commandment in the law is the greatest?" In itself, the question is legitimate and was in fact a subject of debate in rabbinic circles. Here again, however, the narrator reveals the questioner's sinister motivation ("to test him"; note also that the positive interchange between Jesus and the questioner in Mk. 12:29–34 is missing in Matthew). And Jesus' answer itself contains a subtle criticism of the question. Asked for the (one) greatest commandment, Jesus unexpectedly supplies a second, which he explicitly terms "like" the first (a word also missing in Mark). In thus linking the command to love one's neighbor in Leviticus 19:18 to the command to love God in Deuteronomy 6:5, Jesus proclaims that the two are indivisible.

Love of neighbor is therefore a necessary correlate of loving God, and the reader will remember that Jesus' opponents—most specifically the Pharisees—have shown themselves to lack human compassion (12:1–14; 19:3–9). The reader will also know that Jesus has repeatedly invoked the love command and its equivalents (5:43–45; 7:12; 9:13; 12:7), and now

22:40 (again missing in Mark) formalizes its status as the very center of the Law: "On these two commandments hang all the law and the prophets." Love is therefore the hermeneutical key with which one approaches scripture. And even the final phrase, "and the prophets," carries an implicit criticism in it. The questioner speaks only of the Law, but Jesus mentions the prophets also—the writings so rife with God's demand for justice among human beings.

22:41–46 Jesus Poses a Counterquestion

Having effectively escaped the verbal traps of his opponents, and thereby demonstrated his authority, Jesus now goes on the offensive with a challenge of his own. Eliciting from the Pharisees a description of the Messiah as David's son, he asks them how such a designation is compatible with Psalm 110:1: "The Lord said to my Lord, / Sit at my right hand." The Pharisees' inability to answer this question leads to the climactic notation in verse 46: "nor from that day did anyone dare to ask him any more questions."

Jesus' line of questioning rests on three suppositions: that David was the author of the psalm, that the lines were inspired by God's Spirit, and that the two instances of the term "Lord" refer respectively to God and the Messiah. The point is thus to show, through scripture, that the Messiah, although descended from David, is something more than the Son of David. Given the narrator's earlier endorsements of that title, the reader must not take this incident as a rejection of it. But it does mean that it is inadequate by itself. And just as the narrator's perspective on Jesus' entry into Jerusalem encouraged the reader to modify traditional expectations regarding the Messiah Son of David, this climactic incident subtly reminds the reader of the missing component insofar as titles go. God commands the Messiah to sit at God's right hand because the Messiah is in fact Son of God.

At a crucial juncture, then, the reader once again encounters the narrator's claim regarding Jesus' identity as Son of God. But the title is by now no mere abstraction for the reader—a "religious" designation without specific human or moral content, for as in chapters 11–12, the narrator has stressed specific aspects of Jesus' character. He has entered Jerusalem in a triumph that was only paradoxical; in the temple of God he has offered compassion to the lame and the blind and preferred the words of powerless children to the pronouncements of chief priests and scribes; and he has shown from scripture that the love of God cannot be separated from love of neighbor.

The refusal of Jesus' opponents to hear him is thus an indication of their refusal of the compassion of God and their rejection of "justice and mercy and faith" (23:23). They have nothing more to say to him because his verbal victories leave no door open to them except the one they will not enter—acceptance of what he says. Jesus does have something to say, however, and it will show finally that the issue of Jesus' identity is inseparable from this issue of what he stands for in human terms. He will condemn the scribes and Pharisees not for faulty theology but for the content of their characters.

Thinking Today about Matthew 21:1—22:46

Religious Exclusivism and the Problem of Other Faiths

As the narrative nears its conclusion, the rhetoric of absolute good and absolute evil, represented by Jesus on the one hand and the Jewish leadership on the other, grows stronger. In the Matthean world of thought, those who opposed Jesus were totally corrupt. Motivated by fear of losing their own power, they cared nothing about the needs of suffering humanity. Whereas Jesus stood for justice, mercy, and faith, they were unjust, unmerciful, and unfaithful—concerned only with the externals of religion and not its substance.

In connection with an earlier segment of Matthew (see "Powerful Texts, Dangerous Potential," pp. 88–92), I noted the necessity of distinguishing the historical Pharisees from the characters in Matthew's story. I also suggested that one way of dealing with such material is to stress the way in which the church itself manifests the faults that appear in the religious leaders. As we have seen, the theme of a judgment against the church crops up at some very crucial points.

The problem of anti-Judaism becomes far more difficult to mitigate in the present section, however, for here Matthew's Jesus pronounces an absolute judgment of God against the Jewish leaders, stating that the kingdom is taken away from them. Even if we accept the view that the Matthean community is not yet fully separated from the synagogue community (a view I argued against earlier), so that the bitterness is born of a rivalry between two Jewish groups rather than separate religions, a significant problem remains, for in any case Matthew's Jesus pronounces an absolute judgment against his opponents. The kingdom of God will be taken away from them, and the destruction of Jerusalem by the Romans is their visible punishment. At this point an attempt to deal with the problem of anti-Judaism in Matthew (and in the New Testament generally) leads us into broader theological issues, most especially that of the nature of God's action in the world and the relationship between Christianity and other faiths.

In addressing the first of these questions in relation to Matthew 1:1–25 (see "The Power of God as Problem," pp. 24–26), I suggested that we cannot simply dismiss Matthew's witness to God's action in history without defacing the story the gospel tells. I also noted, however, the problematic character of that witness from our contemporary point of view. As we encounter the material in the present section of Matthew, the difficulty takes on a new meaning; and it becomes even more important to explore new conceptualities that can honor both the ancient witness and the demands of our own situation. In 1:1–25, the issue was primarily intellectual, a question of how to deal with claims that stretch our credulity. In Matthew 21:1—22:46, however, a deeply moral dimension of the problem emerges, for here the notion of God's action in history issues in the claim that God condemned the religious leaders of Jesus' generation and destroyed Jerusalem as retribution. Such assertions have led later Christians not only to anti-Jewish attitudes but also to overt acts of violence against Jewish people.

Here again, as at other points in Matthew, we see the need for the contemporary church to be much more courageous than it has often been in facing up to the historically conditioned nature of its scriptures. Although this does not mean abandoning the entire notion of God's action in history, it does mean that we need to bring that notion into conversation with insights derived from our contemporary worldview. We need on one level simply to confess that the gospel of Matthew does not in fact live up to its own ideal of love. We can point out that it appeared in a time of great bitterness, in which both the followers of Jesus and the majority of the Jewish population engaged in condemnatory rhetoric. In addition, we can note that Matthew also speaks of a judgment against the church. But we must also be willing to reject quite explicitly any rendering of the Matthean scheme of God's action in history that asks us to believe that God actually sent Roman troops to destroy Jerusalem and the temple.

These comments are not examples of Christian self-effacement. The problem in Matthew is in principle no different from that in many parts of the Hebrew Bible that speak of God's manipulation of international politics either to punish or to save God's people. Indeed, we find right at the heart of the Israelite tradition, in the stories of the exodus and conquest of Canaan and in the great prophet books, an attitude toward "pagan" religion that distorts the meaning and substance of those ancient modes of religious consciousness in fundamental ways. It is not Christianity alone but biblical religion altogether that must wrestle with this problem.

It is understandable, in light of the seriousness of the problem, that many thoughtful persons in our time find no alternative but to abandon biblical religion or at least to give up altogether any notion that God works in history. The assumption behind the former option is that only those traditions that are ideologically pure are worthy of any sort of allegiance.

We must ask, however, where one can find an ideologically pure tradition, and by what standards we could measure such purity anyway. The second option would seem to forfeit one of the components that has given the biblical tradition much of its power through the centuries, an element that distinguishes it from vapid notions of God as a watchmaker and lawgiver, uninvolved in the lives of human persons and communities.

This commentary (and series) proceeds on a different assumption—that the genius of biblical religion is in fact its ability to work with an imperfect past, a tradition that offers up monumental insights and sources of empowerment while bearing all the marks of human frailty and historical conditioning. Thus, the way to honor that tradition is to appropriate it critically, testing it out in the lives of individual believers and communities and bringing it into conversations with the full range of our human experience.

Such an approach does not result in final answers but calls us to creative thought that can contribute to the ongoing task of applying tradition to new situations. The notion that God acts in human history is deeply embedded in the biblical faith, and it is difficult to imagine authentic forms of either Judaism or Christianity that do not in some way incorporate the notion of the covenant or covenants that God has made with specific historical groups. The root of the problem from our contemporary perspective, however, is that God's covenant with and action on behalf of specific groups have taken the form of exclusivism. This theme is much stronger in Christianity than in Judaism, but it is fair to say that Christian exclusivism is a heightened form of Jewish covenantal thought. In any case, Christians have often believed that if God acted specifically through Israel and then through the church, two implications follow. First, God's revelation to Israel forbids recognizing similar revelations to other peoples. Second, if God acted in Jesus and the creation of the church, God no longer acts through Israel. It is easy to see how the gospel of Matthew has fed such thinking.

If we free ourselves from uncritical appropriation of the biblical thought world, however, it is possible to think of God's revelatory action in relation to both Israel and the church in nonexclusive ways. We can appropriate the genius of the Hebrew prophets, with their witness to God's involvement in history and their radical stands on behalf of social justice, without buying their caricatures of "pagan" religions or their use of sexist imagery. And we can appropriate Matthew's belief that God was at work in the ministry of Jesus and the life of the early Christian movement without accepting the notion that God's action is unilateral, interventionist, coercive, or punitive. Also, we can reject the notion that took the form in the first century C.E. of condemning either the Jewish religious leadership or Israel as a whole.

It will not be easy, when we approach the text of Matthew this way, to deal with passages such as 21:43, except by way of disclaimer. However, we should not overlook a positive potential that arises when we allow such material to function metaphorically. We might, for example, think of many of this country's agonizing experiences throughout its history—such as the Civil War, urban riots, demonstrations over the Vietnam War that ended in bloodshed, and the swelling of our prison populations—as resulting in part from our failure to address issues of social justice in our domestic and foreign policies. Of course, this does not mean that such disruptions are literal, interventionist acts of God; but the notion of God's wrath can perhaps, if introduced with care and bounded by clear disclaimers of literalism, serve as a meaningful metaphor in addressing them.

Such application of 21:43 to contemporary "decisive moments" also suggests a way of approaching Jesus' controversies with his opponents in this section. Here again, those characters in the narrative who reject Jesus can serve as exemplars of universal human failings rather than depictions of the Jewish leadership as a whole during Jesus' lifetime. Christians need not deny that rigid and self-serving attitudes among some of those actual leaders did in fact work together with Rome's oppressive interest in "order" to bring about Jesus' death. But another way of valuing this material is to honor its place in the Matthean plot by connecting the specific attitudes exemplified to the characters' inability to discern God's action in the midst of them. As we have seen, even (or, perhaps, especially) theological questions (22:15–46, "Is it lawful to pay taxes…?") can serve as diversionary tactics in the face of critical moments in history. Thus we should not allow sentimentalism to obscure the bite implicit in Jesus' insistence on a second great commandment. The demand for love of neighbor, incarnated as action on behalf of justice, is a head-on challenge to religion that abstracts itself from the concrete, material lives of human beings in need.

The account of Jesus' entry into Jerusalem raises its own difficulties, but it is also rich with possibilities for the creative interpretation of tradition. It is often associated with the widespread Christian view that Jesus was a different kind of messiah from the one the Jews expected. There is a degree of truth in this contention, but too often it is linked to the notion that Jews were somehow wrong in having the expectations they did. And it is in any case an extreme oversimplification of a complex phenomenon.

The truth is that Jewish hopes regarding God's deliverance in the future took a variety of forms, of which the expectation of a messiah in the strict sense was only one. This notion had not become a formally defined concept in Jesus' time, but at its core was the expectation that God would send an ideal king, a human being, in the line of David, to bring a time of peace, plenty, and security for Israel in the face of its enemies. Because this expectation was an important component in the existing tradition, it is simply wrongheaded for Christians to claim that this expectation was somehow illegitimate.

Matthew's story does encourage the reader to modify certain traditional expectations. But we should beware of the simplistic notions that either the Christian Messiah is peaceful while the Jewish is violent or the Jews expected an earthly-materialistic rule of God while Christians expect one that is spiritual and otherworldly.

To begin with, the expectation of a literal Davidic king was in its own way a hope for universal peace and justice, and on the other hand, the Christian depiction of its own messianism as nonviolent is overstated. For one thing, we have seen that there was a degree of violence in Jesus' action in the temple, and in any case, both this action and Jesus' prophetic words and deeds (note especially 21:18–22 and 22:7) point ahead to the violent action of God in the future. This is a matter to which we must return in detail in connection with Matthew 23—25, the judgment discourse, and it will be important in that same connection to show that the standard distinction between an earthly rule of God and a heavenly one is also misleading.

Despite all these potential pitfalls, the way in which this story and the incidents that follow it challenge the image of a triumphant messiah still has much to say to Christians. But we must let it speak not against a peculiarly Jewish triumphalism but against a universal human one that has certainly infected Christianity. There is great power in the image of a messiah who enters the Holy City on a donkey, whose ministry in the temple is to the outcasts, who is acclaimed by children but opposed by the powerful, and who honors God not through traditional acts of worship but by assaulting the temple. It can help unmask all the idolatrous ways in which we co-opt religious tradition to serve our ideologies of race, gender, nationalism, or economic dogma and all the subtle ways in which we accommodate ourselves to oppressive power.

23:1—25:46: Jesus in Jerusalem

The Fifth Discourse

The Judgment of God and the Close of the Age

The formulary ending at 26:1 marks off 25:46 as the conclusion of Jesus' fifth and final discourse. Scholars disagree, however, about whether chapter 23 is part of this discourse or a prelude to it. Either way, it plays a transitional role. It rounds off Jesus' final debates with his opponents in Jerusalem with a ringing condemnation and signals the end of Jesus' public ministry; but it also pronounces the severe word of judgment that forms the background of Jesus' announcement of the coming eschatological events in chapter 24. I treat it here as part of the discourse, because Jesus speaks continually throughout the chapter; and, despite a shift in location in chapter 24, there is only a partial change of audience. At 23:1, the narrator notes that Jesus is speaking to the crowds and the disciples, and the preceding verse (22:46) has implicitly removed the scribes and Pharisees from the scene. So we must understand Jesus' second-person denunciation of his opponents in chapter 23 as rhetorical: He is lambasting them *in absentia*. Then at 24:1 he begins to converse with the disciples; and in verse 4 he launches his comments about the end of the age, which culminate in a series of warnings in allegorical form and reach a climax in the dramatic description of the last judgment in 25:31–46. Thus, the entire piece is held together by the theme of judgment. Jesus begins by pronouncing judgment on those who reject him in the present, but he closes on the theme of a universal judgment in which he will return as Son of man to hold all human beings—Christians included—accountable for their deeds.

The discourse is designed not only to anticipate Jesus' death but also to give readers in the late first century a perspective on the events that took place in the decades following the crucifixion and resurrection. Both the destruction of Jerusalem in 70 C.E. and the persecutions of the early Christian community appear as predictions on the lips of Jesus, and promises of final vindication of those who are faithful are woven into the injunctions that permeate this material. The words of Jesus thus function simultaneously as prediction, warning, and promise; and they set the stage for the final act of the drama.

23:1–39 Denunciation of the Scribes and Pharisees

In the preceding section, 21:1—22:46, Jesus has entered Jerusalem, disrupted the activity in the temple, told a series of allegories depicting the judgment of God brought on by the people's rejection of God's emissaries, and defeated various opponents in debate. The allegories have placed current events in an ongoing historical sequence that concludes with Jesus' own death, the persecution of the early church, and the destruction of Jerusalem. In addition, the debates have brought the reader to a crucial turn in the plot. The notation in 22:46 that no one dared ask Jesus questions after that brings his public ministry to a close: At 23:1 Jesus speaks to disciples and potential disciples (the crowds) and has only words of denunciation for his opponents.

Strikingly, however, Jesus begins with a saying in 23:2–3 that seemingly acknowledges the authority of the scribes and Pharisees, telling his listeners to do what they teach but not to "do as they do." This introduction frames the issue in terms of the scribes and Pharisees' failure to practice what they preach rather than in terms of the falsity of their teaching, but the discourse that follows attacks (as early as v. 4!) their teachings, as well as their deeds. Not only has Jesus repeatedly challenged his opponents' teaching throughout the story but the narrator also has explicitly denied the authority of the scribes and Pharisees in 7:29.

Some scholars have attributed this apparent discrepancy to imperfect editing, arguing that 23:2–3 ("do whatever they teach you") represents a bit of early Christian tradition that does not reflect the final author's own view. Whatever the ultimate origin of the verse, it makes sense in the present context if we follow Mark Powell's interpretation. Powell begins by noting that in the ancient world, teaching and practice were inseparable, so it would be highly unusual to recommend that one follow the teachings of hypocritical people. Then he suggests that the reference to "Moses' seat" is a metaphor not for teaching authority but for access to the words of Torah, whether through written scrolls or memory (*God with Us*, p. 79). On this interpretation, Jesus says that the scribes and Pharisees know the words of scripture, but their practice shows that they are unreliable as guides on putting it into practice.

In any case, at the beginning of chapter 23 Jesus addresses the crowds and disciples by holding up the scribes and Pharisees as negative examples, and in verses 8–12 he challenges his hearers with a contrasting type of community life. If the scribes and Pharisees prize public recognition and exalt themselves, Jesus' followers should prize the role of servant and deny honorific titles such as teacher, rabbi, and father (understood in the sense of a revered mentor), for only God is father in this sense, and only Christ is teacher. Actually, the Matthean community did apparently know something of special offices within the church (see 13:52; 23:34). But the present passage reflects an egalitarian ideal characteristic of emerging movements, set over against the pomposity and hierarchicalism that tend to develop as movements grow older.

The net effect of verses 1–11 is thus to warn Jesus' hearers and the gospel's readers against the kind of behavior that the scribes and Pharisees manifest, but the bulk of the chapter is a denunciation of these people that leads into Jesus' lament over Jerusalem in verses 37–39. There are thus three levels of meaning the reader should discern. (1) On the level of plot, this material puts the finishing touches on the story of Jesus' rejection: He goes to his death because of the intransigence of Israel's leaders, which is in continuity with their rejection of the prophets. (2) From the perspective of the first readers of the gospel, in conflict with the synagogue communities of their day, Jesus' condemnation justifies their attitude toward those on the other side: They are complete hypocrites. (3) In terms of the internal and ongoing life of the church, the negative image of Jesus' opponents stands as a warning against hypocrisy and unfaithfulness within the church itself.

This chapter contains the gospel's densest concentration of invective against the scribes and Pharisees, but it only gathers together for final emphasis elements of a portrait that has already been painted. Throughout the story, these figures have shown themselves as lacking in compassion, insincere in their religious practice, and utterly incorrigible in their rejection of the emissaries of God. In essence, they stand as the mirror opposite of Jesus himself and the way he represents.

Against this background, the implication of verses 16–21 is not simply that their views on oaths are logically unsound, which is what Jesus demonstrates, but that these views encourage irresponsibility. The logical point is that oaths sworn by sacred objects have an implicit reference to God, who is the one truly sacred reality. But this passage is at one with the following woes that condemn the scribes and Pharisees for paying attention to minutiae and external matters to the neglect of justice, mercy, and faith.

The most uncompromising condemnations come in the first and last woes, verses 13–15 and 29–36. In the first, Jesus calls his opponents children of hell (Gehenna) who not only fail to enter God's rule but also prevent others from doing so, and in the last, he virtually pronounces a sentence to hell. This sentence brings together the two dimensions of the gospel's criticism of Jesus' opponents. In chapter 23, as throughout the gospel, it has been clear that those who reject Jesus are guilty not simply of an error in judgment but of mean-spiritedness. This mean-spiritedness desensitizes them to the workings of God in their midst. Thus Jesus concludes his condemnation of their character by linking them to the refusal of God's missionaries throughout the history of Israel. There is an element of collective guilt in this scenario, but the force of verse 31 is that the members of the current generation, despite their pious attempts to distance themselves from the sins of their ancestors, have in fact repeated those sins. Thus the ironical command to "fill up…the measure of" the ancestors has an air of inevitability about it, but it does not quite constitute the proclamation of a predetermined fate. In fact, Jesus' lament in verses 37–39 would lose much of its power were that the case.

The reader will know that the imminent execution of Jesus, already foreshadowed by the intransigence of Jesus' opponents, will be an important moment in the history of the refusal of God's offers. However, verse 34 actually skips over the crucifixion and directs attention to the persecution of the church. Thus, although the death and resurrection of Jesus constitute the turning point in the drama as a whole, it is really the rejection of the church's message that seals the fate of the generation. In addition, it is important to note that it is this generation, neither the leaders alone nor the Jewish people as such, on whom judgment falls.

The lament in verses 37–39 brings the long history of the rejection of God's emissaries once again into view and subtly injects Jesus' imminent fate into the mix. His declaration that "you will not see me again until you say, 'Blessed is the one who comes in the name of the Lord'" clearly points to his return at the close of the age, which will be described in 24:29 and 25:31–46, but scholars divide on its precise meaning. For some interpreters, it is one more condemnatory statement: The people who reject him now will be forced to recognize him at his glorious return. Another possibility is that it envisions a later repentance, in which Israel as a whole will embrace Jesus as Messiah when he returns. Yet a third is that it reflects a belief, current among some Jews, that the Messiah would come only when the people meet certain conditions. Thus, as Davies and Allison put the matter, "The text means not, when the Messiah comes, his people will bless him, but rather, when his people bless him, the Messiah will come." In other words, the date of Jesus' return, when the world is finally redeemed, is "contingent upon Israel's [eventual] acceptance of Jesus" (*The Gospel According to Saint Matthew*, III, pp. 323–324).

The first possibility is highly unlikely, because the quotation, "Blessed is the one…" (Ps. 118:26) seems singularly ill-suited to express a begrudging recognition. Davies and Allison reject the second on the grounds that such a "straightforward promise of [Israel's] salvation" would be "jarring" after the judgment pronounced in verse 38. Thus the third option is indeed attractive, and it is consistent with my own view that at the end of the gospel Israel remains among the nations ripe for mission (see pp. 75–76, 156–57, and "The Crowds"/"The People," pp. 191–92). In addition, it fits with my reading of 19:27–30, according to which the disciples will sort out the believers and unbelievers in Israel at the end of the age (see pp. 144–45). It is at least possible, then, to read Matthew as holding open the possibility that the majority of the people of Israel will escape final condemnation.

This interpretation of 23:39, however, stands in tension with 24:3–44, which seems to lay out a predetermined sequence of eschatological events, and especially with 24:36, according to which God (but no one else) has knowledge of "that day and hour." Interestingly, however, this verse actually speaks of God's knowledge "about" (*peri*) this matter, but it does not state directly that the date is fixed. In any case, we should beware of assuming a strict consistency in the details of Matthew's narrative, given all the examples we have seen of conflicting currents of meaning.

This same advice applies when we consider that the reading of 23:39 that Davies and Allison propose is also in tension with my own interpretation of 21:43 and 24:34. The latter passage seems to indicate that Jesus' return will come during the lifetime of that second generation. And the former passage seems to indicate that two generations of the people of Israel stand condemned—the one contemporary with Jesus and the one that follows it, in which the postresurrection Matthean community comes into conflict with the Pharisaic leadership. But if this is so, then where does one fit into this scheme a chance for the people of Israel to repent? The question is troublesome, but not in my estimation sufficiently so as to reject out of hand the notion of the possibility of Israel's eventual repentance.

Another enticing feature of verses 37–39 is that Jesus here seems to speak from a vantage point "above" the flow of human history. The phrase "how often have I desired," immediately preceded by a reference to the rejection of the prophets, cannot be reduced to a reference to Jesus' own repeated efforts to call the people to repentance. Thus a number of scholars find here and in chapter 11 an identification of Jesus with the figure of pre-existent Wisdom, personified as female. I have already given my reasons for doubting that Matthew contains such an identification (see pp. 81–82), but there can be no doubt that both in 23:37 and 23:34 (where Jesus says "I send you prophets, sages, and scribes"), he speaks from a standpoint beyond that of his earthly ministry. In 23:34, we can imagine that he speaks specifically as the resurrected one who is inspiring the early community. But 23:37 seems to imply that he is also the one who sent the prophets. Does this then mean that in Matthew, Jesus is after all the incarnation of preexistent Wisdom? Let me answer with a quotation from an article in which I have dealt with this question at some length:

> This is not to say that Jesus speaks as Wisdom incarnate. It is only to say that as Son of God/Messiah, to whom "all things" have been delivered and who can speak of the yoke of the Torah as his own, he occupies a vantage point that is as close as possible to God's own. He can speak for God, who has sent emissaries to intransigent Israel throughout the years…What the reader must grasp is that the rejection of these later emissaries is of a piece not only with the rejection of Jesus but with the earlier rejection of those God sent to Israel. The point is that the Jesus who speaks in chapter 23 is the

middle term in this tragic history; his rejection is the turning point, Israel's definitive rejection of God. His sovereign "I send" and "how often" are important indicators of his unique, transcendent, and divine status; and by placing them in Jesus' mouth the narrator has him assume for the moment a trans-historical posture. The narrator does not, however, invite the reader to speculate on Jesus' pre-existence or his precise relationship to Wisdom. (Pregeant, "The Wisdom Passages in Matthew's Story," pp. 227–28)

In any case, whether the reader identifies Jesus with Wisdom incarnate or not, the major function of Jesus' lament over Jerusalem is not to encourage speculation on the specific nature of his status before God. His high status as Messiah Son of God is something the reader well knows by now, and the present passage assumes rather than argues it. The reader's task at this particular juncture is to grasp that the rejection of Jesus, later confirmed by the rejection of the early Christian mission, was a crucial turning point in the history of God's dealing with God's own people. I would, however, want to qualify the terminology I used above—"Israel's definitive rejection of God"—and specify that although the present generation as a whole "fills up" a long-standing pattern of such rejection, God's condemnation falls not on Israel as such but on its unresponsive component, now represented in the present generation and especially its leadership. The point is, however, that 23:37–39 prepares the reader to hear the more explicitly eschatological parts of the discourse and to approach the narrative of Jesus' death against the background of an ongoing history of God's invitations and the people's refusals.

24:1–35 The Destruction of the Temple and the End of the Age

At 24:1, the narrator reports that Jesus leaves the temple, where he has been engaging his opponents and teaching since 21:12. Coming at this point in the narrative, between Jesus' condemnation of the scribes and Pharisees and the specifically eschatological components of the discourse, this action signifies God's final judgment against Israel's current leadership. If Jesus does not appear in Matthew as Wisdom incarnate (see pp. 81–82, 169–70), his role at this point is nevertheless parallel to that of the Shekinah—God's presence among the people of Israel, often associated specifically with the temple or other sanctuaries. When Jesus leaves the temple, the reader can hear echoes of Ezekiel 10:18, which describes the departure of "the glory of the LORD" from the earlier Temple in an explicit act of judgment against its corruption.

Presumably anticipating Jesus' own condemnation of the temple, his disciples call attention to the grandeur of its complex of buildings; but

Jesus confirms their apparent fears with a prediction of destruction that leads to another question after they have made their way to the Mount of Olives. There, alone with Jesus, they ask the question that launches the eschatological section of the discourse. Treating the destruction of the temple as inseparable from the close of the age when he returns, they want to know both when the expected events will occur and what sign will precede his return.

Jesus' answer to the question of the time frame is clear enough, although it does not appear until the beginning of the third section of the discourse in 24:36: No one but God, not even the Son, knows the time of the end. Less explicit, but consistent with this declaration, is Jesus' denial that there will in fact be a sign that anyone might use to calculate the time of the end. The proverb regarding vultures and corpses in verse 28 means that the "sign of the Son of Man" (v. 30) will be unmistakable. Whether that sign is Jesus himself or an ensign (such as the cross) that he raises, the broad point is the same: When the sign appears, the final act of the drama will already have begun.

This much is clear, but there is much disagreement among scholars when we ask whether any specific event predicted in chapter 24 stands in the past or the future for the original readers of Matthew. And it is in fact exceedingly difficult to know at any given point whether the reference is to the destruction of the temple in 70 C.E. (generally regarded as in the past for Matthew's reader) or to the end of the age.

My own view is that Matthew's Jesus assumes a connection between the destruction of the temple and his return, but distinguishes the two events, thus correcting the disciples' presupposition. Part of the discourse therefore refers to events in the original readers' past and present, but part points to the future.

The prediction in verse 5 of messianic claimants most likely refers to the various would-be deliverers of Israel that arose in the first century, rather than to persons claiming to be Jesus returned in glory. Although we cannot document the use of the specific title "Messiah" in any of these cases, the claimants clearly assumed roles that were "messianic" in the broad sense. Thus, in verses 4–7, first-century readers would naturally think of the tumultuous times that began during the war that led to the fall of Jerusalem and continued into their own present. Likewise, they would see in verses 9–14 a reflection of the difficult period, from 70 C.E. through their own time, in which members of their community would falter under the pressure of persecution and difficulty. To any who were tempted to lose heart in the face of these disappointing developments, verse 14 ("And this good news…will be proclaimed throughout the world…then the end will come.")

would come as a word of grace, for it would reiterate the promise of Jesus' return, give a reason that this event had not yet occurred, and also call the reader to responsibility in the meantime. It is for the sake of a mission to all the world, which Jesus will dramatically commission at the end of the gospel, that the end is delayed.

It is more difficult to be confident about the reference of verses 15–19. In its original context in the book of Daniel, the phrase "desolating sacrilege" referred to a statue of a foreign deity that the Seleucid king Antiochus Epiphanes erected in the Temple in 167 B.C.E. In Matthew, it takes on a another meaning, but it is unclear whether it refers to the desecration of the temple in 70 C.E. or to a parallel event expected just before the eschatological events. In favor of the former is that verse 16 refers specifically to people in Judea, and the counsel to flee to the mountains fits very well the situation Christians must have faced during the siege of Jerusalem. In this case, however, the advice given in these verses would be irrelevant to the Matthean community. Because of the extended injunctions in this section, it seems more likely that at this point the original readers of Matthew, whatever their specific locale (which is probably not Judea), are expected to think of their own future and to apply the advice to their own situation. Also, that the injunctions end with a specific reference to the coming of the Son of man would seem to indicate that the whole passage points to the future rather than anything in the community's past. In their pre-Matthean contexts, on the other hand, these verses would have suggested other references.

Not only the cosmic disruptions depicted in verse 29 but also the tribulations predicted in verses 3–28 are stock items in apocalyptic literature, aptly understood as "birthpangs" (v. 8), because they constitute the difficult but necessary prelude to the new age. Against this background, verse 22 serves the double function of underscoring the horrors of the coming tribulation and also laying the foundation for the admonitions that will come in the final section of the discourse. The declaration that God has shortened the time out of mercy for the elect (the followers of Jesus), presumably so that they do not have to bear more suffering than is humanly possible, constitutes implicit encouragement to stand fast in the face of difficulty.

There is some tension between the notion that God has extended the time and verse 14, which implies an extension of time. But this tension actually serves to underscore a point that is woven into the fabric of chapters 24—25: Although apocalyptic in language and thematic content, the discourse is in no sense whatsoever a timetable of eschatological events. It is, in fact, quite the opposite, by virtue not only of 24:36 ("But about that day and hour no one knows"), but also of the emphasis on the unpredictability of the time of the parousia that will prevail throughout the final section of the discourse. Indeed, as we saw earlier, even this verse does not necessarily imply an already fixed date.

In the present section, however, there are passages that seem to point in the opposite direction—that is, to lay out a series of events that are in fact indicators of the approaching end. This is particularly so of the passage that closes this section of the discourse, verses 32–35, which invites the reader to observe the predicted events and discern the nearness of the parousia. Nevertheless, the reader is left with no really specific indicators, only the broad description of a period of woes that will precede the end. So the net effect is that the reader can neither calculate the end nor even observe a specific series of events transpiring in predetermined order, but can only do what Jesus will continually enjoin in the final section—watch for the end and remain faithful until it comes. But it will be important to note the specific meaning that "watch" takes on as we consider the third segment of the discourse.

Against the background of this emphasis, verse 34 ("this generation will not pass away until all these things have taken place") becomes somewhat less problematic than many interpreters have found it. Despite many attempts to find another meaning for "generation," the most likely interpretation of the verse is that Jesus proclaims that the end will come during the lifetime of those who hear him speak. The question is what meaning this declaration would have had for the Matthean community, probably reading this gospel in 80–90 C.E. My own judgment is that they thought of themselves as belonging to the final generation of human history, which began in the time of Jesus, without being bothered by formal definitions of how many decades a generation constitutes.

24:36—25:46 A Call for Watchfulness and Preparedness

The phrase "that day and hour" in verse 36 refers to Jesus' return at the end of the age (see also pp. 168–69, 171). Thus, Jesus, having distinguished this event from the fall of Jerusalem, now answers the disciples' question in 24:3 about the time of the end; but his answer is that only God—not even he or the angels in heaven—knows when that time will be. This statement, against the background of 24:27–28, constitutes an implicit but forceful prohibition of attempts to calculate the time of the end by observing signs. The reason for the prohibition appears in the verses that follow: One must be prepared at all times. Verses 36–44 thus provide a transition from the prediction of coming events in 24:1–35 to the admonitions about preparedness that complete the discourse, which are clearly directed to the readers as followers of Jesus in the postresurrection community.

The point of verses 37–44, that the end will come unexpectedly, is reinforced by the descriptions of the faithful and wise slave and the wicked slave in verses 45–51. But in this latter section, the imagery suggests specific application to the leaders in the community, for the two slaves seem entrusted with duties toward and authority over their fellows. The good slave provides food for the household, and the wicked one beats the others and neglects his duties.

The theme of unexpectedness in verses 36–44 opens into that of delayed expectation in 45–51; it is the master's delay that entices the wicked slave into irresponsible behavior, and delay figures into the two long allegories that follow. The bridegroom is delayed in the story of the ten bridesmaids, and in the talents, this master returns only "after a long time" (25:19). Despite the opinion of some commentators, however, this does not mean that the gospel of Matthew envisions a long history of the church before the end comes. We have seen that 24:34 reflects the expectation of an imminent end, within the lifetime of the original readers. Also, in 24:45–25:13 the theme of delay is employed in such a way as to work against the notion of a long history. Those who think in terms of delay are the irresponsible characters: The readers of Matthew should be prepared for Jesus' return *at any moment*. The injunction in 25:13—"keep awake" in the *New Revised Standard Version* and "keep watch" in the *New International Version*—does not mean to watch for signs of the parousia but to pay attention to one's own preparedness for the end (see Boring, *Matthew*, p. 451).

But what does preparedness mean? One needs to read the entire gospel of Matthew to answer this question. It means following in the way of the one who is "gentle and humble in heart" (11:29), who has fed the hungry and healed the suffering, and avoiding the hypocrisy, self-indulgence, and greed of those who opposed him (23:25). It means doing justice and mercy and remaining faithful (23:23) and clothing oneself with good works (5:16; 22:11–14). Most succinctly, however, it means obeying the love command that stands at the heart of Matthew's ethic (22:40). And it is, in fact, with a graphic equivalent of the love command that Jesus ends the judgment discourse in 25:31–46.

That ending depicts the final judgment, but each segment leading up to it in the final third of the discourse anticipates it. The "weeping and gnashing of teeth" in 24:51 and 25:30 describes the eschatological agonies of the condemned, and the shutting of the door on the five foolish bridesmaids in 25:10 symbolizes the final closing up of God's rule to those who have excluded themselves. The bridesmaids' pleas at 25:11 are the equivalent of the cries of those who ask in 25:44, "Lord, when was it that we saw you hungry…?" and those who say in 7:22, "Lord, Lord, did we not prophesy in your name…?" In all these cases, persons who expected to be included are in fact cast out. It is clear that in this discourse Jesus is calling the members of the Matthean community to responsibility, holding out before them the dual prospects of reward and punishment. As at other points in the gospel, Jesus makes clear that the church is by no means exempt from the coming judgment: Christians no less than anyone else must give a final account of themselves at the final day.

The majority of recent commentators, however—although acknowledging that the church stands under judgment—read 25:31–46 differently. They point out that the phrase "the least of these" in 25:40 translates the superlative of the same Greek term used in the positive degree in 10:42, "these little ones." Because in this latter instance "these little ones" seem to be Christian missionaries, they take the similar phrase in 25:40 to have the same meaning. On their reading, the final judgment scene in 25:31–46 depicts the judgment of non-Christians based on their treatment of Christian missionaries, just as in chapter 10 those who receive "these little ones" are rewarded and those who do not are punished. In addition, according to some interpreters, the Greek word *ethne*, which the *New Revised Standard Version* renders "nations," should be translated "Gentiles," so that what is depicted here is not a judgment of all humanity but specifically of the Gentiles, who are the objects of the missionary activity commissioned at the end of the gospel. Thus, church members are simply not on the scene at this point; God deals with them separately.

Whichever reading one accepts, the interesting aspect of this judgment scene is that explicit confession of Jesus as the Christ is not the criterion for inclusion in God's rule; that criterion is deeds of love and mercy. So either way, the Matthean emphasis on the love command comes into play as the basis of God's judgment. And even though the Son of man, who is clearly Jesus, is not only the judge but also the referent of the deeds ("you did it to me/you did not do it to me"), the whole point is that he is the *unknown* referent. Neither the sheep nor the goats ministered to the needy because Jesus had identified with them, for they did not know he had. Thus, it is clearly the deeds themselves, and not any attempt to please him, that he honors.

This point holds up on either of the two major readings of this passage. I remain convinced on literary grounds, however, that the sheep and the goats do not represent Gentiles specifically and that "the least of these" are not limited to Christian missionaries. The whole thrust of the discourse has been to enjoin Christians to keep the faith in the face of the coming end; even the preliminary section in chapter 23 focuses on the scribes and Pharisees primarily to present them as negative examples to church members. It would be odd indeed to shift gears at the climax of the discourse and speak not of church members but of those who encounter them on the mission field. On my reading, then, the passage envisions the final judgment of all human beings but is addressed specifically to the Christian community.

To get the full force of the passage, we must ask about the specific identity of those in prison and hungry, and so on. The Christian readers will of course think primarily of their fellow church members, those suffering under the persecutions mentioned earlier in the discourse. But the logic of the passage is that the Son of man is enjoining Christians to do deeds of mercy by applying to them the criterion that will apply to all persons at the final judgment.

This particular way of conceiving the final judgment produces an interesting result. On the one hand, the passage brims over with christological content: The Son of man is the judge of the world and the implicit referent of the deeds of mercy. However, explicit confession of Jesus plays no role in the separation of the sheep and goats. Thus if the judgment of "all the nations" in fact means "all the world," the logical implication is that non-Christians are included among the righteous, not because of their treatment of Christian missionaries but because of their deeds of mercy in general. Yet this possibility is not something that is ever stated explicitly in Matthew, and it would seem to stand in tension with this gospel's strong christological emphasis that is present even in this passage.

The consistent Matthean emphasis on love appears throughout the judgment discourse, figuring not only in the injunctions of 24:36 but also in the indictment of the scribes of the scribes and Pharisees in chapter 23 and even in the description of the woes that precede the end of the age: "the love of many will grow cold" (24:12). This latter passage should warn us, however, against sentimentalizing the demands of love; for the implicit call here is to remain steadfast in love even in the face of extreme circumstances. This point is subtly present also in both the description of the last judgment and the story of the talents.

A popular reading of the latter identifies the coins, the "talents," with human abilities. Such a reading, however, reverses the historical process. The modern meaning of the word *talent* in fact grew out of a particular interpretation of the story: because the master bestowed the talents, and bestowed different amounts on each slave, readers came to think of them as symbols of the differing gifts God bestows on human beings. But as Boring comments (*The Gospel of Matthew*, p. 453), "The talents in this story refer to money (25:18); the differing abilities of the recipients are referred to in other terms (25:15)." Insofar as the talents are identifiable symbols, they signify responsibilities. The point is that the master holds them accountable for exercising these responsibilities—that is, once again, for keeping oneself prepared, doing what is required, in the face of Jesus' eventual return.

The distinctive aspect of the story in its context in the judgment discourse, however, is its implicit recognition of the risks involved in doing what is required. Here the central component of Jesus' original parable shines through the allegorized Matthean story (see "Interpreting the Parables," pp. 98–102, on parables and allegories), for, as Dan Via has noted, the fatal flaw in the third slave's attitude, which led to his disastrous decision, was his unwillingness to take a risk (*The Parables*, p. 118). This theme is implicit in the description of the final judgment as well; for in a time of persecution such as is envisioned in 24:9–14, to minister to persons imprisoned for declaring their faith is not a politically neutral act.

Thinking Today about Matthew 23:1—25:46

The Judgment of God, Inclusivism, and Grace

Judgment is not a theme that plays well on our contemporary stage. For good reason, many contemporary Christians outside fundamentalist or conservative evangelical circles are more likely to think of God's dealings with human beings as therapeutic rather than as judgmental. Burgeoning interest in Eastern religions and "new age" thought has called into question the stark distinctions Christians have traditionally made between good and evil and (most especially) saved and damned. This turn of thought has worked together with a long-standing tendency within modern Western religion to emphasize God's love over against God's wrath, a tendency strongly reinforced by the ascendancy of psychology not only among secular but among religious persons as well.

Here, as at many points in Matthew, it is important to allow both the text's ancient and our own modern points of reference their full due. Excessive emphasis on God's judgment can end in an antihuman attitude toward life, a rejection of human experience in all its richness. The oppressiveness of rigorist forms of Christianity needs no documentation. Yet it is also evident that our contemporary popular thought easily slides into a sentimental, self-indulgent, and self-centered attitude that reduces God to the level of a simpleminded genie catering to the whims of affluent narcissists while tyrants oppress the poor, murder prophets, and ravage the natural world.

Once again, then, it becomes important for the contemporary interpreter not simply to choose one frame of reference over the other but to allow each to challenge the other and to seek ever-new ways of thinking that can embrace key elements of each. This, of course, is a process that cannot be accomplished once for all, but has to take place not just in each new age but in every new reading of the texts.

In another context (see "The Imaging of Evil," pp. 33–36), I have already reflected on the tensions between Matthew's world and our own regarding the reality of evil, the notion of a last judgment, and the question of a final, changeless state as the goal of human history. Let me add here that Jesus' prediction in 24:34 that "this generation will not pass away until all these things have taken place" makes it all the more crucial for theological interpreters to consider alternative ways of honoring these problematic aspects of the text. For, despite the deft movements of many interpreters, one cannot honestly view such a statement as a minor miscalculation, as if two thousand years of human history did not call into question more than the details of a schedule of events.

I have also addressed the problem of Matthean anti-Judaism in other contexts (see "Powerful Texts, Dangerous Potential," pp. 88–92 and "Religious Exclusivism and the Problem of Other Faiths," pp. 160–64) and will add here only the comment that Matthew 23, clearly one of the New Testament's most virulent passages, presents both a challenge and an opportunity for Christian preachers and teachers. The material lends itself well to application to the Christian community, because what it attacks are human, and not peculiarly or even especially Jewish, tendencies. But it is, in my opinion, not enough to make such application. Given our particular place in human history, it is incumbent on every Christian who uses such material at all to disavow in explicit terms the slander against the Pharisaic movement, and by implication all Judaism, that it so clearly manifests.

An issue remains that I have not yet addressed explicitly, although several earlier discussions have set the background for my present comments. At several points, we have seen that Matthew's emphasis on Jesus' status as Messiah Son of God is balanced by the way in which the question of who Jesus is tends to lead into the larger question of who God is, according to Jesus (see particularly "The Point of the Christological Claim," pp. 36–37). In commenting on 13:24–30, 36–43 (see pp. 94–96), I noted an inclusivist strain that stands in tension with Matthew's christological witness: The good and bad seed in the parable of the weeds and its explanation seem to symbolize good and evil persons per se, apart from the confession of Jesus as the Christ. Now a similar inclusivism appears in 25:31–46, especially (but not only) on the reading I have proposed: Salvation seems to depend not on explicit acknowledgment of Jesus but on the deeds of love and mercy that have been so important throughout Matthew's gospel.

Here again the challenge of the contemporary interpreter is to hold together disparate points of view, this time not so much those of the ancient and the modern worldviews but of competing elements within the text itself. Of course the inclusivist element is more compatible with the cultural context in which we live, but the question is whether we can find a way of honoring both that inclusivism and the text's dominant christological witness.

There is no mechanical way of resolving this issue. But if it is true that the Matthean witness to Jesus as the Christ serves the broader agenda of a witness to who God is, then at least one way of holding an inclusivist view of salvation together with the christological witness does suggest itself. And that is to value the christological witness as a kind of confessional hyperbole—that is, to value it more for its imaginative content than for certain literal implications that one might derive from it.

Some elaboration of this suggestion is necessary. The Matthean proclamation that Jesus is the Messiah of Israel, whose death and resurrection bring salvation and open up a mission to all the world, has combined with other elements in the New Testament to foster the doctrine that salvation can be found only in Christ. But in subtle ways, the Matthean witness to Jesus seems to break down, opening into an inclusivist view according to which the criterion for salvation is not acceptance of Jesus but deeds that honor that for which Jesus, as God's representative, stands—that is, deeds of justice, mercy, and love.

If we try, from our contemporary perspective, to bring the two strands of the Matthean witness together, it is possible to include the christological witness within an inclusivist understanding of God's relationship to the world, but not vice versa, for if we maintain that all salvation depends on confession of Jesus as the Christ, then we lose the inclusivist element: God does not in fact honor deeds of love and mercy in whatever context they appear. If, however, we accept the New Testament's confession of Jesus as imaginative rather than literal language, we can understand it not as the declaration of the exclusive irruption of God's grace into human history but as the paradigm of an offer of salvation that is universally present. Such an understanding, however, would in no way involve the denial that it was through a specific person, Jesus, within a specific human context, the history of Israel, that this offer became concrete for the historical community of people that became the Christian church. (On this approach to christology, see Ogden, *Christ without Myth;* Boers, *Theology Out of the Ghetto;* and Pregeant, *Christology beyond Dogma.*)

Some readers may object that such a reading of Matthew results in a doctrine of works-righteousness—salvation by deeds of love rather than salvation by the grace of God. If this is so, however, the problem lies not so much with this approach to Matthew but to the gospel of Matthew itself, for it is the text of Matthew that retains the validity of the Torah (5:17–48), continually exalts the love commandments, and makes ministry to human suffering the criterion of salvation. But to call the Matthean view works-righteousness is not only to judge it by a Pauline standard but also to miss the strong elements of grace that permeate this gospel. In Matthew, as in the synoptic gospels generally, the coming of God's rule that Jesus proclaims is itself a manifestation of grace, and in Matthew in particular, the presence of the risen Jesus with the church (18:20; 26:20) is a strong proclamation of grace. To be sure, Matthew appears "legalistic" if we make Paul's dichotomy of law versus grace definitive. But Paul's views grew out of a particular set of circumstances that were simply not at work in Matthew's context. And a narrow reading of Paul, which falsely judges Judaism to be devoid of a doctrine of grace, has contributed as much to anti-Judaism as has a narrow reading of Matthew.

By way of final comment on the judgment discourse, it is important to observe that the theme of judgment does not play well on our stage because traditional theology has linked that theme to a particular image of God. Many of the biblical images of God are rooted in the practices of ancient Near Eastern monarchs. This is quite natural, given the environments in which the biblical writings appeared. But the consequences of taking these images literally have sometimes been disastrous. Matthew no less than other New Testament writings employs such images. Yet Matthew, no less than other writings in both the New Testament and the Hebrew Bible, also contains powerful countercurrents that, if taken seriously, offer rich possibilities to the contemporary interpreter.

This is not to say that we should reject all aspects of the more problematic images out of hand: Here again, it is important to preserve the richness of the biblical witness. But in the face of a long history in which despotic images of God have served as the sanction for wars of conquest, oppression of racial and ethnic groups, sexism, and the abuse of women and children, it becomes important to mine the biblical texts for the countercurrents. And in Matthew they are evident, most especially in the image of Jesus, in whom the character of God is manifest, as "gentle and lowly," the one who heals the suffering and identifies with all who are in need and whom society rejects.

To honor fully this strain of meaning, however, will involve the interpreter in nothing less than the task of reconstructing the traditional image of God born of the encounter between biblical thought and Greek philosophy, for it is unclear how the notion of an utterly self-sufficient being, unaffected by events in the world, and yet pulling the strings of history in unilateral fashion, is compatible with the God who identifies with the suffering Christ and the wretched among nations and persons. Thus, process theologians have come to think of God as necessarily related to the world, deeply affected by the contingencies of history—as "the fellow sufferer who understands" (Whitehead, *Process and Reality*, p. 351), who redeems the world not through coercion but through the power of persuasion and the decision to include all that happens within the divine life itself.

Reward, Punishment, Judgment, and the Action of God

The potential for anti-Judaism is not the only problem that the theme of God's judgment in the gospel of Matthew brings with it, for biblical thought tends to link the notion of divine judgment to a scheme of reward and punishment that is problematic in itself.

The logic of reward and punishment is straightforward and in many ways appealing. It reflects a belief that if on the human level we can discern right and wrong, such distinctions must somehow be grounded in the universe itself—that is, that the very structure of reality must itself have a moral base. And if the universe is in fact structured in a moral way, this would seem to imply that evil cannot have the final word. Thus the belief that either in the course of history or at its end God rewards those who do good and punishes those who do evil seems to be a logical outcome of the belief that some actions are objectively good and others are objectively evil (that is, that "good" and "evil" are more than mere human preferences). From this perspective, God's action in meting out punishment and reward seems to be a necessary result of God's goodness.

From another perspective, however, schemes of punishment and reward appear actually to work against the notion of God's goodness. If, as much biblical thought would seem to indicate, God's goal is in fact a world in which human beings live in harmony with one another and with the divine purposes—that is, a world characterized by peace, justice, love, and a harmonious relationship with the natural world—then it is unclear how punishment fits into such a scheme. Mere vengeance against evildoers would do nothing to reconcile the world to God. Nor would God's purpose be well served by punishment intended either as example or as discipline. If punishment of one person is intended to serve as an example to another, this would mean that God sacrifices the first person on behalf of the second. And the notion of punishment as discipline tends to enshrine fear as the motivation for doing the good. It is with good reason that psychologists who study moral development consider fear to be the most infantile of motivations for doing what is right.

However, if fear of punishment is a suspect motive for doing the good, so also is hope of reward, for to perform an act of mercy for a neighbor in order get a reward for oneself is not, in fact, actually to love the neighbor; it is rather to use the neighbor for an ultimately selfish end.

It is true, of course, that the gospel of Matthew portrays Jesus himself as speaking in terms of rewards and punishments (see, e.g., 5:12, 22, 30, 46; 6:4, 6, 18; 7:19; 8:11–12; 22:13; 23:32–36), and the passage that ends the judgment discourse (25:31–46, the description of the final judgment) is a striking example. This very passage, however, contains a motif that tends to undermine the logic of reward and punishment. For when those who are designated "sheep" are invited to "inherit the kingdom" because they have ministered to the needs of the Son of man in his suffering, they make it clear that they did not know that it was for him that they did their deeds of mercy. We saw earlier (p. 175) that this means that they are rewarded for the deeds themselves, not because the deeds were done for Jesus. But now we must note that those who did the good deeds did not know that Jesus was the recipient, which suggests that they performed the acts of mercy not in order to get a reward but simply to help those in need. Ironically, then, one is rewarded for acting without thought of reward.

If we bring this insight to other passages in Matthew in which Jesus speaks of rewards, it does not take a great deal of imagination to see that they are best understood in a similar way. Certainly, "blessed are the merciful, for they will receive mercy" (5:7) does not mean "blessed are those who calculate that the best way to get mercy is to give it," for this would violate the very meaning of mercy. One way of understanding the deeper logic of the language of reward and punishment, then, is to say that it is a graphic way of playing up the importance of doing the good by giving it God's sanction in dramatic and familiar terms.

This does not mean that the biblical writers themselves intended such language to function only as a rhetorical device; they most likely believed quite strongly that God metes out rewards and punishments. We should understand, however, the extent to which their belief in a scheme of reward and punishment was tied to specific presuppositions belonging to their ancient environment.

One of these presuppositions was that God acts in the world in a very direct way, so that certain events could be seen as resulting solely from God's intention. That is to say, to these ancient thinkers, God often acted coercively and unilaterally in the world, thus bringing about any desired result apart from anyone else's cooperation. It is true that many passages present God's action in a different way. In Exodus 3, for example, God's deliverance of the people from Egypt seems to depend on Moses' cooperation. Two stories in particular in Matthew suggest that the successful completion of God's plan depends on Jesus' own decision to resist temptation—the testing by Satan (4:1–11) and Jesus' agonizing night in Gethsemane before his arrest (26:36–46). Nevertheless, it is still true that the biblical witness presents God as often acting on the world in a direct and visible way. And this presupposition regarding God's unilateral action undergirds the belief in reward and punishment.

By linking the notion of God's judgment to a scheme of reward and punishment, the Bible also connects judgment to the notion of God's unilateral action. God intervenes, either within history or at its end by coercively enforcing the divine standards of good and evil: The good are rewarded, and the evil are punished. This is not, however, the only way one can understand the judgment of God. For if in some measure reward and punishment seem necessary parts of our social structure—and the degree to which this is so is itself highly debatable—there are other ways of understanding God's judgment of the world rather than in terms of direct, coercive action in the world.

According to process theology, for example (see bibliography on process thought), God's judgment takes place not in the world or in human history but in God's own life. That is to say, God's judgment consists of receiving everything that happens in the world for precisely what it is, whether good or evil. However, God also redeems what happens in the world by always providing for a new future. This means, on the one hand, that God does in fact act in order to affirm the moral base of the universe, but it also means, on the other, that such action does not take the form of retribution. Thus, in the end, the "reward" for performing acts of mercy is nothing other than this—that such actions live on in God precisely as acts of mercy. Conversely, the only punishment there is for acts of oppression is that these actions too live on for precisely what they are.

Thus we have at least one way of honoring the biblical motif of the judgment of God, as well as the deeper intention of the language of reward and punishment, while at the same time taking account of some of the contemporary objections to certain forms that these notions take within the framework of the Bible's ancient worldview. It is important to point out that it is a way that also honors the biblical motif of grace, perhaps more consistently than does the Bible itself. For if process thought holds that God receives all actions in the world for what they are, it also contends that God redeems such actions by always providing new futures in which there is new potential for overcoming what is negative.

When we take literally the notion of a final judgment involving reward and punishment, we actually draw a limit on God's grace; there is a point beyond which it is no longer operative. Yet even the New Testament writing devoted most fully to the notion of judgment contains a surprising hint of the eventual redemption of all things. After a long and bloody account of God's final judgment, The Revelation to John presents a glorious vision of the new world: "On either side of the river is the tree of life with its twelve kinds of fruit, producing its fruit each month; and the leaves of the tree are for the healing of the nations" (Rev. 22:2).

To be sure, the notion of the redemption of all things remains in severe tension with the depictions of judgment earlier in the book of Revelation, and we should note that the gospel of Matthew in any case seems to rest content with a final judgment that brings the redemptive process to an absolute end. But when we bring the ancient worldview into conversation with our own, as we have tried to do throughout this commentary, then new ways of understanding such themes as God's judgment can appear. And these ways often have potential for bringing into more prominent view other biblical strains of thought—most notably, in this instance, God's grace and mercy—which are sometimes obscured by the traditional ways we have approached the writings.

26:1—28:20 An Open-ended Conclusion
Condemnation, Death, Resurrection, Commission

Overview of Events

In 26:1–3, the reader finds a threefold indication that the story is drawing to a conclusion. Verse 1 repeats the familiar formula that signals the endings of the great discourses in Matthew (see p. 10). This time, however, an additional word hints that the teaching of Jesus is now complete: "When Jesus had finished saying *all* these things…" (emphasis added). In verse 2, Jesus refers to the imminence of the Passover feast and his own crucifixion, and in verse 3, the reader learns of a plot by the chief priests and elders to put Jesus to death. Following this introduction, the climactic events unfold.

A woman pours ointment on Jesus' head at Bethany over the disciples' misguided objections, Jesus proclaims the act a preparation for his burial, and Judas makes his treacherous bargain with the chief priests. When Jesus eats the Passover meal with his disciples, he interprets the bread and the wine in relation to his death for the forgiveness of sins, speaks of a coming banquet in the rule of God, and predicts the disciples' failure to stand by him: the betrayal by Judas, the desertion by all of them, and Peter's threefold denial of him. Following Jesus' vigil in Gethsemane, where the disciples cannot even stay awake with him through his agonizing prayer, Judas identifies him to a crowd of armed people, sent by the religious authorities, who arrest him and bring him before the high priest. While Peter proceeds with his denials of Jesus in the high priest's courtyard, Jesus makes no response to the charge that he has said that he was able to destroy the temple and rebuild it in three days. But he answers the question about whether he is "the Messiah, the Son of God" with an implicitly affirmative response that the high priest interprets as blasphemy.

The next stage of the drama, Jesus' trial before the Roman governor Pilate, is interspersed with an account of Judas' suicide and an interlude in which Pilate's wife—having had a dream that convinced her of Jesus' innocence—tries to dissuade him from condemning Jesus. At the instigation of the chief priests and elders, however, the crowds of people meet Pilate's offer to release one prisoner by choosing the "notorious" Barabbas instead. Fearing a riot, Pilate releases Barabbas and hands Jesus over for crucifixion. But Pilate first washes his hands as a declaration of his innocence of Jesus' blood, which elicits from "the people as a whole" the ominous response, "His blood be on us and on our children" (27:25). In the meantime, Jesus has once again implicitly accepted the messianic title (27:11).

The Roman soldiers mock Jesus, then put him to death on a cross at Golgotha, where others continue the mocking: passersby, chief priests, scribes, elders, and the bandits crucified beside him. On the cross, Jesus cries out, "My God, my God, why have you forsaken me?" After another loud cry, he dies, at which point the narrator reports an earthquake, the splitting of the temple curtain, the raising of saints from their tombs, and finally the centurion's declaration: "Truly this man was God's Son!"

The rest of the story moves quickly. A rich follower of Jesus named Joseph of Arimathea buries Jesus in his own tomb and closes the entrance with a great stone, and the chief priests and Pharisees convince Pilate to send soldiers to guard the tomb in anticipation of a claim regarding Jesus' resurrection. On the morning after the Sabbath, two women—"Mary Magdalene and the other Mary"—come to the tomb, where they see an angel descend and roll back the stone. The angel announces Jesus' resurrection and directs the women to tell the disciples to meet Jesus in Galilee; as they proceed on their mission, Jesus meets them and repeats the charge as they take hold of him and worship him. The soldiers at the tomb are dumbfounded at the angel's appearance, and some of them make their way to the chief priests to report what had happened. Then the chief priests and elders bribe the soldiers to put out the false report that the disciples had stolen the body. Following this latter incident, the narrator brings the reader to a mountain in Galilee, where the eleven disciples encounter the risen Jesus. They worship him, and he issues the climactic commission and promise:

> All authority in heaven and on earth has been given to me. Go therefore and make disciples of all nations, baptizing them in the name of the Father and of the Son and of the Holy Spirit, and teaching them to obey everything that I have commanded you. And remember, I am with you always, to the end of the age.

Motifs in 28:16–20

This final passage, 28:16–20, provides a dramatic conclusion to the story, envisioning a mission to the world at large commissioned by the risen Jesus himself. It also draws together numerous strands from the gospel as a whole and thus encourages the reader to think back through the entire narrative.

The reference to *eleven* disciples in verse 16 is a reminder of Judas' betrayal, and it combines with verse 17 to raise the issue of faith for the reader. The notation that "they worshiped him" highlights the prominence of the question of Jesus' identity throughout the story and once again models the proper response. The addition "but some doubted," however, also recalls the common phrase "little faith," which has signaled the real but faltering allegiance of the disciples to Jesus. Even now, standing before the risen Jesus, their faith remains imperfect. Yet Jesus' commission constitutes an affirmation of them. Consistent with the entire narrative, then, the ending presents the disciples to the reader as examples not of perfection but of faith in progress.

The counterbalance to the recognition of imperfection comes in Jesus' promise of his continuing presence with his followers in verse 20. Recalling a similar promise in 18:20 in the discourse on church life ("For where two or three are gathered in my name, I am there among them"), the promise relates specifically to the needs of the continuing church. Jesus' followers know from 10:16–25 that they will face many dangers as they carry out their mission. But here they receive a dramatic reminder that Jesus will be present with them in that task, even as God accompanied Moses (Ex. 3:12).

The disciples are to make disciples of all nations. The command thus constitutes a broadening of the earlier mission, instituted in 10:5–6, that Jesus specifically limited to Israel: Gentiles are now included. The reader is well prepared for this inclusiveness by such passages as 2:1–12; 4:15; 8:5–13; and 15:21–28; even Jesus' description of the limited mission in chapter 10 contains a hint in that direction (10:18). Despite some commentators, however, the phrase *panta ta ethne* in 28:19 should be translated "all nations" rather than "all Gentiles," for the emphasis is on total inclusiveness, not any type of exclusion. And if we take at face value Jesus' words to his disciples in the missionary discourse at 10:23 ("you will not have gone through all the towns of Israel before the Son of Man comes"), it would appear that Israel itself remains among the peoples ripe for mission. If this is so, it is unlikely that 21:43 ("the kingdom…will be taken away from you and given to a people that produces the fruits of the kingdom") means what some commentators argue: that God has now finally rejected Israel as a whole and replaced it with the church (see also p. 75 and pp. 156–57 and "The Crowds"/"The People," pp. 191–92). Jesus' reference in 28:18 to the authority God has given him points back to 11:27 (see also 7:28) and once again reinforces the narrative's claim regarding his status. It also gives the disciples—and hence the reader—reason for confidence; the God whose providential action has been evident throughout the story is the one who is the driving force behind the mission they are undertaking. In a more focused sense, the reference to Jesus' authority also supports the specific task of teaching. Because Jesus has appeared throughout the narrative as the authoritative teacher who fulfills the Torah (5:17–20), they can be confident that what they teach is the truth. This point is reinforced by the symbolism of the mountaintop, which recalls earlier scenes of similarly dramatic import (5:1; 17:1; see also 4:8 and 14:23).

The truth the disciples will teach is not abstract doctrine; in teaching the new disciples specifically to obey what Jesus has commanded, they continue a consistent emphasis on doing, not merely hearing, stated emphatically in 7:21–27. Implicitly, then, Jesus' final command places before the reader yet again the demand for concrete deeds of justice, mercy, and love, even as it contains a strong note of empowering grace in the promise of his presence.

All these elements draw from the earlier parts of the narrative, but the reference to baptism, with its Father–Son–Holy Spirit formulation, leads the reader into new waters. The narrative has developed no explicitly Trinitarian doctrine, and it would be illegitimate to read one into this passage. Nor does the discourse on church life in chapter 18 mention baptism. The command in 28:19 will of course remind the reader of Jesus' own baptism by John in 3:13–17, as well as that John's mission included the offer of a baptism connected to confession of sins (3:6). However, the formulary reference to Father, Son, and Holy Spirit seems to entail something fundamentally different. We can only surmise that the community that was made up of the first readers of this narrative employed this formula in the practice of baptism as a rite of initiation. But the narrator of the story has no interest in elaborating either on the nature and meaning of this rite or on the significance of the formula. The point is simply that it draws the candidates explicitly into discipleship and entails their being taught all that Jesus had commanded.

The final phrase, "to the end of the age," dramatically focuses the reader's attention on the future, but it also draws heavily on the preceding narrative. Both Jesus and John the Baptist had declared that the rule of God/heaven had drawn near, and in the judgment discourse (25:3–31), Jesus spoke of the events that would make that arrival complete. In accepting the commission of Jesus, the disciples—and the reader— participate in the continuing story of God's dealings with the people of Israel and of the world.

The narrative in chapters 26—28 is simple and straightforward on the surface, but a closer reading reveals not only complex connections with the earlier chapters of the gospel but an abundance of internal tensions and ambiguities—all of which contribute to the power, depth, and potential of the story as a whole. One way to trace some of these elements is to focus on the characters and character groups that figure into the tale: Jesus himself, the disciples, the Jewish leaders, the crowds of people, the women from Galilee, the Romans, and, finally, God.

The Characters

JESUS

Throughout chapters 26—28, Jesus appears consistently as God's faithful servant. Just as in the temptation story (4:1–11), a note of genuine contingency appears in the Gethsemane scene (26:36–46). For this account to have its full effect, the reader must allow it to raise the question about whether Jesus might decide not to accept the "cup" that God has placed before him or that God might provide a way around it—a thought that Jesus' own prayer encourages. The prior narrative, however, has presented Jesus as consistently faithful, so that there is every reason to believe that he will remain steadfast, as of course he does. The startling cry at 27:46, "My God, my God, why have you forsaken me?" adds complexity to the image of Jesus but does not negate his faithfulness. Again, the reader must take the words seriously, as an indication of a genuine feeling of abandonment parallel to Jesus' agony in the garden. Yet precisely as a scriptural quotation (Ps. 22:1), these words also signify Jesus' steadfastness even in the face of the subjective feeling of abandonment.

Jesus' use of this scriptural passage also gives it a prophetic quality, consistent with the emphasis on the fulfillment of scriptures that is particularly strong in chapters 26—28. Paradoxically, then, the cry of abandonment actually adds to the reader's sense that all that is happening is part of God's plan.

That plan has the redemption of humanity as its goal. Jesus not only has predicted his death but also has interpreted it at 20:28 in a way that gives it saving significance: it somehow "ransoms" humanity. Moreover, at his last meal with his disciples, he has expanded this interpretation by speaking of the wine as "my blood of the covenant, which is poured out for many for the forgiveness of sins" (26:28). In addition, the use of "this cup" in the Gethsemane scene as a metaphor for Jesus' death encourages the reader to understand it more specifically as a symbol of God's judgment. It thus appears that in submitting to crucifixion Jesus takes on himself the judgment of God in order to liberate humanity from its sins. And recognition of this point directs the reader's attention all the way back to 1:21: "you are to name him Jesus, for he will save his people from their sins."

By the conclusion of the story, however, it is clear that the designation "his people" reaches beyond the Jewish community, for not only have hints of the inclusion of Gentiles appeared repeatedly throughout the narrative but the commission given in 28:16–20 also states explicitly that the mission extends to all the world. The reader can therefore have no doubt that the term *many* in 20:28 and 26:28 is the equivalent of "all."

Jesus also appears, insofar as the human plane is concerned, to be in control of the events that are taking place. In 26:1–5, his prediction that he will be handed over to be crucified during the Passover conflicts with the plot of the chief priest and elders, which is to wait until after the feast to seize him; and it is Jesus' prediction that prevails. It is Judas' betrayal, which Jesus predicts in 26:23–25, that apparently causes the leaders to alter their plans. Jesus has earlier foreseen not only his death but also his resurrection, and he has spoken of the ultimate eschatological events; now in 26:29 and 26:64 he refers again to the latter. As he is arrested and brought before the high priest and Pilate, he neither offers resistance nor plays the role of victim. His silence at some points (26:63; 27:12–14) and prophetic statement at another (26:64) give the clear impression that, ironically, the prisoner is presiding over the events that bring his execution. This irony is paralleled by the ignorance of those who think they are in control and underscored by the taunts of his tormentors in 26:68: "Prophesy to us, you Messiah! Who is it that struck you?" The particularly complex irony here is that the one sarcastically called Messiah really is the Messiah, who has already prophesied all that is taking place.

The theme of the true identity of Jesus, moreover, reaches its climax in these concluding chapters. What Jesus had acknowledged to the disciples earlier (16:16–20), and what the reader has known all along, is now proclaimed publicly in Jesus' implicit acknowledgment of his messiahship.

Human recognition of his status comes in the declaration of the centurion and others keeping watch at the cross: "Truly this man was God's Son" (27:54). In addition, resurrection provides divine confirmation, while the concluding scene on the mountain (28:16–20) provides an image that underscores his worthiness of worship and the authority he has received from God.

THE DISCIPLES

Throughout the entire gospel, the narrator has painted a complex picture of the disciples, summed up in the characterization, "little faith" (8:26; 14:31; 16:8; 17:20; see also 6:30). It is their disappointing actions that have prompted this designation, but "little faith" does not connote "faithless." Jesus has acknowledged the sacrifice involved in their discipleship (19:27–30), and in various ways, he has looked ahead to the time in which they would continue his ministry after his death. He has also addressed the disciples as a privileged circle who receive the secrets of God's rule (13:10–14), apparently accepted their claim to have understood his teaching (13:51–52), and given unqualified approval to Peter's confession of faith (16:16–20).

In chapters 26—28, however, the reader finds the disciples in a downhill spiral. They miss the point of the woman's anointing of Jesus at Bethany (26:6–13), and they fall asleep in Gethsemane despite his pleadings (26:36–46). Judas betrays him outright, and the others desert him at his arrest (27:56). But in many ways the most dramatic instance of their failure comes in the account of Peter's denial, prefaced as it is with his declaration, "Though all become deserters...I will never desert you" (26:33). The statement not only contradicts Jesus' prediction in 26:31 but also places Peter in the prideful position of claiming superiority over the others—a claim made ludicrous by the threefold character and stringent nature of his disclaimer of Jesus.

Precisely at the point of their most shameful actions, however, the narrative provides for their restitution. Having failed on their own, they are nevertheless given a new opportunity by the action of God that Jesus has predicted—the resurrection. In the final scene, they are reunited with him and, like the women before them, worship him. Together with all humanity, they depend on the forgiveness effected by Jesus' blood of the new covenant, and on that basis, they receive the commission to make disciples of all nations.

THE JEWISH LEADERS

From the beginning, the leaders of Israel have appeared in Matthew as totally intransigent, completely closed to Jesus' ministry. Even when the

Pharisees and Sadducees come to receive John's baptism (3:7–10), the reader knows from John's vitriolic response that they are insincere.

Up until Jesus' entry into Jerusalem, it is primarily the scribes, Pharisees, and Sadducees who represent that leadership. With Jesus' entry into Jerusalem, however, the chief priests and elders take on a central role in the plot. It is they who question Jesus' authority as he teaches in the temple in 21:23–27 and who now in 26:3–5 and 27:1 conspire to put him to death. It is clear, however, that the entire leadership constitutes a united front in their opposition to Jesus. For at 21:45, both chief priests and the Pharisees realize that the parable of the wicked tenants in 21:33–44 applies to them; and the narrator's comment at 21:46 includes both groups: "They wanted to arrest him, but they feared the crowds, because they regarded him as a prophet." In 22:15–33, moreover, both the Pharisees and Sadducees are trying to entrap Jesus through debate; and in 27:62–65, the scribes and Pharisees join the chief priests in persuading Pilate to provide a guard at Jesus' tomb. In thus anticipating that the disciples will steal the body and effect a resurrection hoax, the leaders show a complete unwillingness to consider that God might in fact be acting through Jesus.

As the final events proceed, the chief priests also show their utter corruption. They bargain with Judas to betray Jesus (26:14–16) and exhibit a cavalier attitude toward the scriptural prescriptions against the shedding of innocent blood (Num. 35:33–34; Deut. 19:10) in their response in 27:4 to his statement of remorse: "What is that to us?" Together with the "whole council," they show a disregard for justice as they seek false testimony against Jesus (26:59). At the crucial moment, both the chief priests and the elders persuade the crowds to demand the release of Barabbas and the crucifixion of Jesus (27:15–23). But it is perhaps at the cross that the depth of the leaders' depravity becomes most graphic: the chief priests, scribes, and elders lower themselves to the level of a mob by mocking the condemned prisoner on the cross. In the end, they show with a final act of dishonesty that the truth is simply not in them: The priests and elders bribe the soldiers at the tomb to say that the disciples have stolen Jesus' body (28:11–14).

THE CROWDS/THE PEOPLE

From the beginning of Jesus' ministry, great crowds of people have been following him. These crowds seem to be potential disciples: He preaches to them, and they are generally astonished at his teaching, contrasting his authority with that of the scribes and Pharisees. Crowds of people also hail him as Son of David and a prophet when he enters Jerusalem at 21:1–11.

There is, however, a clear distinction between the disciples and the crowds. Their continual astonishment does not constitute actual allegiance to him. And the designation "prophet" is inadequate, whereas "Son of David" remains ambiguous when taken by itself. The crowds, moreover, also show negative traits. In 13:10–17, Jesus explains his use of parables with them by referring to their lack of understanding, foreseen in Isaiah 6:9, which speaks of the dullness of "this people's" heart.

In the end, despite their long-standing interest in Jesus, the crowd at the trial scene follows the leaders by demanding his death. After that fateful decision, Pilate declares his own innocence of Jesus' blood and turns the matter over to them, at which point the narrator states that "the people as a whole answered, 'His blood be on us and on our children'" (27:25).

The culmination of the trial before Pilate is obviously a crucial point in the narrative, and this latter verse has played an ominous role in later Christian attitudes toward Jews. Thus, two considerations are of prime importance for interpreting this passage.

The phrase "the people as a whole" in 27:25 carries a weight beyond that of "the crowd/crowds," but we must be careful in stating what the difference is. Despite the partial interchangeability of "people" and "crowds" in Matthew, and despite the negative use of the term *people* in scriptural quotations, Matthew's Jesus never condemns the Jewish people as such. Rather, he calls the contemporary generation "evil and adulterous" (12:39; 16:4) and "faithless and perverse" (17:17) and names them as the recipient of the wrath of God (23:36). We must understand the phrase "on us and on our children" in 27:25 not as a reference to the Jewish people for all time but as a specific reference to those who rejected Jesus in his own time and those who do so in the time of the Matthean community. (See Saldarini, *Matthew's Christian-Jewish Community*, pp. 32–34. In light of 24:34, however, this would not signify two separate generations.) As problematic as such a notion is for sensitive Christians in our time, it is very different from the often-voiced notion that Matthew's Jesus here pronounces the Jewish people throughout all time guilty of his death.

In any case, having for a time followed Jesus and listened to him, the crowd turns against him. And, lacking the status of disciples, they are not privy to the resurrection appearances but remain subject to the condemnations Jesus has pronounced on an "evil and adulterous generation." Their great mistake was to follow their leaders.

THE WOMEN FROM GALILEE

In 27:55–56, the reader learns of "many women," witnessing the crucifixion from a distance, who had followed Jesus from Galilee and "provided for him." Three are identified specifically: "Mary Magdalene, and Mary the mother of James and Joseph, and the mother of the sons of Zebedee." Only the latter has appeared earlier in the gospel (20:20–23). The narrator assumes knowledge of the other two, but the identity of the mother of James and Joseph is uncertain. Since 13:55 lists James and Joseph among the brothers of Jesus, it is possible that she is actually Jesus' mother. Not only would this be a strange way of referring to Jesus' mother, however, but in 28:1 she is also reduced to "the other Mary." It should also be noted that it is only Luke that refers to Mary Magdalene as the one from whom Jesus had cast seven devils (Lk. 8:2) and only John that reports a special resurrection appearance to her. Also, it is only in John that the women who witness the crucifixion are standing near the cross.

That the women do at least witness from a distance sets them apart from the disciples, all of whom have fled. And two of them—Mary Magdalene and the other Mary—play a crucial role in the narrative. Having come to the site of Jesus' burial on the morning after the Sabbath, they witness the empty tomb, hear the angel's announcement of the resurrection, and are present at Jesus' first resurrection appearance (28:1–10). In Matthew, in contrast to Mark (note Mk. 16:8), their actions serve to model faithfulness for the reader. Not only do they carry out the angel's commission (repeated by Jesus himself at 28:10), but they also precede the disciples in worshiping the risen Christ.

THE ROMANS

Apart from the concluding chapters, indications of Roman power and presence are for the most part sparse and subtle in Matthew, but they are real. The original readers of chapter 2 would have known that Herod ruled as a Roman agent and that after the destruction of the temple the Romans took over the collection of the temple tax (mentioned in 17:24–27) for their own purposes. Moreover, the discussion in 22:15–22 about paying taxes to the emperor is a reminder that Judea is an occupied country.

In some instances, Romans appear in a positive light. Jesus acknowledges the great faith of the centurion whose servant he heals in 8:5–13, and a centurion and other soldiers at the cross confess Jesus as God's Son. Pilate's wife, moreover, acknowledges Jesus' innocence (27:12). Romans can therefore provide examples of Gentile acceptance of Jesus or at least an openness to him. And it is clear that the narrative lays greater blame for Jesus' death on the Jewish leadership than on the Romans: the chief priests and elders not only hand Jesus over to Pilate but also stir up the crowd to demand his death (27:1–2, 20).

On the other hand, Romans and their agents can appear in a negative light as well. Both Herod (Mt. 2) and Herod Antipas (Mt. 14) appear as corrupt and unjust. (But it is only in Luke that Pilate takes Jesus to appear before Herod Antipas, who mocks him but fails to find him guilty; see Lk. 23:6–16.) Roman soldiers taunt and abuse Jesus in 27:27–31, and in 28:11–15 those dispatched to guard the tomb accept a bribe to put out a false story about Jesus' body. As for Pilate, despite the claim of some commentators that hand washing connotes repentance, this act and the accompanying declaration of innocence are best taken as ironical. Although the crowd accepts the guilt for Jesus' death, the narrator's report at 27:26 clearly implicates Pilate: "So he released Barabbas for them; and after flogging Jesus, he handed him over to be crucified." It is, moreover, the soldiers "of the governor" who engage in the abuse in the following scene. Pilate is therefore a tragic figure, aware of the injustice of the execution, but not a sympathetic one.

GOD

There are only two scenes in Matthew in which God functions directly as a character—Jesus' baptism in 3:13–17 and the transfiguration in 17:1–13—and in both cases, it is only God's voice from heaven that the reader encounters. Angels appear at several points as God's agent, however, and throughout the narrative, Jesus himself acts on God's behalf. In addition, passages such as the genealogy in chapter 1 and Jesus' predictions of the future are references to God's action.

The account of Jesus' death and resurrection plays God's absence and God's action off against one another in an intriguing way. At 26:64, Jesus refers to God in predicting his own exaltation, but God remains silent throughout the trial and crucifixion, a point underscored by Jesus' cry of abandonment in 27:46. Immediately after Jesus' death, however, the narrator reports events that the reader will naturally attribute to God: the splitting of the temple curtain, the earthquake, and the opening of the tombs and subsequent resurrection of many saints. But it is Jesus' own resurrection that constitutes God's climactic act and the turning point of the narrative. The God who promised the Messiah long ago through the prophets, ordered the history leading up to his birth, acted through Jesus' words and deeds as well as through angelic emissaries, now brings the story of the Messiah to a conclusion. This does not mean the end of the larger story of God's dealings with God's people, however. For now the risen Messiah, who came to save the people from their sins (1:21), commissions his disciples to include the world at large within the fold of that people. And he does so under the explicit authority of God, who thus continues to act in the world.

Thinking Today about Matthew 26:1—28:20

Competing Currents in a Perfect Ending

The narration of events in Matthew 26—28, culminating in the dramatic recognition scene and commissioning in 28:16–20, makes for a "perfect" ending. Jesus' own predictions of his death and resurrection come to pass, taking the reader through deep tragedy to a glorious triumph that points forward to an eventual final resolution. Accompanied by the spiritual presence of Jesus, the disciples will proclaim his story to all the world in anticipation of the eschatological events he has foretold. The reader is thus assured that the ages-old story of God's dealings with the world will reach a satisfying conclusion. The Messiah whom God promised through the prophets has appeared and completed all but the final phase of his work, and the Rule of Heaven/God has begun to take root in the world and will surely arrive in fullness in due time. In the meantime Jesus' followers, though subject to persecution, can live with confidence as they give themselves to the mission to which he has called them.

The various tensions that we have observed throughout the narrative, however, are by no means dispelled by the ending. Despite its harmonious tone, the final scene itself reveals to the close reader a creative competition between dominant meanings and enticing undercurrents.

CHRISTOLOGY AND THE TEACHINGS OF JESUS

The passage is pointedly christocentric. Jesus reasserts his divinely conferred authority; the disciples worship him; and the Father–Son–Spirit formula increases the reader's sense of Jesus' divine status. In addition, the promise of his continuing presence is clearly the equivalent of a declaration of God's own presence, known traditionally as the Shekinah.

The passage also draws on the preceding accounts of Jesus' death and resurrection for its meaning, and the reader knows to interpret these events specifically in light of the two atonement passages (20:28; 26:28). The Jesus who commissions the disciples at the end is the one whose death and resurrection have ransomed the world and brought forgiveness of sin. In addition, the phrase "end of the age" draws on the gospel's whole complex eschatological prediction to reinforce the apocalyptic aspect of the story's meaning. The Rule of God/Heaven is thus a transcendent reality, transforming the world by God's own action. And the command to baptize adds a sacramental component to the picture. Potential disciples are initiated into the new community. Ransomed and forgiven through the death and resurrection of Jesus, they are thus given a share in the coming eschatological reality.

Focus on these aspects of the ending of Matthew's gospel has led to interpretations of it as a kind of foundational document for a religious community proffering a system of other-worldly salvation. Matthew's long history of predominance as the "church's gospel" is in large measure a product of that reading. Such a reading is by no means wrong—only, in my estimation, too narrow. It ignores important competing currents of meaning that give the story a richer potential.

A strong indicator of one undercurrent appears in the emphasis given to Jesus' teachings. Baptism itself appears as a prelude specifically to the disciples' duty to teach obedience to Jesus' commands. This emphasis is entirely consistent with the gospel as a whole. Jesus' first discourse (chapters 5 through 7) outlines the ethic of God's Rule, and the dramatic judgment scene in 25:31–46 combines with such passages as 13:36–43; 7:12; 9:13; 12:7; and 22:34–40 to produce intimations that inclusion into that Rule is in the end based on love of neighbor rather than on explicit profession of Jesus as the Christ.

Emphasis on Jesus' teachings thus constitutes in some sense a counterweight to the gospel's christological witness. And in doing so it also stands in tension with the atonement motif, for, to the extent that Jesus' teachings are effective in themselves, they presuppose a cosmic situation rather different from that which is operative in the thought of Paul. According to Paul, the world stands imprisoned under the power of sin, and human beings are not fully able to do good apart from an irruption of grace in the world. Hints of a similar understanding appear in the atonement passages in Matthew, but the emphasis on Jesus' teaching—which functions as the definitive interpretation of a Torah God had already given—points in another direction (see "The Judgment of God, Inclusivism, and Grace," pp. 177–81, and pp. 46–51 on 5:17–48).

ATONEMENT, THE VIOLENCE OF GOD, AND THE POWERS OF EVIL

The atonement motif raises serious questions for the modern interpreter to the extent that it might seem to make Jesus himself a victim of God's own violence. However, this problem is partially mitigated by the insight— stressed so often in this commentary (see especially p. 2 and "The Point of the Christological Claim," pp. 36–37)—that in the gospel story Jesus stands on the divine side of the divine-human relationship. That is, the issue of Jesus' identity opens into the question of the character of God. And if Jesus stands for God, then his death appears precisely as a signifier of God's own self-sacrifice.

We may also note that the deterministic strain in Matthew that seems to present Jesus' death as part of God's plan stands in sharp tension with two other elements. The first is a pervading sense of contingency, of an openness that suggests the possibility of a different outcome (see esp. 4:1–11; 26:39, 42, 44), and the second is the presentation of Jesus' death as an act of human injustice (26:59–61; 27:15–26). To the extent that the reader pays attention to the injustice of Jesus' condemnation, the political aspect of the crucifixion will assert itself. And this means that the note of triumphalism in Jesus' comportment during the trial, where he appears "in charge," will have to be balanced with a recognition of his status as victim of humanly ordained injustice. Both ancient and contemporary readers sensitive to oppression will thus be aware of an undercurrent of meaning in which Jesus himself appears as a victim in need of liberation, and the resurrection appears as God's response (see Wainwright, *Shall We Wait for Another?* pp. 101–112). Recognition of this dimension of meaning should lead to reflection on how Jesus' followers today are called to "engage the powers"—that is, to struggle against the perversions in human institutions on behalf of peace and justice, the defining characteristics of the Rule of God (see Walter Wink, *The Powers*, vols. 1–3).

We should also beware of reading medieval doctrines of the atonement into Matthew, however deeply entrenched they have become in the Christian consciousness through the centuries. In the first place, because neither 20:28 nor 26:28 gives the slightest hint of the "mechanics" of atonement, the notion of "ransom" in 20:28 functions more metaphorically than doctrinally. It is only later theological reflection that literalizes the term by asking to whom the ransom was paid and why it was necessary. And this insight lends weight to critiques of traditional atonement theology by Black, feminist, and womanist theologians. (See, for example, James Cone, *God of the Oppressed*, Joanne Carlson Brown and Rebecca Parker, "For God So Loved the World?" and Delores Williams, *Sisters in the Wilderness*.) Interpreters from these perspectives accuse the "satisfaction" theory, especially the "susbstitutionary" variation, of disconnecting atonement from ethics by envisioning a path to salvation that has nothing to do with justice concerns and can even foster abuse and other forms of oppression.

Along somewhat similar lines, J. Denny Weaver (*The Nonviolent Atonement*) has recently made a strong case that the early church's understanding of the atonement in terms of the *christus victor* motif—which envisions Christ as defeating the powers of evil—has firmer New Testament support than the competing theories. In Denny's revised version of *christus victor*, which deletes the notion of God's bargaining with and deceiving Satan, Jesus' ministry of preaching and enabling God's Rule is integrated with his death and resurrection. On the one hand, ethics is restored to the equation, because following Jesus means participating in his opposition to the powers of evil. On the other hand, the death of Jesus appears not as God's intentional sacrifice of the Son but as the unfortunate consequence of a nonviolent opposition to unjust power structures. And the resurrection comes to the fore as the manifestation of God's defeat of the powers of evil.

If we bring Denny's perspective to Matthew, we can see some clear parallels. It is true that the passion predictions (16:21; 17:22–23; 20:17–19) suggest the necessity of Jesus' death, as do Jesus' words at the Last Supper (26:20–35) and in Gethsemane (26:36–45). It is equally clear, however, that the forces that put Jesus to death are not in accordance with God's will; his death remains an unjust act. Early on, Jesus excoriates the unrepentant cities of Galilee and connects their coming fate to their rejection of his message (11:20–24). Likewise the bitter denunciation of the scribes and Pharisees in chapter 23 culminates with a passage (vv. 37–39) that links the coming destruction of Jerusalem, foretold in chapter 24, to their intransigence. And there is no doubt in the parables of the two sons, the wicked tenants, and the wedding banquet (21:28—22:14) that those who put Jesus to death do so in opposition to God. (Note particularly 21:31: "Which of the two did the will of the father?" and 21:37: "Finally, he sent his son to them, saying, 'They will respect my son.'")

Were we to follow this line of logic through consistently, we could understand the crucifixion not as an act of God but as the result of Jesus' challenge, on behalf of God, to the forces of destruction. We would still have to say that it was Jesus' faithfulness to God that that led him to the cross. But this would be the tragic result of his opponents' intransigence, not God's predetermined plan. And the resurrection would appear precisely as God's response to a last, desperate attempt of those who refused to hear Jesus to stand in the way of the Rule of Heaven.

Can we say, however, that in Matthew, Jesus' death functions to defeat the powers of evil rather than as a compensation for sin? Some commentators find the latter notion in 26:39 on the assumption that the "cup" Jesus prays to avoid is a metaphor for God's wrath. Davis and Allison argue (*The Gospel According to Saint Matthew,* vol. 3, p. 497) on the basis of parallels in the Jewish Scriptures and related literature that the allusion is most likely to the coming eschatological sorrows that precede the end of the age. But they find the notion that the symbolism includes the notion that Jesus himself suffers God's wrath uncertain. It is in any case by no means demanded by the text. Nor does 20:28 itself necessarily imply a satisfaction or substitution motif. To the contrary: The more we stress that Jesus' mission in Matthew was in fact to bring God's Rule, and the more we emphasize the resurrection as over against Jesus' death, the more plausible Denny's reading becomes. We cannot say that his reading is demanded by the text, but one can argue with some force that it is in some ways a more faithful extension of the logic of the text than are those readings that derive a substitutionary motif from it.

Whether or not one sees God as implicated in the death of Jesus, the question of the violence of God comes to the fore in the eschatological aspect of the narrative. Both John the Baptist and Jesus announce the coming judgment (see, e.g., 3:7–12; 11:20–24; 21:41; 23:29–36; 25:7–8, 13, 46), and Jesus himself can at one point resort to a degree of violence (21:12–17). Thus the seemingly innocent phrase "end of the age" at the gospel's close points backward to a significant thematic strain in the story as a whole.

God's violence is of course not arbitrary, but appears in large measure as an answer to human violence. The world that God will finally subject to punishment is one in which a king slaughters innocent children to maintain power (2:16–18) and in which religious leaders put to death the prophets God sends them—and, indeed, God's own son (21:34–39; 23:29–35). And yet a violent response to violence still appears incongruous with Jesus' own teachings and practice in Matthew. Here the currents of meaning not only stand in tension but seem quite clearly to clash.

THE WOMEN IN THE STORY

There is also a tension between the concluding scene, in which the eleven remaining male disciples receive Jesus' authority, and 28:1–10 (see Wainwright, *Shall We Wait for Another?* pp. 112–18). In the latter, three women from among the "many" women who witnessed the crucifixion from a distance, in contrast to the males who had fled, receive a double commission of their own. Both the angel at the tomb and the risen Jesus who appears to them on the way send them to give the news of the resurrection to the eleven. These women are the first to know of the resurrection, the first to encounter the risen Jesus, and the first to worship him following the resurrection. Their role is indispensable to the narrative, and yet they are absent in the final, climactic scene in which Jesus confers his authority on his followers.

This latter fact is a good illustration of how a significant strain in the narrative is suppressed by a more dominant strain. Women have played unexpectedly important roles at several points in the narrative. Four women appear in the patrilineal genealogy in chapter 1, and at 9:18–22 Jesus acknowledges the faith of a woman who, transgressively, touches his garment and is healed. Moreover, at two points women get the better end of a contrast with the male disciples: the anointing at Bethany and the story of the Canaanite woman, whose "great faith" is implicitly contrasted with the "little faith" of the disciples. Together with the association of Jesus with the figure of the female personified Sophia (Wisdom) in 11:16–30 and with a hen gathering her brood in 23:34–39, these passages constitute a significant undercurrent that resists the patriarchal framework of the narrative and cries out for recognition.

The Creativity of Interpretation

The tensions that reappear in the final section of the Matthean narrative issue in part from social tensions at work within early Christian communities as they made the transition from the pre-Easter Jesus movement to more institutionalized religious communities. The suppression of proto-feminist elements illustrates one aspect of this struggle. Another aspect can be described as the uneasy combination of a moral story with this-worldly, existential import and a story that presents an offer of eschatological, other-worldly salvation based on a cosmic claim about the story's hero.

We must remember, however, that our ability to perceive these tensions arises largely from the discrepancy between the worldview of an ancient society and the worldview that is typical of our own time and place. That discrepancy need not lead us to force either/or choices among the various strains of meaning. It should rather serve as an opportunity for creative reflection in which we bring our contemporary perspectives into genuine conversations with elements of meaning that are grounded in a worldview of a time and place far removed from our own.

The premise of this commentary has been that it is precisely when we try to hold competing worldviews together in open-ended interaction that the ancient texts can speak most importantly to us. Thus, it is not necessary in reading the gospel of Matthew to choose between an atonement theology and a reading of Matthew that focuses on Jesus' teaching. Feminist critiques of the atonement motif as complicit in the encouragement of abuse through misuse of the call to self-sacrifice make an important point. But there is still redemptive potential in the notions of God's self-sacrificing love and of losing one's life in order to gain it. Neither must we choose between passages that offer an exclusivist christology and others that contain a note of inclusiveness or between Jesus' teachings on nonviolence and Matthew's strong note of eschatological judgment. Nor does recognition of a proto-feminist element necessarily mean rejection of every aspect of the dominant strain of meaning because of its patriarchal taint. What is essential is that we not ignore the tensions, but deal creatively with them.

This does not mean, however, that we must try to hold together utterly incompatible ideas in our own thinking. In the end, the most exciting moment of interpretation is precisely when we find a way of revaluing various strands of meaning—sometimes in a radical fashion—so that all components can work together to bring new understanding.

When we speak of new understanding in this sense, we imply that the time-honored distinction between the interpretation of a text and the application of that text to the reader's contemporary world is not so sharp as scholars and theologians have sometimes claimed. The distinction is real, to be sure; otherwise interpretation would be nothing more than making a text say what we want it to say, and all attempts to *study* a text would be meaningless. Part of what interpretation means is hearing a text when it says something we do not want to hear. But this commentary is based on the premise that the meaning of a text is in some degree open-ended. That is to say, any given text holds the potential for many meanings, and these depend on the point of view from which the interpreter approaches it.

Thus, the gospel of Matthew can, and indeed must, take on new meaning as it is read in ever-new situations by new groups and individuals in different times and places. In fact, this is precisely how it remains a living word throughout the ages. And if this insight is in some measure a product of our own situation at the beginning of the twenty-first century, there is nevertheless a sense in which it is rooted in the practices of ancient interpreters who themselves engaged in highly creative reading. Indeed, the process of interpretation pursued in this commentary is in the end not so different from that envisioned in Mathew 13:52: "Therefore every scribe who has been trained for the kingdom of heaven is like the master of a household who brings out of his treasure what is new and what is old."

Bibliography

Selected Bibliography on Process Thought

Basic Introductions to Process Theology

Cobb, John B., Jr. and Griffin, David R. 1976. *Process Thought: An Introductory Exposition*. Philadelphia: Westminster.

Kaufman, William E. 1991. *The Case for God*. St. Louis: Chalice.

Mellert, Robert B. 1975. *What Is Process Theology: An Introduction to the Philosophy of Alfred North Whitehead, and How It Is Being Applied to Christian Theology Today*. New York: Paulist.

Mesle, C. Robert. 1993. *Process Theology: A Basic Introduction*. With a concluding chapter by John B. Cobb, Jr. St. Louis: Chalice.

Pregeant, Russell. 1988. *Mystery without Magic*. Oak Park, Illinois: Meyer-Stone.

Suchocki, Marjorie. 1982. *God—Christ—Church: A Practical Guide to Process Theology*. New York: Crossroad.

Works on Biblical Hermeneutics and Process Thought

Farmer, Ronald. 1997. *Beyond the Impasse: The Promise of a Process Hermeneutic*. Studies in American Biblical Hermeneutics. Macon, Georgia: Mercer University Press.

Pregeant, Russell. 1978. *Christology Beyond Dogma: Matthew's Christ in Process Hermeneutic*. Philadelphia: Fortress Press/ Missoula, Montana: Scholars Press.

Classic Works in Process Theology

Cobb, John B., Jr. 1965. *A Christian Natural Theology Based on the Thought of Alfred North Whitehead*. Philadelphia: Westminster.

———. 1967. *The Structure of Christian Existence*. Philadelphia: Westminster.

———. 1969. *God and the World*. Philadelphia: Westminster.

Griffin, David R. 1976. *God, Power, and Evil: A Process Theodicy*. Philadelphia: Westminster.

Ogden, Schubert M. 1966. *The Reality of God and Other Essays*. New York: Harper and Row.

Foundational Works in Process Philosophy

Hartshorne, Charles. 1941. *Man's Vision of God and the Logic of Theism*. Chicago: Willett, Clark, and Company.

———. 1948. *The Divine Relativity: A Social Conception of God*. New Haven: Yale University Press.

———. 1953. *Reality as Social Process: Studies in Metaphysics and Religion*. Glenco: The Free Press.

———. 1962. *The Logic of Perfection*. LaSalle, Illinois: Open Court.

———. 1984. *Omnipotence and Other Theological Mistakes*. Albany, New York: SUNY Press.

Whitehead, Alfred North. 1927a. *Religion in the Making*. New York: Macmillan.

———. 1927b. *Symbolism: Its Meaning and Effect*. New York: Macmillan.

———. 1933. *Adventures of Ideas*. New York: Macmillan.

———. 1938. *Modes of Thought*. New York: Macmillan.

———. 1978. *Process and Reality: An Essay in Cosmology*. Corrected Edition. Edited by David Ray Griffin and Donald W. Sherburne. New York: The Free Press. (Original published in 1929.)

Works Cited

Bauer, David R. 1989. *The Structure of Matthew's Gospel: A Study in Literary Design.* Bible and Literature Series, vol. 15. Sheffield, England: The Almond Press.

Boers, Hendrikus. 1972. *Theology out of the Ghetto. A New Testament Essay Concerning Religious Exclusiveness.* Leiden: E.J. Brill.

Boring, M. Eugene. 1995. The Gospel of Matthew: Introduction, Commentary, and Reflections. In *The New Interpreter's Bible,* vol. 8. Nashville: Abingdon Press.

Brown, Joanne Carlson, and Rebecca Parker. 1989. "For God So Loved the World?" In *Christianity, Patriarchy, and Abuse: A Feminist Critique,* edited by Joanne Carlson Brown and Carole R. Bohn. New York: Pilgrim Press.

Caragounis, Chrys. 1989. *Peter and the Rock.* BZNW 58. Berlin/New York: Walter de Gruyter.

Cone, James H. 1996. *God of the Oppressed.* Rev. ed. Maryknoll, N.Y.: Orbis.

Crossan, John Dominic. 1973. *In Parables: The Challenge of the Historical Jesus.* New York: Harper and Row.

Davies, W. D. and Dale C. Allison. 1988–1997. *A Critical and Exegetical Commentary on the Gospel According to Saint Matthew.* Edinburg: T. and T. Clark, 3 vols.

Dodd, C.H. 1961. *The Parables of the Kingdom.* Rev. ed. New York: Scribner.

Garland, David E. 1993. *Reading Matthew: A Literary and Theological Commentary on the First Gospel.* New York: Crossroad.

Hagner, Donald A. 1993. *Matthew 1–13.* Vol. 33a, *Word Biblical Commentary.* Dallas: Word.

———. 1995. *Matthew 14–28.* Vol. 33b, *Word Biblical Commentary.* Dallas: Word.

Harrington, Daniel J. 1991. *The Gospel of Matthew.* Sacra Pagina. Collegeville, Minn.: The Liturgical Press.

Luz, Ulrich. 1989. *Matthew 1–7: A Commentary.* Translated by Wilhelm C. Linss. Minneapolis: Augsburg.

———. 2001. *Matthew 8–20.* Hermeneia—A Critical and Historical Commentary on the Bible. Translated by James E. Crouch. Edited by Helmut Koester. Minneapolis: Fortress Press, 2001.

McFague, Sallie. 1987. *Models of God: Theology for an Ecological, Nuclear Age.* Philadelphia: Fortress Press.

Malina, Bruce J., and Rohrbaugh, Richard L. 2003. *Social-Science Commentary on the Synoptic Gospels.* Minneapolis: Fortress Press.

Miller, Arthur. 1964. *After the Fall.* New York: Bantam Press.

Nolan, Brian. 1979. *The Royal Son of God: The Christology of Matthew 1–2 in the Setting of the Gospel.* OBO 23. Göttingen: Vandenhoeck und Ruprecht.

Ogden, Schubert M. 1961. *Christ without Myth: A Study Based on the Theology of Rudolf Bultmann.* New York: Harper and Brothers.

———. 1982. *The Point of Christology.* San Francisco: Harper and Row.

Overman, J. Andrew. 1996. *Church and Community in Crisis: The Gospel According to Matthew.* The New Testament in Context. Valley Forge, Pa.: Trinity Press International.

Patte, Daniel. 1987. *The Gospel According to Matthew: A Structural Commentary on Matthew's Faith.* Philadelphia: Fortress Press.

Perrin, Norman. 1980. *Jesus and the Language of the Kingdom: Symbol and Metaphor in New Testament Interpretation.* Philadelphia: Fortress Press.

Powell, Mark Allan. 1995. *God with Us: A Pastoral Theology of Matthew's Gospel.* Minneapolis: Fortress Press.

Pregeant, Russell. 1977. *Christology Beyond Dogma: Matthew's Christ in Process Hermeneutic.* Semeia Supplements 7. Philadelphia: Fortress Press; Missoula, Mont.: Scholars Press.

———. 1996. "The Wisdom Passages in Matthew's Story." In *Treasures New and Old: Contributions to Matthean Studies,* edited by David R. Bauer and Mark Allan Powell. Society of Biblical Literature Symposium, vol. 1. Atlanta: Scholars Press.

Ruether, Rosemary Radford. 1983. *Sexism and God-Talk.* Boston: Beacon, 1983.

Saldarini, Anthony J. 1994. *Matthew's Christian-Jewish Community.* Chicago: University of Chicago.

Schottroff, Luise. 1984. Human Solidarity and the Goodness of God. In *God of the Lowly: Socio-Historical Interpretations of the Bible,* edited by Willy Schottroff and Wolfgang Stegemann. New York: Orbis.

Scott, Bernard Brandon. 1989. *Hear then the Parable: A Commentary on the Parables of Jesus.* Minneapolis: Fortress Press.

Tannehill, Robert C. 1975. *The Sword of His Mouth.* Semeia Supplements 1. Philadelphia: Fortress Press; Missoula, Mont.: Scholars.

Theissen, Gerd. 1984. Lokal- und Sozialkolorit in der Geschichte von der syrophönikisschen Frau (Mk 7.24–30). *ZNW* 75.

Wainwright, Elaine Mary. 1991. *Towards a Feminist Critical Reading of the Gospel According to Matthew.* BZNW 60. Berlin: de Gruyter.

———. 1998. *Shall We Wait for Another? A Feminist Rereading of the Matthean Jesus.* Maryknoll, N.Y.: Orbis.

Weaver, J. Denny. 2001. *The Nonviolent Atonement.* Grand Rapids, Mich.: Eerdmans.

Weeden, Theodore J., Sr. 1979. "Recovering the Parabolic Intent in the Parable of the Sower." JAAR 47.

Williams, Delores. 1993. *Sisters in the Wilderness: The Challenge of Womanist God-Talk.* Maryknoll, N.Y.: Orbis.